Toward a New Era of Learning

Untangling Our Next Public Education

Wilson Winnitoy

© 2015 All rights reserved. Collaborative Media Group Inc. / The Innovation Expedition Inc. and The Alberta Teachers' Association.

The rights of Wilson Winnitoy to be identified as the author of this work have been asserted according to the U.S. Copyright, Designs and Patent Act of 1988 and appropriate Canadian copyright law.

Printed in the United States of America.

No part of this publication may be reproduced, stored in or introduced into a retrieval system, or transmitted in any form, or by means (electronic, mechanical, photocopying, recording, or otherwise) without prior written permission of the publisher. Requests for permission should be addressed to *futureTHINK* Press at The Collaborative Media Group Inc., 7608 150 St NW, Edmonton, Alberta T5R 1C8, Canada.

Wilson Winnitoy

Toward a New Era of Learning: Untangling Our Next Public Education

ISBN: 978-1-329-07657-0

Dedication

For Brynne, Liam and Sierra

Wilson Winnitoy is a retired public educator who lives in Ladysmith, B.C. Wilson has over fifty years of experience in teaching, administration, operational and strategic planning, group process design and management, public consultation, and a variety of processes for the collaborative development of solutions to complex problems. He has consulted and presented to educational and non-profit organizations in Canada and internationally.

He served as an advisor and facilitator to the elected and senior leadership of a large Canadian urban school system and, for over two decades, has been a consultant to the Alberta Teachers' Association's Strategic Planning Group.

Acknowledgements

Back in the late 1990s, a hardy and dedicated group of school administrators gathered in my office on many occasions to talk about schools and change. They were the Pioneering Schools Collaborative and I am grateful for those often intense discussions. The idea for this book grew out of them. Interest and support came from many friends and colleagues. I owe thanks to two in particular, Ruben Nelson and Jean-Claude Couture, who urged me on and helped me stay on track. There is probably not a more beautiful place to write than the small village of Pari in Tuscany. David Peat, Maureen Doolan, Eleanor and Andreas Barbieri, and the Pari Center for New Learning offered hospitality, encouragement and advice. Grazie to you all. I am especially grateful to the Alberta Teachers' Association and Dr. Stephen Murgatroyd of the Innovation Expedition for taking an interest and ensuring that this look into the future got into print. Last on the list and first in my thoughts of thanks owed is my family. Thank you Keely and Tayt for your interest and advice, Brent for the sweatshirt emblazoned with, "Ask me about my book," and most of all Joanie for helping me find the ideas and words that would take me forward, critiquing and editing the result, and always offering the loving encouragement that ensured that I would see this through.

Contents

INTRODUCTION 1

CHAPTER 1: WE ALL KNOW THE KIND OF SCHOOLS WE WANT – DON'T WE? 7

CHAPTER 2: VALUING LEARNING 25

CHAPTER 3: THE SCHOOLS WE HAVE – NOW HOW DID ALL THAT HAPPEN? 41

CHAPTER 4: EFFECTIVE LEARNING 69

CHAPTER 5: THE FRONTIER WE ARE IN 93

CHAPTER 6: INTERMISSION, RECAP, AND ON TO 2025 ... 109

CHAPTER 7: BECOMING A THIRD SCHOOLER 147

CHAPTER 8: THE LEARNER AND THE LEARNING 169

CHAPTER 9: TEACHING AS KNOWLEDGE WORK – THE LEARNIST 185

CHAPTER 10: LEARNING IN THE FAMILY AND THE COMMUNITY 203

CHAPTER 11: THE ADULT LEARNER 223

CHAPTER 12: IMPLEMENTING THE THIRD SCHOOLS ... 239

CHAPTER 13: WE NEED TO TALK 241

BIBLIOGRAPHY 257

"While individuals may legitimately judge for themselves whether to look ahead, this cannot be optional for those entrusted with any part of the well-being of others. Firms and institutions are intermediate cases: they must do their best for their customers and their members – those whose best is best will be rewarded in the marketplace. But the right of governments to stop doing forecasting and planning is probably non-existent: in other words, it is their duty to do what they can as best they can. Looking ahead is one of the things they are for." - Wayland Kennet

"…the fact that societies are so enormously conservative with regard to institutions means that when the original conditions leading to the creation or adoption of an institution change, the institution fails to adjust quickly to meet the new circumstances. The disjunction in rates of change between institutions and external environments then accounts for political decay or deinstitutionalization." – Francis Fukuyama

INTRODUCTION

What will our next public education system and its schools be like? It is a good question, but not one, unfortunately, that is on everyone's mind, at least not for now. We are too busy trying to fix the system we have, too busy to look ahead.

We do not have to look very far. Our next public education system, and its new approach to learning, is already revealing itself. It is visible in the pressures from parents and their ceaseless efforts to influence profoundly the quality of the experience their children have in school. It is visible in the creative efforts of many dedicated teachers and school administrators as they surmount, day after day, the dehumanizing tendencies of large-scale mass education. But their eyes are bent so close to that task at hand, seeking and choosing, reacting and repairing, that they themselves are unable to discern the emerging shape of their creation.

Our next public education system is visible in the more-or-less well-intended but clumsy efforts by politicians and various levels of government to reform the schools we have. These often ham-fisted efforts are distracting due to the controversies and unforeseen outcomes that usually surround them. The policy-makers seem unable to take a step or two back from the turmoil and talk to one another. They are too busy fixing what they think is broken to notice the deeper patterns of change that are emerging.

Our next public education is visible in the deeper issues that now surround the schools, issues having to do with the qualities of mind we need to engage with the challenges and opportunities of the times we are in. But our gaze is elsewhere. We are preoccupied with the burning educational issues of the day. We fret about the agendas and biases of the corporate sector, the rising number of incidents of extreme violence and the safety of children, the power of the teachers' unions, the lack of preparedness for post-secondary education and the workplace, and the regular gloomy assessments by the ever skeptical press. The more strident critics of the public schools, less visible in these recent turbulent years, have always seemed transfixed by their own rhetoric. Our public conversations leave scant space for attention, sharing and reflection. There is no sense that we are all wandering into a new territory, a territory that still looks enough like the old that we do not realize where we are and where our journey might take us.

The purpose of this book is to make our contemporary learning journey into a new landscape of public education visible to us.

This is partly a story about the history of our schools and how they came to be the way they are. More importantly, it is an invitation to think about the future of learning and the roles that parents, communities and schools might play in bringing that future to life. It is about how we appear to be losing sight of the deeper purposes of the public schools as they are obscured under the mantle of criticism and proposals for reform, and how we might reclaim and re-create places for learning in a way that we can scarcely imagine. It is a story that arises from the success and possibilities of the public schools of the last century. It is not about their failure. It is about the promise held in the clues to the future in our current public schools, clues that we interpret with difficulty.

This book is a look into the future. You might think of it as one possible storyline in a set of scenarios. If you are familiar with scenario creation, you will know that scenarios are an effective way of nudging us toward stories of the future that differ from our hoped-for or taken-for-granted stories of the future – too often a thinly improved present. Although this book was not written as a scenario study, it argues and presents evidence that there may be a future of learning in our culture that is radically different from the usual scenario – a better-funded, late 20th century public school system under renovation for the 21st century. But more importantly, by taking this leap into a possible future, this book invites others to get in the game of imagining new possibilities for learning.

Just for fun, let us play with the scenarios approach for just a minute. Scenarios are usually developed in quadrants, like a box containing four smaller boxes. The four quadrants arise from the interactions between two of the most important critical uncertainties faced by public education. These distinctive critical uncertainties, each a continuum represented by ↔ or double-headed arrows, crisscross and become the internal ✛ shaped boundaries that turn one big box into four smaller ones. So let us say we have two critical uncertainties:

Will learning remain a process of consumption of packaged and graded curricula and programs, or will it become a process of co-creation by and with the learner?

Will learning retain its base in the public schools, or will it move out into our society with many organizations and agencies supporting it?

Now let's have each of these options become the double-headed arrows that divide our box into four quadrants. Our four possible stories emerge:

1. Learning as consumption of curriculum and programs in the public schools.

2. Learning as consumption of curriculum and programs available from many sources.

3. Learning as co-creation of learning by and with the learner in the public schools.

4. Learning as co-creation of learning by and with the learner with support from many groups of people in our society.

And then our four stories can be written.

Scenarios simplify in order to amplify, and I do not think that it will be that simple. This book will suggest that scenario one is running out of time, two would be a variation on one, and we are headed for some combination of scenarios three and four – the muddle near the middle. My commitment to the reader is that I will present logic and evidence to support that argument, and as much as I can, unmuddle the middle of these converging and diverging possibilities. I will tease out a storyline of the future of learning. If you believe that the future is simply scenario one or scenario two, all fixed up and repainted, I may have just saved you a lot of time and unnecessary reading.

A note of caution here: There is a risk of throwing the learning baby out with the schooling bathwater. The danger lies in either/or thinking. I will argue that schools are becoming toxic to learning. I will also argue that their rebirth is about to occur with a renewed understanding of the purpose and use of formal schooling and instruction. Other examples of misleading either/ors are:

1. Choice versus the common good.//
2. Standards versus choice.
3. Public versus private.
4. Corporate management versus public administration.
5. Inclusion versus elites.
6. Bureaucracy versus entrepreneurship.
7. Discipline versus chaos.
8. Family values versus moral decline.

Formal schooling and instruction, of course, will not disappear. It will be newly understood as part of a massively enriched and dynamic system having numerous tactics and strategies for co-creating and supporting conscious learning.

As you read on, you will encounter references to our First, Second and Third Schools. These three stages or eras of public education are my way of describing long term patterns of change, where we have been and where we may be going. Our First Schools crystallized in the public mind early in the 1900s. There was a high degree of agreement about their purpose and how they should work. Schools built character and imparted skills and knowledge. They prepared youth to be productive workers and members of society and to sustain familiar patterns of family and community life. Teachers were respected authority figures firmly in charge of classrooms where desks were in a row and heads were quietly bent over government approved textbooks. Our assumptions about schools rarely surfaced. They were just not something we needed to talk about.

I went to school in the 1940s and '50s and experienced the conclusion of our First Schools. I taught in the 1960s and experienced the arrival of our Second Schools. Somewhere in the late '50s and early '60s the unwritten agreements about schools began to break down. Conflicts arose over many things we had previously taken for granted from ability grouping to whether blue jeans should be acceptable dress. Words like school failure, crisis and reform began to appear and became a permanent fixture in our public conversations. Assumptions were challenged and schools became something we needed not just to talk about, but to debate fiercely.

This book will suggest that the Second Schools era is concluding. The stresses on our current system are exceeding its ability to cope and to respond creatively and effectively. Our challenge and opportunity is to create our Third Schools and to do it in ways that are much more purposeful and thoughtful than the ways that led us to the first two eras. I will say much more about the Third Schools in the pages to follow.

I write in the hope that a courageous public school system and some of its parents will be willing to bring new approaches to learning into the open by adding them to their menu of educational choices. I believe that once students, parents and teachers try out the new ways of learning that our emerging future is offering to us, they will never turn back. As so often happens, the new must be tried cautiously, and its promise tested against reality, before it can be embraced fully.

I hope for a courageous Canadian public school system because, as I liked to say during my public school career, if someone on the planet gets to create the next form of public education, why wouldn't we choose us? I believe our public school system has the capacity and the commitment. It is the appropriate agency of this change as it exists in the public space and is meant to serve the common good. Part of the learning trust we have given public education is to look forward and initiate change. Here then, as I see it, are our challenges:

> We must rethink the meaning of the values and beliefs that drove the creation of the public schools over 100 years ago.
>
> We must translate them into a new kind of learning that responds to the challenges and opportunities of our time and place in history.

CHAPTER 1: WE ALL KNOW THE KIND OF SCHOOLS WE WANT – DON'T WE?

Given the battles that have swarmed around the schools over the last century, this chapter heading must be a mistake. Or maybe it is not a mistake. Maybe it should just say that we all know the kind of *learning* we want. But wait a minute. In casual conversation in our society, learning is almost always synonymous with schooling. So we'll end up right back where we started, talking about *school* reform. Or will we?

The Ideal

Let's begin with the words of an eloquent American, W.E.B. DuBois:

> Of all the civil rights for which the world has struggled and fought for 5,000 years....The freedom to learn...has been bought by bitter sacrifice. And whatever we may think of the curtailment of other civil rights, we should fight to the last ditch to keep open the right to learn, the right to have examined in our schools not only what we believe, but what we do not believe; not only what our leaders say, but what the leaders of other groups and nations, and the leaders of other centuries have said. We must insist upon this to give our children the fairness of a start which will equip them with such an array of facts and such an attitude toward truth that they can have a real chance to judge what the world is and what its greater minds have thought it might be. (as quoted by Linda Darling-Hammond in *The Right to Learn: A Blueprint for Creating Schools That Work*, p.1).

Some say that our North American schools have a European parentage and can be traced back to places like Prussia and to writers and thinkers such as Pestalozzi and Rousseau. Be that as it may, in the mid-1800s in Canada and the U.S., some thinking was done and actions taken that were very important for the birthing of public education. The last 150 years have seen the unfolding of a coherent philosophy of public schooling in Canada and the United States.

In Canada, Egerton Ryerson shaped the ideal and pioneered the advent of a universal education system. His vision consisted of the traditional three basics of public education: that it should be public, compulsory, and free. As a former minister of the Methodist Episcopal Church, and in keeping with his times, he threw in a healthy dose of moral and patriotic instruction as well, although his schools were to be "non-discriminational." (Desmond Morton, p. 55) A superintendent of education for 32 years, his ideas had a profound and positive effect on the early stages of the public school system in Ontario, and, in turn, Canada (*The Canadian Encyclopedia*).

In the United States, a similar vision is attributed to, among others, Horace Mann and the common schools movement of the mid-1800s. Mann was instrumental in bringing about the adoption of the Prussian system of compulsory public schooling in the United States. As Maxine Greene points out, Mann, the first, and for many years, secretary of the Massachusetts Board of Education, threw in a healthy dose of his own value system – calling for education to "ensure control of the passions by morality and intelligence." (*The Dialectic of Freedom*, p. 32) Leonard Waks states that there have been four themes with variations that have permeated the last 150 years of American public education. They are: (1) the promotion and the reproduction of democracy; (2) the provision of equal opportunity; (3) the promotion of social cohesion; and (4) vocational preparation to promote national economic productivity and hence the common good (*Choice, Charters and the Common School*, AERA Annual Meeting, 1996).

The ideal of common school, as embodied in our Canadian public education system, has been an ideal worth struggling for. In tandem with our moderately centrist form of government and our socially and fiscally balanced approach to the economy, it has provided significant and tangible benefits to Canada. One thinks of our commitment and our capacity to create social cohesion, natural justice, mosaic communities, innovation and productivity. It has been worth the huge struggles over ends and means, and the human and financial commitment to bring it off superbly well. Some areas have been woefully inadequate, such as native education, but on balance our schools, through decades of challenging change, have made a significant contribution to the shape of our nation.

Our public school system, under the umbrella of government and public administration, has shown constancy of commitment to its mission of ensuring that education would be, in Ursula Franklin's terms, an "indivisible good" in which all could share.

> Normally one considers it the obligation of governments, whose institutions are funded through a taxation system, to attend to those aspects of a society that provide indivisible benefits – justice and peace, as well as clean air, sanitation, drinkable water, safe roads, equal access to education; public institutions, from courts and schools to regulatory and enforcement systems, developed to do these public tasks. In other words, there is historically the notion that citizens surrendered some of their individual autonomy (and some of their money) to the state for the protection and advancement of "the common good – that is, indivisible benefits. (*The Real World of Technology*, p. 70.)

The ideal, the common good, and the indivisible benefits are all still valid to most Canadians today. The problem is that the era in which a 19th century system design worked to deliver the good is ending. Our world, the lived reality we share and our great legacy, the institution of the public schools, are drifting further apart. Our success was necessary and appropriate in the 20th century. The amazing resilience and adaptiveness of our schools now works against us as the clock ticks us further into the 21st century, and we struggle to repair and renew a system of the previous century.

What we all know

Many times over the years, I have attended parent meetings, the ones that so often occurred under the fluorescent lights and around the trapezoidal tables of school libraries where talk turned to kids and learning. I have also, many times, listened in on conversations among friends or in coffee shops where parents, and often students, talked openly with each other about the schools they desired. I believe there was and still is considerable agreement on what schools should be like. It takes a bit of digging into, sometimes beneath the language and behind the complaints about the behaviour of teachers, the problems of their children, or the zany rules of schools, but some common themes do emerge.

We all want schools that increase, not diminish, our natural curiosity and motivation to learn. We want schools that know the difference between learning and training, between educating and schooling. We, of course, want schools that get results. But we also crave schools that embrace the mystery and complexity of each child's learning. Here is a lament from someone just out of high school:

> For me, learning is thinking, creating, understanding. It is about nourishing rather than numbing the mind. For years I have learned more in the summertime, when I am free to think on my own terms, than in the school year. The pen in my hand means something more than a final exam. It stretches beyond standardized testing and into my creative spirit. (Evan Morgan, *Dead Students Society*, *Maclean's*, September 2nd, 2002.)

And here is where we run into two significant challenges.

The first challenge is that the schools we want are not the same school for every child. We want shape-shifting schools that are both reassuringly familiar, kind of like a better version of the ones we went to when we were kids, and able, somehow, to pull off the magic trick of slipping comfortably like familiar old clothes over the unique shape of each child's learning. This often expresses itself in a yearning for that special teacher who will pay attention to my child. "I've heard there's a really good one in Grade Three. Oh, I hope our Megan gets her and not that other one."

The second challenge is that even if schools could pull off the ultimate magic trick for any institution and shift their shape for every person, they might still miss something very important. That very important something is the array of forces outside the lives of children and schools that are calling for a new kind of learning for a new era – forces like information technology, do-it-yourself careers, fragmented civic and political involvement, diverse ways of being a family, a male, a female…well, we've all seen the lists.

More on these two challenges later.

So, beyond the fundamentals, it is difficult to find agreement. And in their desperate search to find a school that will serve the needs of their own child, many parents feel forced to try to bend an entire classroom, grade or school to their will, and then, in some cases, to leave in frustration for another school or school system. In hearing their stories, I know that in most cases the public schools they left could not possibly have provided the personalization, the custom fit of content and teaching approach, they were looking for. I can also discern through their stories the kind of warmth or coldness of the listening and responding that occurred as they pleaded, badgered and insisted in their search for a lever of change.

But I have had to acknowledge that more will be expected of the schools in the future. For profound reasons, having very little to do with the competence of staff and the effectiveness of schools, public education will not be able to respond.

Beyond the rhetoric of failure and reform

It would be unwise, if not impossible, to dismiss the storms of conflict and controversy that have swirled around public education for the last several decades. They have consumed huge amounts of space in the public press, innumerable conference agendas and the minds and hearts of those who care about our school systems. This wall of rhetoric has shut off the light and obscures the heart of the matter. It is this: We spend too much time fighting over how to build a better yesterday and ignore the common ground we stand on and the challenges and opportunities that lie ahead. We stomp around angrily on the very puzzle pieces that could be used to create a picture of tomorrow's learning.

We may have spent ourselves. I have noticed in clipping articles to my "schools crisis" and "schools reform and restructuring" files that although the familiar themes remain, the pace has slowed and the vitriol has been diluted. Or perhaps more worrisome, we are resting and gathering our strength for a new attempt to return public education to its mythic past golden age. It is worrisome indeed when one of the best friends of the public schools, Seymour Sarason, writes of "the predictable failure of educational reform":

> I came to see what should have been obvious: the characteristics, traditions and organizational dynamics of school systems were more or less lethal obstacles to achieving even modest, narrow goals. How does one deal with the abstraction we call a system embedded in and reflective of a society that created and nurtured that system? Can such

> a system be altered from within? Does it require changes and pressures from without, or does it require some kind of transactional readiness from both sources? And how do we determine whether we are tinkering with and even bolstering the system rather than changing it? (Seymour B. Sarason, *The Predictable Failure of Educational Reform*, p. 12.)

Other commentators anticipate the anger and disappointment of the public when the current efforts to reform public education are judged to have failed. A few years ago, a business leader in the British Chambers of Commerce described the situation in schools as a "national disgrace" and said "the system was in the 'last chance saloon' after 'endless' government initiatives" (*BBC News*, April 16th, 2007).

We desperately need to get past the finger pointing and hand wringing. We are missing numberless opportunities to create new systems for learning by building on existing strengths and new insights. We are avoiding constructing a new conversation in the public space in Canada and the U.S. about our renewed and re-energized cultural commitment to learning, and the best ways to express this public trust given changing conditions. We need to take seriously the proposition that new forms of learning are emerging in our schools, homes and workplaces, and that by thinking and designing forward, not backward, we can all reap enormous benefits, especially for our children. We need to heed the words of Nel Noddings, another researcher who cares deeply about the future of our schools.

> At a time when thinkers in many fields are moving toward postmodernism – a rejection of one objective method, distinctively individual subjectivity, universalizability in ethics, and universal criteria for epistemology – too many educators are still wedded to the modernist view of progress and its outmoded tools. Too many of us think that we can improve education merely by designing a better curriculum, finding and implementing a better form of instruction, or instituting a better form of classroom management. These things won't work. (*The Challenge to Care in Schools*, p. 173).

The new, fortunately, is becoming visible. We need to pay attention.

We have an opportunity

We have a clear and present opportunity to create something better – better learning for us and for our children. And the best news is that better is not only possible, but also probable. I do not write in the hope of staving off some disastrous turn of events. I write in the hope of drawing our attention, earlier than it might otherwise be drawn, to the good and exciting work that lies ahead. A new kind of learning "will out," or to say it in a new-agey way, will "manifest" in our schools, homes and communities. The signals are there, so the transition to a new level of learning has already begun. Parents and teachers are making some remarkable efforts and taking on huge challenges. Attempts to accommodate choice and diversity and new technologies are but a few examples.

Some pain is inevitable. There have been and will continue to be false starts and seeming failures. A new map will help us to see some directionality in these efforts, how they connect, and where our efforts should focus next. What follows will, I fear, be an initial, crude and incomplete map. It will also, I hope, be as intriguing and potentially useful to us as were the early maps that guided explorers and navigators into different places on our planet.

A new way of learning, when viewed from this aerial mapping height, will appear to be much more messy and convoluted than the way we do things now. "Unimaginable," you say. "How could things be more tangled than they are now?" Well, given our time and place in history and the new world we are moving into, this complexity should not surprise us. Nor should the need to act toward the future as we think about the way things might be. I suspect that is why so many change efforts are now underway.

> While new understandings can create a heightened sense of the need for change, and a direction in which an organization may feel it needs to go, new actions help to get it there. The conventional way of thinking about organizational change puts these in a sequential order. But from a chaos perspective they often need to be reversed. New action can catalyze new understandings. (Gareth Morgan *Images of Organization*, p. 270).

Some writers about change have summed it up more strongly by saying that we need to act our way toward new ways of thinking rather than thinking our way toward new ways of acting. This may be especially true for new ways of expressing learning as a cultural value and a societal priority, as public education is one of the most complex, deeply institutionalized, and potentially turbulent systems to engage with change.

The thing to keep in mind is, we can do it – we can thoughtfully and responsibly co-create this profound change. One very important objective of this work of making new maps is to show that from a learner, parent or teacher point of view, the new way of learning points to and leads us toward vital processes that make sense and are manageable.

Toward Conscious Learning

For those of us (mea culpa) who slept through more schooling than we care to admit, these words may call up guilty memories rather than a contradiction. For most of us though, the question would be: How could learning be anything but conscious? One cannot learn unless one both attends and pays attention. The mind may wander, but one must be fully present if learning is to occur. The tricks that many of my favourite teachers had in their repertoire were designed to catch us with our minds unleashed and reel us back into the lesson underway. Constant vigilance was required for both, but it was especially hard work for *my* teachers.

Conscious learning might be another way of saying that the lid of the mind must be open before anything can be poured in. However, we all know that much more is needed for responding to the challenge of learning than passively ensuring the lid of the mind is propped open. "Mindful" does not mean "full mind" or "no more room", and we are becoming mindful of our learning in important new ways. Students and parents are now awake to the issue and the search for sources of good teaching and learning is on.

So how is the idea of conscious learning relevant here? What we are searching for, I think, are those unique and rare contexts for learning that awaken our minds and engage our consciousness fully. This means more than just being on heightened alert. The mind is engaged with learning in new ways, ways that are more deeply thoughtful and interactive. Tantalizing? This idea will be explored more fully, with respect to learning, in chapter four.

But, back to that word conscious, and how it fits with learning.

I will deal with the question of conscious learning briefly, using three ideas about consciousness that are important for what follows. I am thankful to Merrelyn Emery, a great teacher from Australia, for presenting two of these significant features of consciousness in a workshop I attended some years ago.

The *first* is that *we are purposeful and are ideal-seeking.*

The *second* is that *we are capable of seeing ourselves as actors in our own lives.*

And another feature, thanks to the writings of Edward O. Wilson:

The *third* is that *we are, thanks to evolution, well equipped and driven to figure things out.*

As ideal-seeking critters, we know that better is possible in our own lives and many, if not most of us, become relentless seekers of the better, of an improved state of affairs for us and for the world we live in. And because we've been given the gift of reflexivity, the capacity to see ourselves as actors in our own lives, we can learn to see how we do the seeking, how we create and develop theories of our own life stories, and test them in our lived lives. And because we're wired to solve problems, to figure things out, we like to learn how to learn and how to dig out good learning, to sift and excavate it like gold from the rivers and caverns of our life's journey.

So, hello. This is us, and learning that consistently falls short of embracing these challenges lets us down in a big way.

Since Merrelyn Emery's workshop, I continue to find echoes of the first two powerful ideas. For example, in his remarkable book, *Sources of The Self*, Charles Taylor makes reference to ideal-seeking:

> ...we come here to one of the most basic aspirations of human beings, the need to be connected to, or in contact with, what they see as good, or of crucial importance, or of fundamental value. And how could it be otherwise, once we see that this orientation in relation to the good is essential to being a functional human agent? (p. 42).

And staying with the philosophers, here is another voice with some thoughts on our inner will to be authors of and not just characters in our life story. This is from Hannah Arendt's 1964 lecture on *Labor, Work, Action*.

> However, only man can *express* otherness and individuality, only he can distinguish himself and communicate *himself*, and not merely something – thirst or hunger, affection or hostility or fear. In man, otherness and distinctness become uniqueness, and what man inserts with word and deed into the company of his own kind is uniqueness. This insertion is not forced upon us through necessity…. It is unconditioned; its impulse springs from the beginning that came into the world when we were born and to which we respond by beginning something new on our own initiative. (Peter Baehr *The Portable Hannah Arendt*, p. 178).

Arendt says that we live in a "web of human relationships…woven by the deeds and words of innumerable persons," and as we live and act, we change forever that web of human relationships in ways impossible to predict. Although we are not solely the authors of our life's stories, "it is precisely in these stories that the actual meaning of a human life finally reveals itself." (pp. 179-180).

Emery and Arendt might disagree on the degree of self-authorship of our life's stories. For Walter Truett Anderson, the beautiful image of Escher's hands, each drawing the other, each drawing a hand drawing a hand, comes to mind. The set of hands may not be acting alone, but the imagery is about the capacity for self-awareness and reflexivity (*Reality Isn't What It Used To Be*, p. 255). It is a powerful image, and the capacity to be reflexive in the more complex aspects of our lives seems to be growing in importance.

But, there is more at work here, another "hand." In his book *Consilience*, Edward O. Wilson states:

> The most distinctive qualities of the human species are extremely high intelligence, language, culture, and reliance on long-term social contracts. In combination they gave early *Homo sapiens* a decisive edge over all competing animal species, but they also exacted a price we continue to pay, composed of the shocking recognition of the self, of the finiteness of personal existence, and of the chaos of the environment (pp. 224-225).

And so, we are led to an inevitable truth. The truth is that this is not a simplistic either/or issue of life authorship in the sense of control – either I'm the captain of my ship or I'm not. It is about something remarkable on offer – choice and mutuality in the complex dance of life. We cannot, indeed, choose to be the solitary authors of our life's story, but we can choose our stance and the form of engagement. We can discover, as many have before us, that the times and places of our lives in which we can claim authorship are always larger than our darker moments would lead us to believe. And, being conscious learners means being driven to learning at deep levels around profound questions of importance in our own lives. Here's how Mark Kingwell picks up the theme of our reflexive capacity and searching intelligence:

> Given the ability to reflect on the conditions of our own existence, a double-edged gift we apparently enjoy uniquely, humans are both social and contemplative by nature. We form associations and have intentions, not just instincts. We make judgments about the world and ourselves. We possess character, which surrenders its secrets to rational insight. In short, we pursue happiness actively, for it is the end of human actions, that for the sake of which all things are done. (*Better Living: In Pursuit of Happiness from Plato to Prozac*, p. 329).

There are significant implications in all this for the kind of learning experiences we should seek to provide, without compromise, for young people, and for ourselves.

Remembering Learning

Occasionally, over the years, I have led workshops and discussions where the topic was schools and learning. I sometimes asked people to remember an experience of learning something important to them, a learning event that stands out in their memory. It could be something that they remember learning in conventional situations such as school and youth groups, or with family and friends. It could be something learned in an unusual or even a strange situation, perhaps where something unexpected occurred such as a vehicle breakdown or being stranded in a big and unfamiliar city. I then asked them to recall, if they could, the feelings associated with that event.

Some remembered feelings of threat and danger, where the learning occurred as result of a mistake or lack of understanding. These feelings were particularly acute when the screw-up or ignorance was displayed in front of someone in authority or important to impress. This is the kind of learning where we can remember that someone, perhaps a grimly patient parent or teacher, saying, "I'll bet you won't make that mistake again," or "That's a good lesson for you."

Most of the memories were more positive. People remembered having mixed feelings ranging from stress, probably arising from seeking a puzzle piece, an answer, or a resolution, to an "aha" moment when something previously murky became clear, to a feeling of elation as the new insight was gathered into the mind and put to use. I can remember situations where I seemed frozen in an intense focus, my eyes and attention riveted on something that I needed to understand. Most of us agreed that after the learning happened, there was usually a sense that the learning mattered because it made a difference. Something worthwhile would have been incomplete or an opportunity would have been missed if the learning had not happened.

In discussion, we almost always reflected on the world of difference between *needing* and *wanting* to learn and *having* to learn. The feelings of indifference and boredom, all too often associated with classroom instruction, were rarely associated with learning. We wondered if it is true that, as someone put it years ago when reacting against the alternative schools movement, searching for schooling that is exciting and fun is like searching for the Holy Grail. It is an ideal and doesn't exist in the real world. Schooling must inevitably consist of dull routines and stuff that just is not that interesting. Teachers simply have to overcome this painful reality with interesting lessons and motivating teaching styles. In other words folks, just get over it. There is no yellow brick road to the Emerald City of learning.

Maybe, and maybe not.

Harrison Owen in his book *The Power of Spirit* describes what happened when a friend of his asked a large group of people to describe a "deep learning moment...when they really learned something powerful."

> All the people answered the questions with some variant of the following: Prior to the moment of powerful learning there was a general feeling of dis-ease, what the Germans might call *angst*, which is usually translated as "anxiety," but anxiety of a sort with no particular point of reference: something is happening/going to happen out there and I don't know what it is. In the moment it was experienced as total confusion: chaos. Nothing made sense and everything was strange and

different. Once the moment had passed, there was a feeling of relief at a minimum and, more typically, triumph. The world, although superficially the same, was very different. Profound learning had taken place, made all too clear in the radical perception of difference (pp. 26-27).

This is the kind of learning we might expect people to seek, given the features of human consciousness discussed earlier. The important outcome, central to the theme of this book, is not only knowing that learning has taken place, routine and conventional, or deep and profound, but also the conditions that caused the learning to occur and the role of the learner in creating those conditions.

How do we come to see and know ourselves as the creators of learning in our own lives? This challenge is a major focus of the rest of this book. But one more perspective on the opportunity that awaits.

Children Learn What They Live

"Children learn what they live" is the title of a poster (Author unknown, boardofwisdom.com) that used to hang in many Calgary public school system offices and classrooms, particularly in the elementary schools. Many examples were given, and they all had to do with the formation of what we call character. Children learn confidence, justice, and how to like themselves if they live among people who value and encourage those characteristics. This poster was not about subject matter or content. It reminded us that the central characteristics of a good person and a good mind result from being able to live and practice those ways of being in one another's lives, whatever the environment.

The theme of this poster will be a central theme of our next era of public education.

As we move to meet the challenges and opportunities of our times, we will create new ways of living our learning for all age groups. For young people in particular, we will create a new public system of learning that will enable them to grow into reflexively self-managed learners and develop the capacities for the co-creation and co-design of learning opportunities with other resourceful people. For younger children, special learning supports or "scaffolding" will be needed as each child moves in unique self-paced ways toward the threshold of active awareness and self-management. For all learners, the new scaffolding will ensure that the requirements of the public interest are met, usually expressed as a curriculum and testing systems.

We will also deal with the reality that the public interest is no longer expressed in the rigid hierarchies of the system and the industrial-era design of grades and classrooms.

On the surface, some of the places and spaces of learning will look the same. But the processes of creating learning will be strikingly different, from the foundations on up. The processes will be redesigned to ensure that every young learner has the best possible chance to develop 21st century and not 19th century uses of the mind, as the best teachers have dreamt of for years. A new way of living the learning will create new levels of engagement for young minds that currently happens to the very lucky minority in very special schools and classrooms.

These efforts will transcend current issues about preparing students for the workplace or to be active citizens. We now have the opportunity to create the kind of learning that will prepare adaptive minds to operate in new contexts where old assumptions about work and citizenship and other current categories are under challenge or are no longer valid. The public learning systems of the future will align with the growing cultural need for good minds and lively intelligence, or they will be pushed aside and circumvented even more rapidly than is happening now.

Gizmos in the Cloister

Whether or not we have positive images of the next Canada (or United States, or Britain), there are clear signals that we are reaching toward and struggling with a new cultural maturity. This is particularly true for our young adults. No longer willing to be caught up in the myth of progress, where things just get bigger, better and faster, we are reaching out to embrace what will certainly be a challenging and difficult societal journey. We are awash in information about global forces and the increasing complexity of everyday life. It can all be seen as an incentive to think about possibility, rather than a deterrent.

We don't just yearn for but fully expect that there should and will be:

- ➤ Acceptance of our responsibility to our environment with appropriate changes in our behaviour (although we are finding climate change a bit daunting),

- ➤ Powerful ethical declarations and new laws to accompany scientific and technological breakthroughs,

- ➤ A move forward from narrow-minded government accountability and what Steven Clift calls "drive-by" democracy to participatory governance and citizenship,

- ➤ Opportunities to manage our physical and mental well being, such as ways to balance and integrate home and work life, and

- ➤ Careers that we can design and that offer personal as well as financial rewards.

These are just a few examples of our growing belief that our speeded-up white water lives can be filled with promise, not portents of disaster.

But as all this occurs, there are futile and inappropriate efforts to insulate our schools from the churning going on in our culture. A good example is the effort over the last decade to ban cell phones and other high-tech gadgets from the classroom. There have been fears about cheating and violations of privacy. There have been incidents of students calling parents during class time to complain about their teachers, resulting in sometimes angry confrontations at the classroom door.

In so many ways, we try to keep the myth of the little red schoolhouse – the false front of the public schools – alive. I am reminded of an old and sad saying from the ancient days of the Soviet Union and Leonid Brezhnev when state-owned farms and factories were still in operation, but there was often no money to pay the workers. The Soviet workers' saying, heavily ironic, was, "If the managers continue to pretend that they are paying us, we will continue to pretend that we are working." The modern public school teachers' analogue could be, "If the culture continues to pretend that it wants the kind of schools our Moms and Dads went to, we'll continue to pretend that that's what we are."

It is time to break away from the old myth. We need to move forward from a system designed to write on the blank tablets of young minds to a system designed to invite young minds to write their stories of learning on the blank tablets of their futures.

Open Systems and Schools

Emery, an Australian teacher, researcher and writer, uses a very simple and powerful diagram to illustrate her open systems approach to participative strategic planning (*Participative Design for Participative Democracy*, p. 235). The diagram sets out her view of systems that interact with their environments. There are two, sometimes three, concentric rings, with the system, perhaps an organization or a community, in the central circle and the operating environment encircling the system, sometimes including both the immediate task or work environment and the larger global environment.

Emery's open systems diagram illustrates the dynamics at work in our current situation and of some of the major themes of this book.

Emery says that the "System…has a history, a character, a distinctive competence," and that "Human Systems contain the potential for ideals." Of the environment, she says that it "presents constraints and opportunities." The system circle and its encircling environment interact. Emery says that we make plans and we change the environment, and we learn from the environment and it changes us. It is a graceful ballet (or awkward stumble) of purpose and change. A word of caution here. Emery is describing an *open* system that interacts with, influences, and responds to its local environment. As Don Beck and Christopher Cowan point out, "If you push against a CLOSED system, know that you are asking for real trouble because it will push back." (*Spiral Dynamics*, p. 78).

So let's imagine that we are standing in an outer circle, in the environment, and looking into the system circle in the centre. We see an institution designed with ideas from the 19th century, reshaped by the forces of the 20th century, trying to come to grips with the conditions of the 21st century. We see the heroic actions of teachers and parents trying together to make going to school one of the peak experiences of a child's growing up. In spite of their best ideal-seeking efforts, we see many schools becoming unhealthy places for young minds to seek and to grow. And we see the increasing crippling effect of the design assumptions and the culture of schooling on the developing and needed capacities of young people to apply their minds to the complexities of modern life.

Now let's stand inside the middle circle and look out into our environment, particularly our own society and culture, but also the whole world. We see our western countries and a planet of increasing complexity, with huge forces at work and the potential for significant change in shorter periods of time. We see people expanding their consciousness, to use an out-of-date phrase, and developing new muscles of the mind. Some reach out voluntarily to create new opportunities to learn and develop their repertoire of knowledge and skills and apply them to deep and personal commitments. We also see that the "shock/maintenance learning" and the "human gap" identified by the Club of Rome report of many years ago is still at work. (*No Limits to Learning*, pp. 10-12). Many of us are responding to the emerging forces and pressures by trying to make today work better.

In spite of the struggles of our best and brightest teachers and students, and our committed parents, the system and its environment are growing out of alignment. As Thomas Homer-Dixon puts it:

> We can see how our world is, in many ways, becoming more complex, fast-paced, and unpredictable. As a result, the problems we face are getting more complicated as well, and ... we need longer and more elaborate sets of instructions for technologies and institutions that can effectively solve them. Or, to put it in terms of complexity theory: the greater complexity of our world requires greater complexity in our technologies and institutions. (*The Ingenuity Gap*, p. 194).

And so we must begin paying serious attention. Behind the classroom doors our teachers are burning out as they manufacture complex responses to complex learning challenges. The system is letting them down. As the organizational theorists and leaders have warned us, when the complexity and rate of change on the outside of the middle system circle exceeds the complexity and the rate of change inside the middle circle, as Jack Welsh, the former CEO General Electric put it, "the end is in sight."

This book will argue that the end and the beginning are both in sight because both are here.

CHAPTER 2: VALUING LEARNING

It's High and It's Timely

I probably can't stress it enough: This book is not a re-telling of the all-too-familiar media-driven story of school failure and futile or frustrated reform. The story we are in is not that simple. Inconveniently, there are no outright good or downright evil heroes or villains. Despite policy makers' dedication to metrics such as high-stakes testing and graduation rates, there are no simplistic, binary (it is or it ain't) measures of success. The emerging future of education is a far richer story of possibility and opportunity – for teachers and for learners of all ages. More importantly, the timing is right. The forces and dynamics at work in our culture are setting the stage and offering the choice of a different future. The chances of success are good even in the face of substantial concern about some of the changes I will be describing.

The current situation in Canada is an invitation to action. Here are some of the reasons.

The attention being paid to learning as a cultural value and asset is at an all time high. It is being connected to prosperity and social survival along with familiar pillars such as "investment climate" and "spending on research and development."

> Education is one of society's most important endeavours and the key to economic success, social transformation and opportunities for individuals to enhance their existence. But it is also one of society's most fossilized, rigid and change-averse institutions. It is still rooted in a medieval model that does not serve all students, or society, as well as it could. But a fundamental shift is easier than most people realize. It is not just about sprinkling a bunch of personal computers into classrooms. It's also not about uniforms, standardized tests, breaking the stranglehold of teachers' unions or eliminating tenured professors. What must happen to education is that its very modus operandi must change. And those nations that realize this will leave all others in their dust, economically and socially (Diane Francis, *Maclean's,* March 5th, 2001).

This connection between schools and economic and social health is not new. But the clear and arresting words are, "…its very modus operandi must change." What *is* new is the theme that the fundamental transformation of our schools is essential if the benefits of education, that is, learning, are going to arise. The importance of learning is becoming "mission-critical" according to many commentators. Writing more recently, Richard Florida offers another take on the urgency:

> …many of our schools are giant creativity-squelching institutions. We need to reinvent our education system from the ground up – including a massive commitment to early-childhood development and a shift away from institutionalized schooling to individually tailored learning. This will require a level of public and private investment of a magnitude larger than the widespread creation of public schools and modern research universities a century ago (*The Globe and Mail*, November 29th, 2008).

There is a strong message here. It is that we do not need to repair our schools; we need to rethink how they work. The consequence on offer is that if we do not do this soon, and well, we will have given a hostage to fortune in a highly competitive world.

An important fault line between beliefs and outcomes is being revealed here.

In the past, our beliefs about and societal investment in learning have been transposed onto the system that we created to deliver learning: the public school system. Support for the public schools as a system has been equated with supporting education generally, as well as the values we believed were embodied in the public schools, values such as economic growth, equity and social justice. To support the public school system was to support our beliefs about learning and the common good. Notice the echo of this in the phrase "the common school." This entanglement of system with values has permeated our conversations and debates for some time.

> Canadians value their education system and want to see it properly funded. That's the finding of a public opinion poll conducted on behalf of the Canadian Teachers' Federation (CTF). The CTF-commissioned poll found that 80 percent of Canadians support

increased funding for elementary and secondary public education (*The ATA News*, August 27th, 2002).

Alberta's Commission on Learning continues this entanglement of system and values in the *Highlights* section of its 2003 report:

> ...education will become even more critical to individual Albertans, to their communities, and to our province as a whole, especially with the growing importance of skills, knowledge and ideas to the future of our society and Alberta's role in the global economy. Albertans are strong supporters of their public education system. However, it will only remain one of the best systems in the world if we take deliberate actions to keep it that way (*Every Child Learns, Every Child Succeeds*, Alberta Learning, October 2003).

To keep it that way! Of course, the writers did not mean, "To keep it the same." Even so, it's hard to reconcile the language above with Diane Francis' warning and its implications.

We keep spending money on the existing system even as our skepticism about the effects of more dollars rises.

> Despite a cash infusion this spring for basic education, a new poll shows Albertans are no more satisfied with the public school system than they were two years ago. And almost three-quarters of the 800 people surveyed by Ipsos-Reid in the poll...said more money should be put into public schools. In the spring provincial budget, spending for K-12 education went up by $287 million (*Calgary Herald*, September 6th, 2005).

Albertans are not alone.

> And with the challenges of globalization becoming everyday more apparent, Britain's record on education declines steadily, despite a doubling of spending from £29 billion ($62 billion, using current exchange rates) in 1997 to £64 billion ($138 billion) projected for 2008. The Organisation for Economic Cooperation and Development last year claimed a quarter of the British population aged between 25 and 34 are "low skilled" in terms of educational attainment, five times the numbers in Japan (*Maclean's*, June 11th 2007).

A report from New Philanthropy Capital said the government had not improved truancy levels over the past 10 years despite spending £1bn on the problem. But Education Secretary Ruth Kelly said the money had been well spent (*BBC News*, September 6th, 2005).

In the meantime, quietly in the background, the fault line between our system of schooling and our values and beliefs about learning is widening.

Three Bowls of Public Education

Imagine a nested set of three stainless-steel bowls, the kind of all-purpose containers most of us have around the kitchen. No, this is not about how Goldilocks dished up some learning to the three bears. We'll use these containers to represent some pieces of the puzzle we are trying to solve here.

The big bowl at the bottom that cradles the next two represents our cultural value and societal investment around learning. It is the least visible or tangible of the three bowls, but it is there and is very important. When we hear Diane Francis and others talk about the importance of learning, giving children a good start in life, developing productive and engaged citizens, and transmitting a core of values and beliefs, they are talking about that big bottom bowl. They are talking about a central value of our culture. It would be unwise to assume that they are also talking about the next bowl, the middle one.

The middle bowl represents the institution and the systems we created to embody and put into action the high cultural value we placed on learning. We in Canada created the institution of the public schools over one hundred years ago. We needed a way to bring to life our beliefs about childhood, learning, and coming of age and to carry those beliefs into our lives. And so we created the public school system and it, in turn, created the myriad of authorities and bureaucracies that have successfully ensured that generations of Canadians received a good education, part of a "good up-bringing" as my parents called it. And in the spirit of mixing bowls, we continue to "mix up" the system with the big idea beneath it, the public schools with the values and beliefs they represent.

And what about the last bowl, the small cozy one cradled at the top? It has teachers and students in it, and sometimes parents and other adults. It represents what John Goodlad, in a book title, referred to as "a place called school." It is, very simply, the classroom, that place where a teacher and some students get together to do education. A place called school and its classrooms, that place we all have clear memories of, is the actual if somewhat dated, physical reality of our century and a half-old values and beliefs about learning. The classroom, with its classic mix of the teacher and the taught, is the intention of the middle bowl, the institution of the public schools, created to deliver on its promise – to ensure a good education for everyone.

When I started school in the mid-1940s and walked through the doors of the red brick Albert School in Regina, I disappeared simultaneously into all three bowls. My parents and their friends, and our culture at that time, made no distinctions. The culture, the institution and the classroom talked the same game and stood for the same things. I had disappeared into the institution our society had created and given absolute power to take charge of my learning. And that was as it should be. The schools represented the traditions, wisdom and grandeur of the state. If I got into trouble at school, I was almost automatically in trouble at home. The responsibility of the school, that we have called "in loco parentis" or "in the place of the parent," was invested with enormous confidence and trust.

We blurred our view of the three bowls and treated them as one handy tub in which all our ideas and assumptions about public education blended. Up into the 1940s, those ideas and assumptions cohered and resonated with one another. But then, some signals of change began to appear. By the 1950s, Hilda Neatby, a professor of history at the University of Saskatchewan, was challenging our assumption that we, or anyone, really understood what it all meant.

> Canadians have a great traditional respect for education and this respect has, at the cost of much material sacrifice, spread education over a vast country and through every group of a very varied society. But it is no longer easy to say exactly what education is. We all burn incense at the altar, but if faced with the challenge "Ye know not whom ye serve," it is fairly certain that we would answer, not with one clear voice but with an indistinguishable babel of sounds (*So Little for the Mind*, pp. 5-6).

Neatby was taking aim at the claims and the influence of progressive educators and reformers. This was not a new battleground; its roots were in the 1930s.

What was new was that Neatby no longer saw this just as a clash of pedagogies, or academic theories about how schools should work, a clash mostly kept out of the public view. She saw the fundamental structures of belief underpinning public education fracturing. She believed that there was a serious question about whether the interests of society were still being well served. And by shining her critical spotlight ruthlessly on the administrators, her detested "experts in education" in the middle bowl, she pushed us toward thinking more clearly about each of the three, our values and beliefs, the system's purposes and leadership, and the realities of the classroom.

In the process, Neatby became one of the first popularly read critics of public education. Many more would follow.

In spite of *So Little for the Mind*, our trust and our schools and the comfortable assumptions surrounding them lasted for a few more years. Somewhere in the 1960s it all truly began to change. The three bowls started to pop free of each other. The lines between them became less fuzzy and each became independently visible and subject to suddenly intense scrutiny. The familiar world of public education changed forever.

The End of a Covenant

When the world of public education changed, something very old, seemingly solid but suddenly fragile, began to fracture and break. My parents, and to a lesser degree, my generation, had accepted an unwritten agreement or covenant, one that, of course, had the force of law behind it. The unwritten agreement was that we would, at the coming of the legal entry age, not eagerly or reluctantly but unquestioningly, consign our four and five year-old children to the system of public education. We would, in a sense, stand back and let the system do its work. After all, it represented what we all stood for – discipline, good hard work and, depending on which system the child ended up in, Protestant or Catholic values.

Simply put, that deal is off. And what a deal it was. We didn't disparage public systems back then with language like "state run." The government owned and ran the public schools, and we were all invested in them and had a stake in their continued success. True, school systems were monoliths and ran along tracks of their own making. Nonetheless, for my parents, if there were ever any problems, a brief phone call to the principal or the teacher over at the stately, red brick Lakeview School would sort it all out, or sort me out, very quickly. In the Regina I grew up in during the 1940s and '50s, educators were almost automatically accorded the highest respect. Teachers and principals were seen as people of high integrity and commitment. Of course, there were some rigorous social expectations that went along with those generous assumptions.

My generation of parents was beginning to feel just a little less casual about the expectation of entrusting our children to the system. And in the background of pop music, we were hearing a new rattle of warning in the culture. Our two entered their public school, not the little neighbourhood one that did kindergarten, but the big one a school bus ride away, in 1975 and 1979. They were too young to know that Pink Floyd and Supertramp were telling them about school and becoming like bricks in someone else's wall, too good girls and boys who lived lives of all work and no play. But their Mom and Dad noticed, and we were intrigued. Songs about the dark side of going to school were a new thing – school was never an issue, musically speaking, for Frank Sinatra or Peggy Lee. So we paid attention to the pop-culture images of schools, but took them simply as good artists expressing the sometimes florid spirit of the counter-culture. Even the gentle, rose-tinted perspective of W. O. Mitchell had revealed some issues about whether schools were good places for kids – well, boys, at least (see his *Who Has Seen The Wind*). And being educators, we were brushing up against the ideas of Jonathan Kozol and Ivan Illich.

So as our family of four gathered in the evening at the dinner table, we would ask about school and how things were going. We expected to know if anything was truly amiss and to sort it out as my parents had through conversations with sensitive and attentive teachers and administrators. Our kids' schools resolved any problems pretty well on their own, and we usually accepted those resolutions, although they left us a bit uncomfortable at times. For my generation, whose children entered school in the '60s and '70s, in spite of some discomfort, not much had changed from the previous generations. And after all, as the school reform ferment of the '60s had promised us, weren't all these big systems creating fundamental changes, quietly, on the inside?

Well, as it turned out, not really. And as it now turns out, the old deal is going, going, and gone. As one writer put it, "Trusting one's beloved child to a stranger and a group of littler strangers, not to mention a system, is unsettling at best." (*The Globe and Mail, Tracking the Teacher*, September 3rd 2005).

This does not mean that parents today have turned their back on their public schools. It does not mean that they are all walking away in anger, looking for choices outside the system. In fact, it means that parents want not more, but something different from the public system, that which it cannot easily deliver. *It means that more and more parents are in search of an engagement with learning in the hope that they may yet find it in the public schools.* The system never stopped delivering public education as it was designed to do. It never stopped improving and adapting to learners. Rather, the world in which these efforts worked faded away far more rapidly than any of us could have imagined.

Now, in the 21st century, parents are saying as loudly and as clearly as they can that they want to be co-creators of learning for their children, as they are increasingly co-creators in their work, careers, health, recreation and spiritual life. Amazingly, they are saying this in a world of new family and economic pressures that will make the goal very hard to achieve. Yet, through endless phone calls and parent-teacher conferences, and hours invested in home or charter schools, they are seeking new ways to do learning together in the public space. They are asking for new ways that are consistent with current pressures and demands on families and the emerging demands on the minds of our learners. They believe it can be done. They are looking for and will flock to the schools and systems that figure it out.

Living in Two Worlds

For now, very few schools or school systems are able to be figuring it out. They are too busy scrambling just to keep up.

Until the "new order" of learning and role of schools is identified and established, parents will continue to put pressures on schools, pressures that are often inconsistent and, as a result, both puzzling and vexing. These pressures will continue until the fundamental issues around the future of learning and our public schools are seriously addressed. In the meantime, parents will be forced to be of two minds and to continue living in two worlds or realities of schooling at once. These two mindsets and realities are not entirely contradictory, but they do make uneasy partners and complicate the search for solutions by parent groups and schools.

On the one hand, or mind, there is the school as the educational version of a public utility. Here, the challenge for parents is to intervene in a way that is consistent with how the existing schools work and their standing in the community. Parents are taking steps to ensure that their neighbourhood and community schools are working well. And if they are not working well, parents are ready to go looking for schools that are. They seek to serve or at least influence the processes of school governance and program delivery. They ponder the rankings and comparisons of schools offered in the media and talk to other parents about the quality of education in their school. They no longer have an automatic and enduring trust in the schools as institutional representations of the official story of learning in our culture. They demand results and accountability.

On the other hand, or mind, there is the school as the local learning boutique. Here, the challenge for parents is to act as an advocate for the learning and futures of their own children. Parents are now taking extraordinary steps to bend the will of the schools toward their own children. They trust their own judgment as parents to know what is and works best for their children. They closely monitor their children's programs and engagement with classroom activities. They telephone, email and meet with the teacher and the principal as often as it takes to satisfy themselves that absolutely everything possible is being done to create a good learning situation for their children, even in poorer or so-called high-needs communities. In some cases, they are even doing this in real time as their children call them from the school during lessons and email them at home and at work.

In other words, do whatever it takes to ensure that our school is effective and one of the top-rated *and* do whatever it takes to ensure that our children's unique needs are met. Most parents know that the solutions sometimes contradict each other – for example, drill and practice for higher test scores versus encouragement for learning excursions outside the required curriculum. Many simply assert that a good school should be able to do both. Parents are caught in a strange twilight zone where they anxiously scan the school ranking tables in the newspapers but fret about the damage that standardized tests and high-stakes testing may be doing to the minds of their children by forcing learning into boxes and straight lines. They hope that their schools are weeding out incompetent teachers but worry that the schools are too homogenized to respond to the uniqueness of their child, or to attract good minds. They carefully watch the distribution of resources for new technologies but want a human touch in their child's teaching.

The public press helpfully keeps the pressure up and adds confusion by sporadically remanufacturing the crisis in public education, offering solutions from the past and warning about our compromised future, usually our economic future, if we don't do something drastic – and soon. Although the media's attention has turned, in recent years, to health care, and lately to the banks and financial markets, it will soon return to the schools. It will return because the geology of this issue is volcanic, and quietly, just beneath the surface of our society, the heat and pressure continues to build underneath the dome – the idea of the centrality of learning.

This sense of being caught in between, of being in a transition between old and next, is one of the most powerful symptoms that a new reality is trying to present itself. I will make this clearer when I describe the shape of the frontier we face.

We're Going To Change…Um…Something

Through the last several decades, many parents have worked with their schools on school improvement, and in more recent years, to adapt teaching to their own child. The main weapon in this educational activism has been meetings, not militancy or marches. Some parents and students took a more radical stance that had its first expressions in the counter-cultural sixties. Their efforts provoked responses from school systems that enabled some of their ideas to go into the mainstream, such as alternative schools and locally developed curriculum. Those efforts also influenced the way many more parents and students viewed change in their schools and school systems and possibilities for appropriate action.

The more radical approaches of parents and students to get the kind of changes they wanted have gone through a number of stages. To make them more distinct, I will tie them to decades. This oversimplifies, but it maps well against my own experience, and I suspect there is evidence to support these stages.

The '60s – We'll Change The System

A popular song in the '60s was *Enter the Young*. Both the music and the lyrics conveyed the boundless energy and hopes of a new generation of young adults, a generation we call the baby boomers. The stakes were high. The young were going to challenge and change some deeper societal assumptions. They took aim at issues like definitions of success and the good life, and oppressive and dishonest institutions that they felt were ruining personal growth and creativity. Whole school systems were going to be transformed or disappear; the children would be freed from going to school and would grow into creative, caring and authentic adults. The ferment of that decade expressed itself at the end, around 1970, in book titles such as *New Reformation, Our Time Is Now: Notes from the High School Underground,* and *The Soft Revolution.*

The '70s – We'll Change Our School

"The system," however one conceived it, turned out to be remarkably durable. Its industrial-era design assumptions were not to be easily softened or erased. Attention turned to creating change and alternatives within systems that turned out to also be remarkably porous, in spite of their rigidity. This decade saw the fullest flowering of the alternative schools and early plans for school choice programs within school systems. Some colleagues and I designed such a program for the Calgary Board of Education in 1974. Its intent was to invite people to create choices within the system so that they were not forced to look outside the system. In the language of the time, it was called a "demand-side" process; by 1980, it had pretty well been converted to a "supply-side" process, enabling the system to set the priorities and guide the design of large-scale options. And maybe, also, to say, "Hey, trust us, we really do know best."

The '80s – We'll Change Our Teacher

This was the decade in which serious efforts were underway to close the distance between the school and the home. Programs such as the Calgary Board of Education's Parents as Partners program sprang up. These efforts brought parents into the schools in ongoing and intense ways that were well beyond occasional volunteering. Parents became frequent, and in many cases, astute observers of the school culture and teaching styles of teachers. They became clever negotiators around the choice of teachers and changes to the ways that the teacher interacted with their child. By 1990, the parent involvement movement efforts were losing their initial energy, schools were feeling put upon, and parents were getting increasingly frustrated with being so close to the classroom and being able to effect so little change. School councils were buffering parents' impact on teachers. By 1994, a lead story in *This Magazine* was titled "The Irate Parent Industry" and warned, "Look out kids! Mom and Dad want to fire your teachers, cancel recess, and bring back the basics." (September-October, 1994).

The '90s – We'll Change the Learning

The change in the 1990s becomes most dramatic when viewed through the lens of media attention to the schools. The river of advice on how to influence decision-makers, start an alternative school, reform your own school, or change teaching strategies diminished from a full roar to a steady rumble and became part of the background hum of activism and debate. The issues and choices became more finely grained and the possibilities more upbeat. The dominant theme shifted to how children grow, develop and learn, and what roles are played by parents, family and the community. Magazines were filled with advice on how parents could help their children become better learners, assess the approaches to learning on offer in their schools, and turn their homes into supportive places for the work of the schools. Feature articles addressed learning disabilities and processes of innovation in admittedly stretched and overcrowded schools.

By the turn of the decade, as the millennium washed over us, the radical and harsh critiques of systems, schools, and teachers were fading. Articles cautioned parents about pushing their kids too hard, especially in the early years. Parents and their children were being portrayed as a team, a team that could get good at supporting learning at home and innovation in the school. A 1999 cover story in *U.S. News & World Report* was headlined: "How Kids Learn: Faster than you think – but don't push too hard" (September 13th 1999).

As each new wave of change occurred, it carried the old ones forward too, so that there are still people who seek to fundamentally change the system or create alternative schools. But as we move further into the 21st century there are many more who are focused on their day-to-day involvement in their child's or their own learning. Their numbers are growing, as is their interest in how good learning can be created for them and their children.

On a Quest for Good Learning

We are on a quest for good learning, at different levels of meaning and in a myriad of ways. At the level of society, we talk more and more about the centrality of learning to the future success of Canada, whether more narrowly in terms of economic success or in terms of broad social goals. We want to maintain our leadership and the quality of our work in areas such as agriculture, the arts, science and technology. We know that Canada has a distinctive history and set of competencies to build on and offer to the world. Michael Ignatieff summed a few of them up rather nicely, as reported by Christopher Flavelle, at a federal Liberal Party policy convention back in March 2005.

> They are: the emphasis on 'peace, order and good government' in our parliamentary democracy; recognition of minority rights in the Charter of Rights and Freedoms, but with an insistence that ethnic nationalism yield to civic nationalism; and a tradition of progressive experimentation in social programs (*The Walrus*, May 2005).

Wanting to sustain what we're good at and meet the challenges of the future, we have come to value learning and the creation of good learning as much as we have valued the old and worn change levers such as economic development, taxation policies, fiscal strategies, and human resource development. When committees, public gatherings, and think tanks ponder the future of Canada or its cities and regions, learning and its proxy, education, are high on the list of critical factors. The quality of our post-secondary system gets frequent mention; sometimes even the public schools rate a mention.

At other levels closer to home, the search for the right school or teacher and the best choice for our children go on with unflagging energy. In ways hard to map and understand, the myriad efforts of system reform and parental diligence and the initiatives of dedicated learners have the potential to connect the three "bowls" of learning back together. The desire at the grass roots for participatory and co-created learning connects with the new cultural emphasis on good learning as the basis for social and economic well-being. What we all want for Canada, we seek day by day for our children and for ourselves as learners even in the midst of the 'business as usual' around credentials and good test scores. And because we have not yet designed systems to support this new learning, choice continues to be one of the main themes.

But choice with a difference. Our beliefs about choice are shifting, whether as a consumer of material goods, health care or learning. As Robert Reich has pointed out, "the logic of mass production dictated sameness." And:

> The emerging system is starkly different. I have detailed elsewhere the shift, starting in the 1970s and escalating since, from high volume to high *value* production, from standardized to more customized, rapidly improving products and services…(*The Future of Success*, pp. 16, 17).

Depending on how much you love coffee, the following may be a trivial or very non-trivial example, but as of March 2004, Starbucks had "more than 19,000 ways it can serve a cup of coffee" and "five kinds of milk to stir into it." (*USA Today*, in *Social Studies*, *The Globe and Mail*, March 11th, 2004). By 2006, Starbucks had raised the number to 87,000 different combinations. And then there's that dizzying array of television channels that feed into our homes. Everywhere we look, our range of choices is being expanded, and the demand for more choices just keeps growing.

Some observers worry about whether the quest for choice is in conflict with the ideal of a commons, closely related to the ideal of the common school, which is constructed through difficult decisions about values:

> And so, often through the illusion of choice, by believing that we have a choice, by acting as though we have a choice, we make sense of what has happened, we put our own stamp on it, and we insert our story as part of the larger shared narrative. Weaving our story into the larger narrative is an important part of constructing public life.
>
> The difficulty arises when by telling our own story; we unfairly and rudely preempt the tales of others. ...By exercising our right to choice, we may limit the meaningful choices of others (Janice Stein *The Cult of Efficiency*, p. 222).

And indeed, some worrisome effects have already occurred in school choice efforts and pilot programs in the U.S. The opportunities to choose were increased for some and were diminished for others. It is important to remember that the desire and the impetus for choice in the public schools is more a symptom than a solution. Charter, private, and corporate efforts to offer effective and competitive choices in schooling will continue, but they are signals about the emerging change rather than the change itself. And, interestingly, these efforts may lead us deeper into the real task, the creation of a learning commons in Canada and, further, a revitalization of our understanding of and commitment to the commons as a space for citizen involvement and debate.

Toward a New Public Good

The shift will be from traditional public education to a learning commons. It will happen because of new systems that support the co-creation of learning by parents, students, educators, and the community. This development of a learning commons will engage us all in searching and deepening our beliefs and understandings about learning, new ways of working together, and a revitalized focus on the common good – a good that can no longer be assured through traditional institutions.

Continuing to tinker with and reform the public schools we have will not deliver the kind of systems we need to support learning in the 21st century. At best, it would be simply a classic case of too little, too late. At worst, it would distract us from the real work and ensure that opportunities were squandered. The efforts through the last few decades have been heroic, but we are stuck with outdated and, by contemporary standards, seriously flawed system design assumptions. How we got there will be addressed in the next chapter. There is agreement about the challenge in many quarters.

> Indeed, it would not be an exaggeration to say that a major priority for the next five to ten years is the development of radically different approaches to teaching and learning. We might describe the challenge as the invention of a new pedagogy (Michael Barber, *The Learning Game*, p. 270).

Fundamentally new system design assumptions are needed that will help us define and deliver the forms of learning we will be doing together in our society over the next many decades. They are slowly emerging, written into but masked by the changes we see happening around us.

If all of this adds up, substantial numbers of Canadians are ready to go to work with each other. We are ready to begin identifying and refining these new ways to do learning – not privately or alone at home, but together in the public space. There may be a significant percentage of parents who would like to shelter their children at home or have them associating with their own kind in island-like schools based on class, religion or other factors. There may be students who want to learn at a distance or online with very little contact with other students. I suspect that most parents and students know that the most robust, challenging and rewarding forms of learning will be developed in concert with others who share the same values about learning and the energy to create change. Sometime soon, beyond the current crop of home schooling collaboratives, school-change coalitions and associations promoting specific approaches to public education, parents and students will begin getting together with educators and other supporters to get on with this work.

It is a journey about recreating and redesigning learning in the public space, the societal enterprise we have called public education. And this journey will occur in the public space because there are many things at stake and complex issues to address.

> Canadians, like those in many other post-industrial societies, value not only choice and all it brings with it, but also justice, fairness and equity, however we understand and give meaning to these values. The conflict among these values is often intractable and incommensurable. It is because these conflicts are intractable that we turn to conversation in public space, and to those we choose to govern, to set legitimate rules for a conversation that is not about interests, but about principles and values. The legitimacy of this conversation rests on recognized, fair, inclusive and open procedures for deliberation and persuasion, where those who join in reflective discussion are neither manipulated nor intimidated (Janice Stein, *The Cult of Efficiency*, p. 225).

We have been launched on this journey by the combined force of changes in the world and our own desire for something better. As the work encounters barriers and conflicts, we will find that we are recreating and redesigning how open and inviting public spaces and healthy citizen dialogue can serve us as we apply shared ideals to challenges. The search for good learning is inseparable from the search for the public good, a renewal of the particular form of the commons that has distinguished Canadian society.

CHAPTER 3: THE SCHOOLS WE HAVE – NOW HOW DID ALL THAT HAPPEN?

Teaching In the Machine

Back in a time when trains pulled by steam were still new, dusty black Model T's stuttered and barked along Canada's dirt roads, cooking was fueled by wood, and people read by the fluttering light of candles and coal oil, we created a shared mindset about what life in a public school is like. Our basic ideas of what "real" schools look like have changed a little since then, even with the addition of computers. The classic ingredients are classrooms with students sitting in rows, a neatly dressed teacher in charge of instruction at the front of the room, a quantity of textbooks, displays on the wall (if you're my age, you'll remember those maps with the chocolate bars in the corners), and an atmosphere of quiet industry dappled with energetic teacher-led discussions.

These were what I call our "First Schools."

Around the turn of the last century, the story of reality that shaped our school system was narrow in scope and widely shared. Schools were meant to be crucibles of character, turning most young men into reliable and trainable workers while preparing a few for professional careers, and young women into dedicated and skillful homemakers. Without having to consult or compare notes with each other, churches, youth groups and schools could support each other. They worked from similar assumptions. Where I grew up, they often shared the same leadership.

The values were obedience, discipline, good character and a grasp of the basic book learnings that would prepare youth for family and work. A very small percentage went on to finish secondary schooling and higher education. As the *Alberta Teachers' Association's magazine* reports:

> School attendance was itself often a matter of concern because school-aged children were a ready source of labour on farms; so many parents were inclined to send their children to work in their fields as soon as they were physically able.

And indeed, one autumn day in the early part of the last century, my grandfather marched into a classroom in a high school in Yorkton, Saskatchewan, and ordered my father to go back to the farm with him and help with the harvest.

> A student's education was considered adequate if he or she mastered the "3 Rs" – reading, 'riting and 'rithmetic, the equivalent of Grade 6-8. Attending high school was still a rarity (*The ATA Magazine*, Winter 2005).

If we roll forward a few decades, *The Canadian Encyclopedia* reports that by 1939, "There were 40,000 students, representing 5% of the population between the ages of 18 and 24" enrolled in Canada's twenty eight degree granting universities (p. 1, 873).

Into this world stepped two people, Frederick Taylor and John Dewey. There were other significant contributors to public education, but these two are important to this story.

A professional bureaucracy, modeled after railways and postal systems, administered schools. Administration meant predictability and stability. The epithet "faceless bureaucrats" was actually a compliment. Good administration *was* invisible. The machine bureaucracy was supposed to run so smoothly that you would hardly know it was being tended. Frederick Taylor was the American inventor of Scientific Management; the man, as Drucker puts it, who thought of applying knowledge to work, thereby launching a 100-year long "productivity explosion" in the developed economies. (*Post-Capitalist Society*, pp. 34 to 40) Because much of Taylor's research was based on time and motion studies, his method became known as the "stopwatch method" (Raymond E. Callahan, *Education and the Cult of Efficiency*, p. 29).

Callahan observes that Taylor was "an outstanding, creative engineer, as well as a fine scientist", but unfortunately, educational administrators who "*showed no real interest in, or ability to carry out, such painstaking research*" applied his theories to schools. (*Education and the Cult of Efficiency*, p. 40, italics in original). And so the stopwatch man's efficiency theories were somewhat blindly applied to schools and school systems to make them more time saving and cost effective. "School plants" were studied thoroughly to ensure they did not waste time or energy, chalk or toilet paper.

Graded and ability-grouped students and compartmentalized curriculum fit into this industrial model. Standardized schools were the foundation of educational progress. What Larry Cuban and David Tyack have called the shared traditional beliefs or "grammar of schooling," a kind of cultural template or DNA, the public face of public education, became cemented into place (*Tinkering Toward Utopia*, pp. 87 and 135).

John Dewey brought an interest in active and socially relevant learning to this smoothly humming machine world. The result was a movement called progressive education and a wave of experimental schools. The schooling machinery remained intact but the point was made that learning should connect with the real world, even if the world had to be artificially recreated within the walls of the school.

Dewey gave us many profound insights, but for my purposes here, at least the following two ideas. He gave us the idea that schools could be different; that they need not conform to some sort of industrial template or master plan. And he gave us the language and ideas that marked the beginning of a decades-long struggle, the struggle of learning, being able to coexist with schooling in the machine bureaucracy, and the struggle of good teaching to transcend the system. Another piece of the "grammar of schooling," the more private face of public education partially hidden behind the public facade, was formed.

With some variations on the themes, these two stories about creating places for learning have been with us ever since. A quick glance at the early history of North American high schools offers us some good examples of opposing views in the tug of war over how schools ought to work.

Ten Academics and Seven Cardinal Principles

Although high school education became universally available early in the last century, at mid-century, the completion rate was still around only 40 percent. Many efforts were made to define a purpose for high school education that balanced the needs of the culture and the needs of the student. In these early efforts, the student was viewed as a passive consumer and the curriculum as a commodity. The curriculum and school culture was a good fit for a select sub-group – those who were academically inclined and persevered in order to go onward to higher education. There's some feeling that things really haven't changed that much.

> As one survey of American schools after another has confirmed, students are rarely invited to become active participants in their own education. Schooling is typically about doing things to children, not working with them. An array of punishments and rewards is used to enforce compliance with an agenda that students rarely have any opportunity to influence (Alfie Kohn, *Choices for Children: Why and How to Let Students Decide, Phi Delta Kappan*, September 1993).

Tyack and Cuban in *Tinkering Toward Utopia* describe two major reports on the high school developed in the United States. Inevitably, the influence of these reports would have been felt in Canada through teacher training, journals and professional meetings.

The first report came from the Committee of Ten, led by Harvard President Charles William Eliot. The Committee consisted primarily of university academics. They saw their task as tidying up a messy landscape of subjects and courses in order to provide "coherent intellectual training" (p. 50). Tyack and Cuban add:

> ...Eliot and his colleagues believed that all secondary students would be best served by a rigorous academic training, one that offered them some choices of classical or modern subjects. The Committee of Ten saw the high school as an agency for honing intelligence for its own sake but also as an institution for preparing students for careers in a complex and interdependent society. In the next generation, however, secondary education would begin to become a mass institution with a significantly broader mission (*Tinkering Toward Utopia*, p. 50).

The second report was a position paper on the high school entitled *Cardinal Principles of Education*, Tyack and Cuban point out that this time the authors were "mostly specialists in the new field of education" (p. 50).

> Worried about the high drop-out rate of students, educators believed that the high school should offer different training for pupils of "widely varying capacities, aptitudes, social heredity, and destinies in life." The report stressed "activities," "democracy," and "efficiency," and seemed to relegate traditional academic subjects and pedagogy to the scrap heap. It provided an influential rationale for an expanded

and differentiated curriculum that was supposedly adapted to the "new students" of the day (*Tinkering Toward Utopia*, p. 51).

In the same way that the Committee of Ten's report shortly came under attack by progressive educators for its limited view of learning, by the 1950s the exhortations of the Cardinal Principles were being blamed by critics for "the erosion of intellect and the trivialization of culture they saw as endemic in high schools" (*Tinkering Toward Utopia*, p. 52). One of the most stinging attacks came from a university teacher that I remember very clearly for her tough-minded cross-examinations of particular students, the same Dr. Hilda Neatby who made an appearance earlier in this book. Neatby could be very hard on those students she knew were training to be teachers. Years later, in her book *So Little for the Mind*, I found out why.

> The bored "graduates" of elementary and high schools often seem, in progressive language, to be incompletely "socialized." Ignorant even of things that they might be expected to know, they do not care to learn. They lack an object in life; they are unaware of the joy of achievement. They have been allowed to assume that happiness is a goal rather than a by-product.
>
> While business men express themselves in their usual forthright way, university professors explain in more academic language the deficiencies of those whom they are required to produce in three or four short years, invested with a cap and gown, prepared to take their place, in traditional language, as the intellectual leaders of society. These intellectual leaders of the future literally cannot read, write, or think. They are good at word recognition, but to "read, mark, learn and inwardly digest" even simple material is beyond them. They can write, and often type, but too often they cannot construct a grammatical sentence. They can emit platitudes, but they can neither explain nor defend them. They are often as incapable of the use of logic as they are ignorant of its very name. Yet these high school "graduates" are not stupid, or ill-intentioned, or incurably indifferent to what they have never learned to call their duty. They are only lazy, ignorant and unaware of the exacting demands of a society from the realities of which they have been carefully insulated (*So Little For The Mind*, pp. 11-12).

I am sure that Hilda Neatby would prefer to spin in her grave, horrified, rather than actually confront a first-year history class of today – all several hundred of them. But I'll use her diatribe against the soft intellectual climate of the public schools, which she concedes may be an "indulgence in emotional exaggeration," to usher in what I call our "Second Schools."

The Struggle Surfaces

When we gaze into the late fifties and early sixties, we begin to see more clearly the ideas and forces that have shaped the last several decades of public education.

In the late 1950s, John Goodlad published his book *The Non-Graded School*. Goodlad proposed that students should move through the curriculum at their own pace, not in lock step with the rest of the students in a graded classroom. It was a frontal attack on the industrial model of schooling. Non-gradedness was not new, but the idea that all public schools should be reformed in accordance with a grand design, rather than a few experimented with, was new. The book had a major impact and launched reforms in hundreds of schools, mostly elementary, around North America.

At about the same time, the two themes of reform encircling the struggle of learning to transcend schooling began surfacing in the high schools. Their braided paths began in the late 1950s with the launching of Sputnik by the Soviets in 1957 and the emergence of the counter-culture on North American campuses in the early 1960s. On the one hand, the schools were accused of failing to teach the traditional disciplines with rigour, and on the other hand, schools were accused of being mind-numbing and irrelevant to the lives of students.

In 1960 in the U.S., the Students for a Democratic Society (SDS) was founded, initiating some years of intense activism and peaking on December 2, 1964 when 1,500 people at Berkeley occupied Sproule Hall and refused to leave until student activists previously arrested were released. Instead, 773 more students were arrested. Students battled onward for guarantees of greater choice in programs and participation in the running of the university. The impact of this trickled into Canada. It even affected my efforts in the mid-sixties to be the staff advisor to my high school's student newspaper. I found myself caught in the middle of a huge and growing gulf between traditional administration (my school principal) and student power (my student editor).

When the Soviets launched the gleaming little basketball-sized satellite called Sputnik, they also unintentionally launched the first great postwar outcry about the deficiencies and failures of the North American high schools. Waves of new curricula, particularly math and science, began to hit the schools. By the end of the 1950s, waves of reform were rolling across school districts all over North America. Most of the waves originated in the U.S., but many of the shores they washed up on were Canadian.

Within a decade the two stories in our ongoing 20th century struggle had morphed into the now familiar reform agendas. On the one hand, reform as community building and teacher empowerment. On the other hand, reform as scientific and business management. These two themes can be hard to disentangle because in some respects they sound the same. For example, both themes can sound like they are saying, "Free the teachers! Free the teachers from the bad systems they are caught in." Well, they need a closer look.

Reforms based on research into teaching and school leadership have addressed the complexity and richness of possibilities in teaching and learning. Reformers have:

> ➢ Tried to remove the boundaries and boxes in the highly regulated environment of the classroom.

> ➢ Experimented with time and organization so that teachers could focus on individuals and small groupings of students.

> ➢ Invited teachers to share their craft in teacher-managed teacher centres.

> ➢ Asserted that any assessment of teaching effectiveness requires profound knowledge of the learner and the contents of her or his portfolio of growth – growth in many dimensions, knowledge based more on judgment than on measurement.

Reforms based on research into business and management practices have addressed the rapidly rising cost of education, the lack of productivity and the unsatisfactory performance of graduates. Reformers have:

> Characterized teachers as trapped in old systems run by professional bureaucrats and therefore unable to produce results.

> Experimented with choice and moving money directly to the schools and students.

> Urged school systems to stop prescribing methods and organization and to get clear and firm about results.

> Advocated high-stakes testing as a superior and reliable way to assess results and return on investment.

It was a busy few decades. The sound and the fury, although weakened in hurricane-speak to a category four or three, still echoes through the schools.

Advocates on both sides continue to promote their reforms. Innovations such as multi-aged groupings and school-business partnerships form uneasy relationships. Teachers try to sort out the implications of simultaneous proposals for standardized national curricula and tests, and for self-managing schools with student-centred curricula and an array of assessment strategies. The struggle to hold the two stories together has begun to take a serious toll on the schools. With variations, the themes of Taylor and Dewey continue to haunt us right up to the present day. Here's Linda Darling-Hammond writing about "the policy problem" in public education and how overregulation is making teaching "steadily less attractive to talented college students."

> These contrary impulses reflect the two competing theories of school reform currently at work across the country. One theory focuses on tightening the controls: more courses, more tests, more prescriptive curricula, more regulations, and greater enforcement through systems of rewards and more sanctions. The other seeks to build local capacity through stronger teacher education and the development of schools as inquiring, collaborative organizations (*The Right To Learn*, p. 94).

Over the years I have collected magazines whose covers reveal other perspectives of the struggle. I keep them in a file called "Crisis," a name I applied some years back when the word was much favoured by the press in connection with public education. (The word crisis has migrated, and we now hear much about health care and economic crisis.) Their covers display some of the stages in these stories.

- The June 1970 issue of *The Atlantic* is headlined "Murder in the Schoolroom," announcing the beginning of a three-part series by Charles Silberman that, we are promised, will tell us "how the public schools kill dreams and mutilate minds." A young boy sits slumped over his desk in an attitude that could be death by boredom. He is caught in a soft corona of light holding back an encircling mysterious darkness. The large area of relentlessly parallel wooden floorboards of his antique classroom makes him appear small and lost.

- The October 1976 issue of *Saturday Night* is headlined "The Ignorant Canadians." A smiling child stands in front of a blackboard clutching her school supplies. The large notepad features the image of Mickey Mouse. We are warned: "In fifteen years this child will have a B.A. She may not be able to write, spell, talk, think straight – or get a job. The process will cost you about $38,000. Is there anything you can do about it?" (Hilda Neatby arises from her grave and applauds.).

- The cover of the April 20th, 1981 issue of *Newsweek* is a tad more direct, promising to tell, in a special report, "Why public schools are flunking." The cover features the image of a yellow eraser-topped pencil, sharpened and ready for work. It is tied tightly in a knot.

- A baseball bat-wielding Principal Joe Clark dominates the cover of the February 1st, 1988 cover of *Time*, and we are asked, "Is getting tough the answer?" Clark thinks that the answer is yes, delivers some tough love, and sells the film rights to his life story, but as the article promises to explain, the "critics are up in arms."

- By 1990 and the Fall/Winter special edition of *Newsweek*, things have mellowed a bit and we are offered a "Consumer's Handbook" focused on "How to teach our kids." Bart Simpson and his mischievous friends dominate the cover and there is no threatening baseball bat in sight.

- The January 11th, 1993 issue of *Maclean's* offers to explain "What's Wrong At School" and "Why Many Parents Give Failing Grades To

Their Children's Teachers," and the September-October 1994 cover of the schools-friendly *This Magazine* features a pair of grim parents who are "Troublemakers" and "Back-to-Basics Bullies."

➢ By the end of the 1990s, *Time* is much more upbeat, offering images of smiling, adjusted and achieving kids and stories such as "What Makes A Great Student?" (October 19th, 1998) and "So You Want To Raise A Superkid…" (April 30th, 2001).

➢ In 1999 and a few years later, three magazine issues, featuring more upbeat images on their covers, offer help to parents no longer much interested in reform but on the lookout for the best schools. *U.S. News & World Report* offers a special report on "Outstanding American High Schools," (January 16th, 1999), *Newsweek* covers "America's Best High Schools" (May 16th, 2005), and *Maclean's* tells us about "Canada's Best Schools" and "What makes them great (it's not money)" (August 29th, 2005).

➢ A year later, the pressures hitting students and their schools come under scrutiny. *Harper's* depicts a teacher sitting with her students, all rather formally dressed as in the good old days, with the headline "Grand Theft Education: Literacy in the Age of Video Games" (September 2006), *Time* shows us an empty desk with a book and an apple (the fruit, not the computer) and tells us "How To Build a Student for the 21st Century" (December 18th, 2006) and *Maclean's* shows us a student slumped at her desk and declares "Homework Is Killing Kids" (September 11th, 2006).

➢ But then, moving on to the 2010s, *Maclean's* grumbles in tones rhetorical, "Why is it *your* job to teach your kid math?", and peremptory, "Stop Brainwashing Our Kids" (March 19th, 2012) (November 5th, 2012), perhaps signaling that the schools are in for a new round of chastisement.

The issues surrounding school reform played out similarly, although not identically, in the U.S. and in Canada. I think that these magazine covers tap into general themes characteristic to both countries. During it all, the schools continued to be responsive and to innovate. These changes gave a sense of momentum but somewhat obscured the permanence and contradictory nature of the two stories of reform.

The Sound and the Fury

In the 1960s, educators became preoccupied with systems theory. As a graduate student at the University of Oregon in 1971, I got to try my hand at using programmed learning techniques to write units of curriculum…in poetry! In the 1970s, we school bureaucrats discovered modern management and what Donald N. Michael calls planning "technologies" (*Learning to Plan and Planning to Learn*, pp. 75-76). We entered the age of acronyms such as MBO and PPBS. And then, in the 1980s we discovered leadership. Some school administrators, having been steeped in what they liked to call "best knowledge and best practice," created sermons and parables about good teaching and learning. They practiced leadership by carrying their inspirational messages to the classroom. They became, in Bruce Mickleborough's memorable words, a "secular priesthood" (In a speech to the Alberta Teachers' Association Fine Arts Council Conference in 1971). We proudly rode each new wave. One of our school board administrators was frequently heard to assert that managers managed things and leaders led people, and therefore leadership was a more worthy calling than management.

If you were a teacher, you kept your head down, your hopes up, and undoubtedly wished that all of the above would do any of the above well – and well away from your classroom. But it was soon heads up, for technology was on its way with fresh new acronyms, CAI and CMI, and computer literacy, hardware, software, and the World Wide Web. And changes in governance with parent involvement (arm's length), parents as partners (still arm's length), then school councils (elbow length). And changes in teaching and learning with integration of special needs, honouring diversity, and right/left brain research. And changes in roles with teachers as researchers, teachers as leaders, and parents as teachers. And changes in process with advising, facilitating, mentoring, coaching, students having voice, and advocating. And changes in legal/legislative frameworks, community expectations, and demographics.

Thirty-five years on, we still have the story of the familiar industrial age school with its traditional calendar, self-contained classrooms, subjects, grades and report cards. We still have the story of the endless adaptations to social and family changes, new curricula, technology, rising expectations and scarce resources. On the one hand, the school as an efficient and productive machine and on the other hand, the school as an inclusive, caring, learning community.

In the early part of the 21st century, it might be said with Dickens that we have the best of times and the worst of times. As Robert Theobald, quoting a colleague, said, "Things continue to get better and better, and worse and worse, faster and faster." And he adds, "I am both despairing and profoundly hopeful (*Reworking Success*, pp. 7 and 92).

We all know about the getting faster so what's getting better?

Public education in the early part of the 21st century is an unparalleled success story. Since World War II, it has held an increasing percentage of students, absorbed cultural diversity, expanded the range of things taught, responded to technology, survived the battles over reform, sustained overall performance, delivered greater percentages of graduates to post-secondary and remained open and accountable. Its severest critic can walk in the door of almost any school office on almost any school day, ask to talk to the principal or someone in authority, and likely get a polite hearing and maybe even a tour of the school. As Michael Barber says about teachers in the U.K., and he could be describing teachers in Canada or the U.S.: "…there are teachers up and down the country who are changing the world. The sheer, determined professionalism of many teachers is magnificent and rarely conveyed convincingly to the public" (*The Learning Game*, p. 224).

And more pointedly from a Canadian academic, Charles Ungerleider:

> Our neglect of public schools is perverse and malicious. We make impossible demands upon them and strangle them financially. We create trivial changes for the sake of ideology and avoid necessary changes for lack of fortitude. We say their graduates don't measure up and make fatuous comparisons between one public school and another. We belittle their accomplishments. And some Canadians just ignore them.
>
> The paradox is, that despite this treatment, Canadian public schooling has never been more successful. Our public schools are more successful today than they were a decade ago, and more successful

than comparable jurisdictions elsewhere in the world (*The Globe and Mail*, September 2nd 2003).

The problem is not that the schools failed. The problem is that they succeeded. They adapted and are trapped by their success.

What's worse?

It is the price we are paying for still trying to live in both stories of schooling at once. The price is getting higher and higher. Stress is an increasing problem. The traditional roles of teacher and principal are rapidly becoming unsustainable. An article in the *Victoria Times Colonist* warns that, "Various factors are drawing teachers...out of schools and into more tranquil tutoring centers...." (Sarah Schmidt, March 27th 2003) Organizations like the Alberta Teachers' Association are concerned about the number of teachers who plan to leave teaching early in their careers and the remarkably few who would recommend teaching as a career to their children. Robert Reich points out the drop in women entering college who were planning to become schoolteachers from nearly 40 percent in 1968 to 10 percent only six years later (*The Future of Success*, p. 126) The ratio of men to women in the classroom in American schools has been declining and is at a 40-year low (*The Christian Science Monitor*, March 15th, 2005). As the stress grows, so does the issue of teachers' working conditions, which are inevitably linked to students' learning conditions. Working conditions have become a significant battleground in teacher union negotiations.

Schools are developing informal complex systems to keep up with the complexity of change in our society, but there is an increasingly dangerous imbalance nonetheless, particularly in information technology, professional autonomy and support for diverse student needs. The love/hate relationship between the system and its public, although less strident, is still intense. The gaps between our societal conversations about what schools are for, the gaps between a Conference Board and a school board, a parent council and the parents of a student, still create unnecessarily polarized views and angry debates.

Signals from a Dark Heart

There are increasingly strong signals of social breakdown in our schools.

In spite of the dedicated efforts of teachers and principals and the brave talk about learning communities, the efforts to construct healthy learning environments are being increasingly haunted by a growing heart of darkness in our schools. They are in danger of becoming unhealthy places to spend one's formative years. There is a sad irony here. I noted earlier how schools are trapped by success – their capacity to adapt and their overall success in dealing with sweeping change. Schools ought to be the world we dreamed of when youth of my generation suffered through lectures, blackboard notes and worksheets. Most teachers take great pride in making their classrooms into exciting places and engaging their students with learning.

The simple fact is that teachers, students and parents, even given their best efforts, can no longer compensate enough for the essentially 19th century system design assumptions the public schools are built on. In the early grades, it's mainly the parents who feel the frustrations. Many teachers yearn for a better way of being in a learning relationship with children. But as a rule, children are simply not expected to be moving toward the co-creation of learning. A few years ago, Ana Serrano, a key figure in Canada's new media industry, speaking with Myrna Kostash about a new media training program, said, "Our teaching methodology is that H@bitat is not a teaching but a learning space" (*The Next Canada*, p. 82). An interesting distinction, and creating a "learning space" is an attractive idea, but most teachers are charged with and accountable for creating a teaching space. They do, when they can, convert and infuse it into a learning space, the source of many of the magic moments we remember with our favorite teachers. While students may begin to fight back, bully and disengage at increasingly earlier ages, generally they handle their gently regimented days quite well. Sadly and ironically, many public school critics see greater and not-so-gentle regimentation as the answer to any and all problems.

We may have locked ourselves into those 19th century design assumptions in subtle and powerful ways. In *The Ingenuity Gap*, Thomas Homer-Dixon discusses how our high-stakes "meritocratic" standardized testing programs tend to replicate I.Q. tests. They are used as "institutionalized gatekeepers" to allow certain people to move upward in the social hierarchy and achieve power and influence.

> Over time these people, through their decisions and actions, tend to reproduce the institutions and procedures, including the testing procedures, that empowered them, thus putting more of exactly the same kind of people into positions of influence (*The Ingenuity Gap*, p. 219).

It is in the teen years where the 19th century clashes most violently with the 21st. Students appear to be withdrawing their participation in the fiction of needing to be somewhere specific every day at a very specific time so that one specific person can impart some specific bits of knowledge and information to them. They are increasingly angry and frightened at being forced into the company of other young people who feel the same – and equally frustrated about having to be there every day. The considerable capacities of schools to entice and engage young people have very little distance and flex left in them.

> i-at-ro-gen-ic...*adj.* (of a neurosis or physical disorder) caused by the diagnosis, manner, or treatment of a physician or surgeon (*Webster's New Universal Unabridged Dictionary*, p. 704).

Schools are becoming emotionally and intellectually toxic. In medical parlance, they are becoming iatrogenic – producers of the very conditions they seek to overcome, conditions that are toxic to learning. The very qualities of mind and flourishing of consciousness that our culture is now lifting its eyes and its expectations toward are being defeated by the antique design principles of the public schools.

For many, it has been merely vexing and a source of wry nostalgia or grim humour.

> The book that has so intrigued Fortune and other media outlets is called *Most Likely to Succeed at Work: How Work is Just Like High School*, by two San Francisco communication consultants, Wilma Davidson and Jack Doherty.
>
> "School is never over," Doherty argues, and says just look around any office: the sucking up, the bullying, the gossiping, the flirting, the backstabbing...'
>
> The more you look around, the more you realize it's high school for grownups." Roy McGregor, *The Globe and Mail*, October 28th 2003.

and:

> Medford High School, whatever its appearances, was not a school. It was a place where you learned to do – or were punished for failing in – a variety of exercises. The content of these exercises mattered not at all. What mattered was form, repetition, and form. You filled in the blanks, conjugated, declined, diagrammed, defined, outlined, summarized, recapitulated, positioned, graphed. It did not matter what: English, geometry, biology, history, all were the same. The process treated your mind as though it were a body part capable of learning a number of protocols, then repeating, repeating. If you'd done what you should have at Medford High, the transition into a factory, into an office, into the Marines would be something you'd barely notice; it would be painless (Mark Edmundson, *The Teacher Who Opened My Mind*, Utne Reader, Jan-Feb 2003, p. 74).

The sad irony here is that the condemnation of a clearly conventional high school is contained in a tribute to a teacher who stood apart from the mind-numbing routines and invited out the desire to learn. As Noddings observes:

> Schools today are not supportive places for children with genuine intellectual interests. With rare exceptions, they are not supportive places for students with *any* genuine or intrinsic interests (*The Challenge to Care in Schools*, p. 60).

In the last two decades there has been an increasing wariness of difference and free expression. The origin of this wariness is likely a mixture of fear about the possibility of extreme situations in schools and frustration over the difficulty in predicting and preventing these kinds of events. Certainly in the U.S, and to some degree in Canada, this mixture led to the introduction of so-called zero-tolerance policies which, in turn, led to greater restrictions and penalties such as suspension and expulsion.

On March 9, 2004, 14-year-old students' rights and freedoms of expression in Canada had a bad day. Two events were covered on that same date in *The Globe and Mail*. The first is an editorial entitled, *Where's the danger in a student's kirpan?*

> In saying that public safety takes precedence over religious freedom, Quebec's highest court stated the obvious last week. But in barring a

> 14-year-old Sikh student from wearing his kirpan, a ceremonial dagger, to his public school, the Court of Appeal made a grievous error. It accepted the most speculative of dangers as a reason for undermining religious freedom, a freedom explicitly protected in both the Quebec and Canadian charters of rights. ... In theory, the wearing of kirpans violates well-intentioned school policies against the carrying of knives or weapons. In practice, however, when an Ontario human-rights inquiry headed by Gunther Plaut examined this issue in 1990, it found not a single incident of kirpan-related violence in a Canadian school in 100 years (*The Globe and Mail*, March 9th 2003).
>
> (That student, Gurbaj Multani, won the right to wear his kirpan from the Supreme Court of Canada, but by 2013 was considering leaving Quebec due to the restrictions being proposed in the Charter of Quebec Values. *The Globe and Mail*, October 22nd 2013).

And just to give parents who are anxious about their sons' skills with eye-liner something more to worry about:

> Grace Yates figured her 14-year-old son Kevin was just going through a phase when he grabbed some makeup, marked heavy lines under his eyes that appeared to drip black tears down his cheeks and headed off to school. ... But when officials from Kevin's junior high school in Calgary called home recently to complain that the Grade nine student's appearance was bothering other students, and threatened him with suspension and perhaps even expulsion, Mrs. Yates was enraged. 'At first I couldn't believe it,' she said. 'It's not like he's slashing tires or skipping school.' Now, Kevin and his family are locked in a fight with Bob Edwards Junior High School and the Calgary Board of Education over what's an appropriate appearance in the classroom (*The Globe and Mail*, March 9th 2004).

But then, Kevin's Mom didn't go to school when being a "Goth" became associated with gunfire in the school cafeteria. And, according to the news story, Kevin's principal found herself under some serious pressure from other parents, pressure that had little to do with style and much to do with their children being at risk. Of course, being 14 years old isn't what it used to be when I started teaching. I suspect we are somewhat baffled by the worldly and otherworldly lives of teens.

David C. Berliner and Gene V. Glass have more recent examples of bizarre over-reactions to children. They describe the suspension of a five-year-old for making a "terroristic threat" involving a bubble gum; a six-year-old ordered to reform school for bringing a weapon to school, his new Cub Scout utensils; and a 13-year-old suspended for tossing a rubber band, a weapon, onto his teacher's desk, thence assault with a weapon. Extreme examples, but illustrative of the fix the schools are getting into. (*50 Myths and Lies that Threaten America's Public Schools*, p. 133). Berliner and Glass go on to say that "most school systems recognize that zero-tolerance policies have not lived up to the promise to make schools safer" (p. 137). Some recent data show that school suspensions are dropping, in part because school systems are restricting the kinds of offences that can lead to expulsion.

In Extremis

All of this leads us on a brief journey into two nasty back alleys of school life, bullying and violent crime. Although it is *extremely unlikely* that children or youth will encounter a shooting or hostage taking in their school, the fact that such incidents do occur at all is a source of parental fear and protectiveness and student wariness and stress. In some communities and neighbourhoods, social stress and breakdown is felt to be severe enough that violent events in schools are just waiting to happen.

Many competing arguments and reasons are given. Poverty, poor parenting, family breakdown, peer pressures, television, movies, video games and other factors all get their share of the blame. Interestingly, very few commentators raise the issue of the institutional environment of schools as a cause. Many, in fact, call for greater discipline if not outright regimentation and more reliance on the juvenile justice system. Maybe, just maybe, it is time to admit that the forced mixing of kids in what are still, in spite of the best efforts of teachers, quasi-'total institutions' (Goffman, *Asylums*), creates a volatile tipping point toward brutality and violence. It is the place where the postmodern video-gaming generation meets the industrial-schooling machine, a clash of cultures bound to produce frustration and anger. Certainly schools are much more open and accommodating than they used to be, but like some computer models of global warming warn us, it seems that only a few degrees rise in the school climate, particularly where there are heat waves of bullying, can produce spectacularly violent storms. The temperature has been rising for some time.

In 1974, Congress mandated that the U. S. Department of Health, Education, and Welfare conduct a national survey to examine the prevalence of school crime and identify the perpetrators. The study, *Violent Schools-Safe Schools: The Safe School Study Report to the Congress*, found that 40% of the robberies and 36% of the assaults on teenagers took place in schools. The highest rates of victimization were found in junior high schools, the perpetrators of the crime being students. More than 100,000 teachers were threatened with physical harm, and each month an estimated 5,200 teachers were physically attacked. Teachers were five times as likely as students to be seriously injured (School Safety: What's Being Done and Where Is It Going? *Issues Challenging Education*, Horizon Site, University of North Carolina at Chapel Hill).

If memory serves, that report to the U.S. Congress crossed my desk in Calgary in the mid-70s. It was an impressively thick volume and an eye-opener. The first serious actions to secure schools against crime and violence occurred in the U.S. later in that decade. We became used to the shocking images of police and their dogs patrolling school hallways. Students were locked in and were not permitted exit and re-entry during the school day. These early attempts to create security in schools were countered by calls for greater democracy and consultation with students and parents. Codes of behaviour were developed using collaborative processes. Student courts were convened to mete out justice on specific misbehaviours.

Interestingly, since that report was written, in Canada and the U.S., the rates of violent crime have fallen. The crime rate in Canada has fallen to its lowest point since 1972 (*The Globe and Mail*, July 26th 2013). However, there has been a trend toward rare but extreme incidents of violence in schools. We now live in the lengthening shadows of Taber and Columbine. The shadows not only include the murders of young people, but the often-angry reactions focused on the lives of schools. Zero tolerance, in spite of doubt about its effectiveness, remains in vogue, and a comfort to those who think that the courts are too lenient with youth and there should be "adult time for adult crime." Security issues are paramount and distort the community life of schools and the relationships between students and teachers. This is a plea from a large organization of teachers and head teachers in the U.K.:

> Pupils should undergo 'airport-style' spot searches for knives and guns in an effort to cut the level of violence in schools, a teachers' union says. The NASUWT, which has 223,500 members, wants 'zero tolerance measures put in place, in light of a 'growing weapon-carrying culture'. Last November, Luke Walmsley, 14, was stabbed to death in a school corridor in North Somercotes, Lincolnshire. NASUWT general secretary Eamonn O'Kane said police should screen pupils using X-ray equipment. "Unfortunately, such strategies are necessary, now that the increasing use of weapons in crime on the streets is threatening to disturb the relative calm and security of schools (*BBC News*, February 25th 2004).

It is important to remember that in spite of the rise in extreme violence such as shootings in schools in recent years, violent incidents in schools are still rare. The rate of youth violence in our society generally does not seem to be increasing. A 1998 *Utne Reader* article cites a 1997 study by the National Centre for Juvenile Justice stating that "today's violent youth commits the same number of violent acts as his/her predecessor of 15 years ago." The same article cites a 1997 Justice Department report that states that violent juvenile offenders "are not significantly younger than those of 10 or 15 years ago." (*Utne Reader*, Sept.-Oct. 1998). The article laments the "draconian" crackdown on kids and the policy mantra of zero tolerance, a mantra that may be running out of steam according to an article in *The Globe and Mail* entitled *Why tolerance for 'zero tolerance' is running out* (January 13th 2007). A report in *The Christian Science Monitor* tells of a significant reduction in school violence:

> Between 1992 and 2002, violent crime in schools fell 50 percent, from 48 victimizations per 1,000 students in 1992 to 24 per 1,000 in 2002, according to the joint report from the Bureau of Justice Statistics and the National Center for Education Statistics. It's a striking decline - one that mirrors a national drop in crime overall (December 6th, 2004).

In an update almost a year later, the *Monitor* observed the same trend.

Some Canadian data suggest that children may be the most at risk after they walk out of the school in the afternoon. Statistics Canada reports that:

> Police data showed that during the 2003 school year children aged six to 13 were at the greatest risk of physical assault during the four-hour

period between 3 p.m. and 7 p.m. About four out of every 10 physical assaults occurred during this interval (*The Daily*, April 20th, 2005).

Far more worrisome is the dramatic rise in the last two decades of youth tormenting youth.

> It is estimated that bullying incidents happen in the average school every seven minutes in the yard, and every 25 minutes inside – each lasting about 37 seconds. The technique can include hitting, kicking, swearing, name-calling, mocking, racial comments, any repetitive and aggressive behaviour that leaves its victims in tears, or withdrawn in fear (Anne Trueman, Back To School, *Vancouver Sun*, August 15th, 2002).

A 1999 victimization in schools study of over 2,000 secondary students done by the Canadian Research Institute for Law and the Family found that "more than half (54 percent) said they had been victimized at least once within the past school year" (*Calgary Herald*, April 20th, 2002). Many teens have switched schools; some have taken their own lives. Back in 2002, shocking reports told of one teen who tried to kill herself twice in the same year, and another teen, Dawn-Marie Wesley, who succeeded. She hanged herself after being threatened on the telephone by one of her tormenters (*The Globe and Mail*, March 30th, 2002). More recently, we have all become familiar with the tragic stories of Amanda Todd and Rehtaeh Parsons, suicides and victims of relentless and vicious online bullying. The Canadian Institutes of Health Research (CIHR), citing a number of research sources, states "at least one in three adolescent students in Canada have reported being bullied recently" and looking at the school experiences of adult Canadians, "38% of males and 30% of females reported having experienced occasional or frequent bullying" (see http://www.cihr-irsc.gc.ca/e/45838.html). And now the problem has leapt into cyberspace with the rising incidence of cyber bullying. *Maclean's* cites the Media Awareness Network's report that "a quarter of young Canadian Internet users report having received material that said hateful things about others" (*Maclean's*, May 24th, 2004). The CIHR reports that "girls are more likely to be bullied on the Internet than boys" and "the most common form of cyber-bullying involved receiving threatening or aggressive e-mails or instant messages, reported by 73% of victims" (see http://www.cihr-irsc.gc.ca/e/45838.html).

Almost every school now has some kind of program or student engagement aimed at raising awareness about the damage of bullying and taking steps to stem the tide. Their efforts are being met with calls to do more and invoke criminal prosecution. But the tide is heavy and deep and has been running the other way for some time. As a result, teachers do not feel safe, nor do the students. "A survey of violence against teachers in Scotland's schools has found an average of three incidents each day in term time" (*BBC News*, November 2nd, 1999). *USA Today* reports "70% of students (grades one - eight) in an online poll conducted by Scholastic publications say they don't feel safe in school" (March 15th, 2001). It is important to stress again; that violence is not out of control in our schools. But the fact is that schools increasingly breed the kinds of fears, frustrations and behaviours described here. There are no easy explanations such as kids are kids, same as they have always been – we have just started paying attention. It is time to ask the question: Is the institution itself rapidly becoming the critical part of the problem? Some sobering signals to ponder:

- Alongside the monkey bars, lockers and lunch rooms, several hundred school districts in the United States now feature police officers patrolling the corridors armed with tasers, high voltage stun guns (*The Globe and Mail*, May 27th, 2004).

- It is a sign of the times that schools are practicing lockdowns – a 21st century take on sixties' bomb drills when schoolchildren dived under desks to protect themselves from the fallout of nuclear attack – as they have fire drills for years (*The Globe and Mail*, October 18th, 2004).

- In the United States, about 160,000 children miss school every day for fear of being bullied, according to the National Association of school psychologists. Some of these children endure rides on buses where bullies have the run (*The Christian Science Monitor*, April 19th, 2005).

- A middle school in Boulder, Colorado, banned hugging, suggesting that students high-five instead, and a high school in Pennsylvania prohibited students from carrying any kind of bag aside from lunch bags, which will be inspected. The Clovis, New Mexico, police locked down a middle school, closed off several streets, and placed officers on rooftops before discovering that what they thought was a weapon carried by a student was actually a thirty inch burrito (*Harper's Weekly*, May 3rd, 2005).

➤ Four in 10 Ontario teachers have been the targets of verbal abuse, physical threats or intimidation by their students, according to a study being released today." "The verbal abuse, racial and sexual slurs, and threats of physical assault have been so severe that more than 20 percent of teachers say they have sought professional help, the survey found (*The Globe and Mail*, September 26th, 2005).

➤ The terrifying ordeal of a teen-age girl who was allegedly sexually assaulted and harassed for 18 months in her own high school may have lifted the lid on a little-discussed aspect of youth violence in Toronto (*The Globe and Mail*, November 14th, 2005).

➤ Six boys at a small Alaskan school were arrested last weekend on suspicion of planning to carry out a Columbine-style massacre. ...The arrests came two days after five teenagers in Kansas were arrested on suspicion of planning a similar massacre last Thursday, the seventh anniversary of the Columbine high school killings... (*The Guardian Weekly*, April 28th, 2006).

➤ ...a 13-year-old boy was treated at a psychiatric hospital after a ... now well known, humiliating video of him posing as Star Wars character Darth Maul was illegally obtained and downloaded by classmates ... (*The Tyee*, May 21st, 2007).

➤ LOCKDOWN, Threat forces security alert at two Regina high schools; afternoon classes cancelled for hundreds of students (Headline from *Regina Leader-Post*, April 20th, 2007).

➤ The percentage of teens who say they attend high schools with drug problems has increased from 44 percent to 61 percent since 2002, according to a study released...by Columbia University's National Centre on Addiction and Substance Abuse (*The Christian Science Monitor*, August 17th, 2007).

> Parents have a new item to add to their kids' back-to-school supplies list: the bulletproof backpack. The response, says [MJ Safety Solutions], has been overwhelming (*Calgary Herald*, August 21st, 2007).

> …another tactic has been borrowed from the private sector: club bouncers and other tough nuts are being employed as temporary teachers to keep classrooms in order. Recruitment agencies are actively scouting for the bouncers, along with ex-soldiers and former police officers. Applicants do not need any teaching qualification to cover for absent regular staff (*The Guardian Weekly*, April 17th, 2009).

> A B.C. high-school student's English assignment about an automatic firearm for protection in a post-apocalyptic world with zombies and cannibalism led police to close the school last Friday after Internet gossip misinterpreted the story as a threat (*The Globe and Mail*, March 23rd, 2010).

> Shock and anger spread yesterday through a rural Massachusetts town where a prosecutor has charged nine teenagers with bullying an Irish immigrant girl who later committed suicide (*The Globe and Mail*, March 31st, 2010).

> Using technology designed to protect U.S. troops, a Maryland company that makes bulletproof whiteboards has contracted with a university seeking to offer its professors greater protection in the event of a school shooting (*CNN*, August 17th, 2013).

A sad sample but so it goes. Has the picture changed in recent years? There are varying reports, hopeful and discouraging, on the kind and number of incidents, along with a consistent sense that the school day has changed for the worse for many of our young people.

> Half of all 14-year-olds in British schools are being bullied, and so-called cyber bullying is now the most common form of abuse, according to a survey.

> The study, by the National Centre for Social Research, was based on a sample of 15,000 children. Researchers found that many teenagers try to stop their parents from getting involved or telling their schools.

Cyber bullying – sending abusive or mocking messages by mobile phone, email or on websites – is now as common as the age-old teenage practice of name-calling (*The Guardian Weekly*, November 20th, 2009).

The percentage of American children being bullied by peers has dropped sharply, likely because of the success of anti-bullying campaigns, according to a U.S. study. The study, funded by the U.S. Department of Justice, found that the percentage of children who reported being physically bullied over the past year had declined from nearly 22 percent in 2003 to under 15 percent in 2008. The percentage reporting they had been assaulted by other youths, including their siblings, dropped from 45 percent to 38.4 percent. (*CBC News*, March 4th, 2010).

For students across the country, lockdowns have become a fixture of the school day, the duck-and-cover drills for a generation growing up in the shadow of Columbine High School in Colorado and Sandy Hook Elementary School in Connecticut. Kindergartners learn to hide quietly behind bookshelves. Teachers warn high school students that the glow of their cell phones could make them targets. And parents get regular text messages from school officials alerting them to lockdowns.

School administrators across the country have worked with police departments in recent years to create detailed plans to secure their schools, an effort that was redoubled after the December 2012 shootings in Newtown, CT.

Even without a direct threat, schools will default to a lockdown. A high school in the San Francisco Bay Area was locked down last week as the police in the area hunted for a carjacking suspect (*The New York Times*, January 16th, 2014).

A *CNN* news report takes a look at incidents involving "a minor or adult actively shooting inside or near a school" in the 18 months between the December 2012 Sandy Hook shooting and a more recent shooting at an Oregon high school. *CNN* followed up on claims of 74 incidents over that period of time and found that only 15 of the 74 incidents were comparable to Sandy Hook and the Oregon high school. "That works out to about one such shooting every five weeks, a startling figure in its own right." The *CNN* list excludes "personal arguments, accidents and alleged gang activities and drug deals" (*CNN*, June 19th, 2014). To add to the pressure, lawsuits against school boards for failing to protect their children from violence and bullies are becoming more frequent. As school boards and governments struggle to find ways to deal with bullying, some researchers are concerned that anti-bullying programs do not work as well as they should.

The climate of fear, and perhaps a yearning for bulletproof backpacks, is not restricted to youth or the hallways of their schools.

> ...Britain has become a place increasingly fearful of its teenage population, a forthcoming report will warn. Britons are more likely than any other Europeans to blame young people for antisocial behaviour, according to extracts from a study by the Institute for Public Policy Research (IPPR) released last weekend. They are also less inclined to intervene if they find teenagers causing trouble. Last year more that 1.5 million Britons thought about moving house to escape young people hanging around, and 1.7 million avoided going out after dark for the same reason, the report finds (*The Guardian Weekly*, October 27th and November 2nd, 2006).

This is a sad commentary on the state of our schools and our views about youth. It should be a wake-up call, not an invitation for further rounds of condemnation.

Light in the Shadows

All of the above might seem to be saying that the kids have somehow "gone bad." Well actually, they have not. Here's Neil Howe and William Strauss responding to research that finds today's young people more selfish and narcissistic than previous generations.

> No matter what teens say on surveys, there is scant evidence that they act more selfishly. In fact, the trends in youth behaviour support the opposite conclusion – that Millennials have much greater regard for one another, their parents, and the community than Generation Xers or baby boomers had at the same phase of life (*The Christian Science Monitor*, March 5th, 2007).

Howe and Strauss give a number of examples of counter trends. They would not surprise us. We all know or have heard of teens that volunteer, play a helping role in their own communities and just make sure they are there for each other when there is a need, such as the Boston teens who founded Interfaith Action (now YouthLEAD), a program that builds "relationships among religious faiths in their community" (*The Christian Science Monitor*, October 24th, 2007). Students are the first in line to express a yearning for schools as a safe and secure place to be. They do not want draconian rules, but they do want standards and expectations with reasonable and certain consequences for people who ignore them. They do not want to live in a climate of enforcement and fear, but they do want their schools to be free from intruders, bullying and violence, such as the Vancouver secondary school students who have launched an experiment in restorative justice (*Vancouver Sun*, November 19th, 2009). They want to know that there is an appropriate justice system operating in their school, preferably collaborative so that students have helped shape it, and that it is communicated and practiced. Many are concerned that their schools will go a bit overboard and add dollops more security and zero tolerance to the fragile blend of safe and caring.

The debates do and will continue. How well do we understand these complex places called schools? The hopes and fears of students echo in the minds and hearts and the writings of legions of academics who study the schools. The struggle continues to understand the schools we have.

We have a growing torrent of challenges emerging across a wide spectrum of change, improvement and development in our schools and school systems. The myriad research centres, foundations and faculties are working with energy and commitment to shed more light on student learning, school improvement, and systems of support. They bring their quests for profound knowledge into the schools and change the ways that teachers and students work with each other. Very few issues have escaped their attention. In spite of the inevitable frustrations over moving theory into practice and creating professional learning communities in schools, they constantly look ahead over the incoming waves and white caps toward new research challenges.

At the American Educational Research Association's annual meetings, which I attended for many years, research from around the world was shared at often packed sessions, with note scribbling academics sitting cross-legged on the floor or standing against the walls. Americans learned about the fate of Thatcherian school reforms in England while Canadians heard about the successes and failures of teacher evaluation and accountability policies in the United States. It was all great, except...

I was always haunted by a feeling that we were all talking about something we had inherited from a distant past, even when the topic was very contemporary, such as online learning. That a huge amount of effort was going into small increments of improvement in the schools. That we sat in the swelling and lengthening shadows of the huge challenges looming over the schools. That so much more was needed and still needs to be done. While acknowledging the improvement in educational research in the U.K., Michael Barber states:

> ...there is no sense anywhere of a research strategy in education: where are the frontiers of our knowledge about education? (*The Learning Game*, p. 220).

Where indeed? Especially when the whole enterprise may be facing a massive frontier that calls many, if not most, of its foundational assumptions into question.

In the meantime, the search for ways to make the current system more effective must continue. It would be a breach of trust to do otherwise. And every day, legions of students set out for school hoping that it is the day that something special happens to make education just a bit more exciting and meaningful in a safer and more caring space.

CHAPTER 4: EFFECTIVE LEARNING

What is the kind of learning we seek? What are the characteristics of learning we are coming to value as a culture? How does a new approach to learning connect with being creative? Or productive? It is time to say more about these questions.

It would be inappropriate to try to provide even a brief history of learning or developments in learning theory when so many better sources are available. But it is important to understand that our view of what we regard as good learning is shifting. Our beliefs about our cultural context and the importance of learning, the sources of influence on learning, and the ways learning can be developed and be part of our lives, are expanding. The following is intended to provide a glimpse of some shifting patterns. We have benefited greatly from the work of pioneering scholars, but we are no longer as inclined, for example, to use Skinnerian behaviourism as a basis for designing systems of human learning and growth. The pioneers and the researchers have given us our foundation, but we are moving on.

The voice of respected educator and researcher, Nel Noddings, helps us to see with greater clarity what is needed:

> Classrooms should be places in which students can legitimately act on a rich variety of purposes, in which wonder and curiosity are alive, in which students and teachers live together and grow. I, too, believe that a dedication to full human growth – and we will have to define this – will not stunt or impede intellectual achievement, but even if it might, I would take the risk if I could produce people who would live non-violently with each other, sensitively and in harmony with the natural environment, reflectively and serenely with themselves. To make real changes in education and escape the dull tick-tock of pendulum swings, we have to set aside the deadly notion that the schools' first priority should be intellectual development. Further, we must abandon the odd notion that any institution – family, school, church, business – has one and only one stable, main goal that precludes the

establishment and pursuit of other goals (*The Challenge To Care In Schools*, p. 12).

There is an inspiring vision! How do we get from here to Nodding's there? And what might learning be like when we get there?

Old Learning for an Old Consciousness

In the mid-1960s, John Carroll described, in a much-quoted article, a multi-layered and integrated model of school learning. Carroll was attempting to untangle a messy web of concepts in educational psychology and to capture, in a simple model, the factors that affect success in school learning and their interaction. Early in the article, he defines the concept at the core of his model, the learning task.

> The learner's task of going from ignorance of some specified fact or concept to knowledge or understanding of it, or of proceeding from incapability of performing some specified act to capability of performing it, is a learning task. To call it a task does not necessarily imply that the learner must be aware *that* he is supposed to learn or be aware of *what* he is supposed to learn, although in most cases it happens that such awarenesses on the part of the learner are desirable (*A Model of School Learning*, Teachers College Record, 1963, 64, p. 723).

Carroll goes on to caution that his model is not intended to apply to goals that "do not lend themselves to being considered as learning tasks." Examples he gives are "attitudes and dispositions" such as "tolerance for persons of other races or creeds, respect for parental or legal authority, or attitudes of fair play." These are "thought to be largely a matter of emotional conditioning or of the acquisition of values and drives." He also cautions that "in actual school practice, the various tasks to be learned are not necessarily treated as separate and distinct…" (p. 724).

Carroll's ideas were enormously important and led to the development of teaching innovations around "time on task" and "mastery learning." Although the model was not about learning theory as normally understood, it was a powerful tool for designing individual learning processes. It was designed to address the kinds of learnings that are most easily assessed by diagnostic, classroom, and standardized tests.

Looking back at Carroll's model reminds us that much has changed. Notice the siloed or fragmented depiction of how the mind, learning and the classroom work. Although awareness is said to be desirable, the learner, at least in theory, may not even need to be aware of the need for or the content of the learning. Some kinds of learning involving values and beliefs can be seen as disconnected or separate from the learning of content. And the family and the community are distantly or indirectly connected to the learning.

Notice the distance between Carroll's model and Nodding's ideas about "a dedication to full human growth" given in the quote above.

Carroll's model is still a powerful analytic tool and in actual classroom practice some of the "disconnects" mentioned above are dealt with. But, as one writer has put it, "changes in the global economy of the last 30 years and the need to focus on additional outcome measures beyond the achievement in basic skills, point to the need to broaden the scope of important variables" (W. Huitt, *Overview of Classroom Processes*, Educational Psychology Interactive). The Carroll model fits with an era when we could comfortably view the school as something that can be understood more as an efficient machine that delivers learning and less as an organic part of child and family life.

Far from disdaining Carroll's work, we do, as they say in science, stand on the shoulders of giants. But time moves on. Let us have a look at a more contemporary view of learning.

Mindful and Mindless

I am grateful to Ellen J. Langer for the above distinction, which is explored thoroughly and with great clarity in her book *The Power of Mindful Learning*. Early in her book, Langer offers a list of "seven pervasive myths, or mindsets, that undermine the process of learning."

1. The basics must be learned so well that they become second nature.

2. Paying attention means staying focused on one thing at a time.

3. Delaying gratification is important.

4. Rote memorization is necessary in education.

5. Forgetting is a problem.

6. Intelligence is knowing "what's out there."

7. There are right and wrong answers (p. 2).

Langer goes on to say that "These myths undermine true learning. They stifle our creativity, silence our questions, and diminish our self-esteem."

Although Langer does not carry her thinking forward and express it as possibilities for new systems to deliver mindful learning, her theories and findings are of great importance in shedding light on how learning happens. Their effect in any learning environment would be significant. And, Langer cautions, "The ideas offered here to loosen the grip of these debilitating myths are very simple. Their fundamental simplicity points to yet another inhibiting myth: that only a massive overhaul can give us a more effective educational system" (p. 2). I agree that it would be wrong to perpetuate this myth. I hope that some of the things I have said about getting past the battles over school reform make my position clear. We should stop trying to overhaul, massively or otherwise, the system and its people. We should step forward into a new world of possibilities for learning.

The problem in part is that we are trapped in our metaphor of the school system as a machine that delivers learning. The myths that Langer describes are almost predictable if our system design mentality is oriented to command and control processes in a machine bureaucracy. They stand in sharp contrast to what we know about learning in our lived lives, our tacit knowledge of good learning. We should ask why, if the myths are so fraudulent and the answers so simple, we have uncritically accepted them for so many decades. We should ask why teachers have had to struggle for so long within this machine metaphor to foster and nurture learning driven by curiosity and initiative.

A gentle revision to professional practice, using research such as this, is well and good. It is part of the process of continuous improvement. The implementation of changes that are research-based is central to the work of any profession. We would be unwise, however, to leave in place a system that has shown its great capacity to grind innovation down and return us to crude and simplistic arrangements for providing schooling.

New Learning for a New Consciousness

With these two time-bound and contrasting views of learning presented above in mind, I would like to return to the three characteristics of human consciousness that I mentioned in Chapter One. I would like to say more about how these characteristics relate to the kind of learning I am about to describe.

You will recall that I described three characteristics of human consciousness: being purposeful and ideal seeking, seeing ourselves as actors in our own lives, and being genetically shaped and equipped to figure things out. These central characteristics have undoubtedly been available to us through most of human history. At times, they may have been latent, languishing without encouragement or development, or quelled by the kinds of social and organizational contexts people lived in. Individual variation has played a role too. Through time, from before the worlds of Stonehenge and tipi circles to the wired global village, we have seen an increasing expression of these central qualities of being human.

In our contemporary world, we are reaching for yet higher levels of human development and cultural maturity. It is dawning on us that we require new uses of the mind and an increasingly robust and adaptive intelligence to enable us to take advantage of the problems and opportunities of our time and place in history. We need young minds that are willing not only to take responsibility for their own learning but also to learn how to create learning for themselves, both new learning and new personalized versions of learning already out there. We need young minds that, as they mature, embody a 21st century version of traditional wisdom – they see what needs to be done for the greater good and set about doing it without having to be given permission. After all, many feel that young people are far too adept at finding out all the wrong things. Let's give them the support and the opportunity they need so that they may direct their considerable talents and energy toward the daunting puzzles and prognoses of our times.

I will say more about change in the next chapter. Here I will just say that this emerging sense of urgency about learning arises from feeling driven more than feeling in control. The number and intractability of complex problems intimidates us. As Thomas Homer-Dixon puts it:

> ...most of us feel, at least on occasion, that we are losing control; that issues and emergencies, problems and nuisances and information – endless bits of information – are converging on us from every direction; and that our lives are becoming so insanely hectic that we seem always behind, never ahead of events. Unexpected connections among places and people, among macro and micro events, connections that we barely understand in their true dimensions, weave themselves around us. Most of us also sense that, just beyond our view, immense, uncomprehended, and unpredictable forces are operating, such as economic globalization, mass migrations, and changes in Earth's climate. Sometimes these forces are visible; more often they flit like shadows through our consciousness and then disappear again, behind the haze of our day-to-day concerns (*The Ingenuity Gap*, p. 16).

And Ronald Wright:

> Our main difference from chimps and gorillas is that over the last 3 million years or so, we have been shaped less and less by nature, and more and more by culture. We have become experimental creatures of our own making.
>
> This experiment has never been tried before. And we, its unwitting authors, have never controlled it. The experiment is now moving very quickly and on a colossal scale (*A Short History of Progress*, p. 30).

On a global scale, we are moving, haltingly, from what Walter Truett Anderson called "global theatre" toward a truer sense of a global civilization.

> It is a world coming together – a global civilization, the first that has ever existed, emerging into being before our very eyes – but one that seems to be, at the same time, in the process of falling apart. It is doing neither and both; it is becoming a system that is not organized according to belief as we once knew it. We may not yet have a global civilization that we can recognize as such, but we clearly have a global theatre: for the first time ever, all people are more or less capable of knowing they inhabit the same world, and more or less aware of what is going on in it (*Reality Isn't What It Used to Be*, pp. 232-233).

We can no longer sit safely sequestered in front of various glowing screens and dispassionately watch events. Thanks to readily accessible media, we are now reminded daily of our many real connections to the planet. Our views are informed by talented and committed people who take us much closer to events than our eyes or cameras carefully focused on the world could. We are invited to ponder the connections from Africa to our sense of justice and compassion by Stephen Lewis and Romeo Dallaire; connections from China and Africa to our personal health by doctors and public health officials who study the threats of SARS and Ebola; connections from the U.S. and Japan to the jobs in the automobile, housing and lumber industries by economists and cabinet ministers; connections from tar sands and burning rain forests to our climate, air and water by David Suzuki; and connections from the Middle East and other parts of the world to our own beliefs and sense of safety and security by Janice Stein and Gwynne Dyer.

We are increasingly aware that we as individuals and Canada as a society have important decisions to make in the near future about how we will live with one another in an increasingly precious country in an increasingly smaller world. We know that we cannot and should not run in front of events. We also know that dropping out and living more simply will not magically put a protective moat around us and keep the bigger world at bay. We are coming to realize that new uses of the mind are required. We should not be surprised, for there have been signals.

A Club of Rome report, *No Limits To Learning*, sounded a prescient warning at the end of the 1970s about the growing "human gap" that learning, with increasing urgency, would have to bridge. The "human gap" is "the distance between growing complexity and our capacity to cope with it." The authors emphasize that the fundamental shift in the human predicament or "world problematique" arises from the fact that "contemporary complexity is caused predominantly by human activities," and not by the forces of nature as in past eras (pp. 6-7). Note the compelling voice of urgency and hope from three and a half decades ago:

> The fact that contemporary learning contributes to the deteriorating human condition and a widening of the human gap cannot be ignored. Learning processes are lagging appallingly behind and are leaving both individuals and societies unprepared to meet the challenges posed by

> global issues. This failure of learning means that human preparedness remains underdeveloped on a worldwide scale. Learning is in this sense far more that just another global problem: its failure represents, in a fundamental way, the issue of issues in that it limits our capacity to deal with every other issue in the global problematique. These limitations are neither fixed nor absolute. Human potential is being artificially constrained and vastly underutilized – so much so that for all practical purposes there appear to be virtually no limits to learning (p. 9).

This is an analysis that is still relevant and has been powerfully picked up in the work of Thomas Homer-Dixon looking at the contemporary contours of the "Ingenuity Gap." David Orr, writing about education, the environment, and the "human prospect," frames the challenge this way:

> It is time, I believe, for an educational "perestroika," by which I mean a general rethinking of the process and substance of education at all levels, beginning with the admission that much of what has gone wrong with the world is the result of education that alienates us from life in the name of human domination, fragments instead of unifies, overemphasizes success and careers, separates feeling from intellect and the practical from the theoretical, and unleashes on the world minds ignorant of their own ignorance. As a result, an increasing percentage of the human intelligence must attempt to undo a large part of what mere intellectual cleverness has done carelessly and greedily (*Earth In Mind*, p. 17).

This quote may sound like the finger pointing I seek to avoid. A spirited attack on "education that alienates us from life" lifts the debate, for me, to a different level. It forces us to confront the issue of what good learning is and what it is for.

Good Learning – One Perspective

As I suggested in the first chapter, we have a clear and powerful sense of the kind of learning we seek and many are working toward, especially parents and older students. The new basics, the new centralities of reflexive and wise uses of the mind require a new imagination and design for a system that supports the co-creation of good learning. We do not need a superstructure to be imposed on top of the system we have now. Any new design should "soak up" and incorporate the best that we have learned from the past about educating young minds – and older ones too. Its purpose would be to invite young minds to new levels of development consistent with the capacities of human consciousness as I have described them. It would prepare intelligent minds to actively engage with a very much "smarter" planet and one facing huge challenges.

What would that learning be like? How would it address the challenges we face?

Some years ago, I offered the following ideas about learning as a contribution to a scenarios project being done by the Alberta Teachers' Association. Much of the thinking and discussion about changes in the environment of the ATA begged the question: What kind of learning are we aiming for? This list is not intended to be a rebuttal to the myths that Langer describes, but it does represent a distinctly different mind-set. My list is about some characteristics of learning that would cause us to see it as an expression of personal commitment and engagement with the larger community – learning as an individual and common good. We might call it "good" learning.

RELEVANCE Learning connects to the learner's lived reality and is critical to the success of future learning and action.

REFLEXIVITY Learning expands consciousness and understanding of the processes of learning, creates learning about learning and increases the capacity to adapt and create effective learning processes.

EMANCIPATION Learning increases freedom from canned or institutionalized learning systems and reduces dependence on external support.

CHARACTER Learning inspires courage, persistence and integrity in response to challenges and opportunities, even in the face of great obstacles, and creates connections to community.

WISDOM Learning connects information to knowledge and points to deeper truths that affect values, beliefs and life choices.

New systems are emerging that will support good learning. The process will be gradual and complex because of the intertwining of old and new. What we have known as curriculum and content will still be a necessary ingredient but will be provided in ways that are consistent with the characteristics of learning as described above. In some cases, because of the complexity of the content or the learning style or other life commitments of the learner, the content will be packaged and delivered as in the past. And, yes, there will still be assessment and accountability. But, a caution from David Orr:

> At the heart of our pedagogy and curriculum is a fateful confusion of cleverness with intelligence. Cleverness, as I understand it, tends to fragment things and to focus on the short run. The epitome of cleverness is the specialist whose intellect and person have been shaped by the demands of a single function…Ecological intelligence, on the other hand, requires a broader view of the world and a long-term perspective. Cleverness can be adequately computed by the Scholastic Aptitude Test and the Graduate Record Exam, but intelligence is not so easily measured. In time I think we will come to see that true intelligence tends to be integrative and often works slowly while one is mulling things over (Orr, p. 30).

If there is a central characteristic in my description of good learning, it is reflexivity. It is the one characteristic that enriches and enlivens all the others, but will not automatically emerge even if all the others are present in the current system. Take away reflexivity, and many of our best schools are already swarming all over the list. On the other hand, very few of our best schools, if any, would assign a final and critical graduation task; a written analysis, an essay question, in which each learner describes what has been learned about learning, one's own capacity to learn, the means to sustain and improve that capacity, and the new ideas and knowledge she or he has added to society and the planet so far and hopes to be adding in the future. As the saying goes, while school may be multiple-choice, life is an essay question.

Walter Truett Anderson identifies reflexivity as one of the five fundamental characteristics or "metatrends" of the postmodern worldview – "ways of looking at reality/unreality that are evident in actions people are taking in relation to politics, religion and culture." Anderson says that they are metatrends because "we experience them not only as changes, but as changes in the way things change" (*Reality Isn't What It Used to Be*, p. 254).

Anderson's full list of metatrends is:

> We can see a growing awareness of the multidimensional, relativistic quality of human experience…The most important part of this is thinking-about-thinking itself, reflexivity: the mind's ability to see itself, and to see itself seeing itself (Anderson offers M. C. Escher's "famous drawing of a hand that is drawing a hand that is drawing the hand" as a beautiful illustration of this key idea.)

> Second, and following from the above, people develop a different sense of identity and boundaries. We live in the age of the fading boundary, the twilight of a mind-set that structured reality with sharp lines.

> Third, we come to accept the centrality of learning to the life of every individual, to every society, and to the species as a whole…It is not so much the constant filling-in of a picture as an ongoing process of reality construction in which it frequently becomes necessary to step out of the picture, and sometimes to drop the old picture entirely.

> Fourth, we come to accept morality, and moral discourse, as a living and central element in human existence. We see our interpersonal relationships as collaborative efforts in constructing values.

> Fifth, we inhabit all kinds of [social constructions of realities] in new ways (*Reality Isn't What It Used to Be*, pp. 254-260).

Anderson is describing a new world of the mind into which good learning should fit rather comfortably even though the learning itself might be somewhat less than comfortable. The power of the mind to do this work is depicted with great clarity by Edward O. Wilson in *Consilience*.

> Mind is a stream of conscious and unconscious experience. It is at root the coded representation of sensory impressions and the memory and imagination of sensory impressions.

> Consciousness consists of the parallel processing of vast numbers of such coding networks.

> All together they create scenarios that flow realistically back and forth through time. The scenarios are a virtual reality. They can either closely match pieces of the external world or depart indefinitely far from it.

> They re-create the past and cast up alternative futures that serve as choices for future thought and bodily action (*Consilience*, p. 109).

The kind of streaming, processing and choice-making described here, this "self-organizing republic of scenarios" as Wilson describes it (p. 110), offers a way of understanding the inner workings of reflexivity. It offers a way of mapping an integrated higher order consciousness. It helps us to see the potential we have to employ reflexivity while engaging, with a high level of self-awareness and connectedness, with our lived world and the lives of other people.

We need ways of learning that will resonate deeply with who we are and the many possibilities we contain. As Walt Whitman said in *Song of Myself*, "I am large, I contain multitudes" (*Leaves of Grass*, p.51, p. 95).

Conscious of Learning

What does reflexivity look like when it is emerging and present in our lives? How do we think and act when we can see ourselves having knowledge and beliefs about our learning and constructing better and better ways of carrying on this most fundamental of human activities? The first thing to stress is that the capacity to be more self-conscious and think with reflexivity is not, as described above, restricted to learning. We are looking at a signature quality of mental life that opens our eyes to and illuminates all dimensions of our lives. The purpose of this book is to draw our attention to the emerging critical need for mature and adaptive thinkers in our culture and how this development is being frustrated by the structure of the schools that we have. The focus here is on learning, but the effects of this capacity play out in the many dimensions of our lives.

It is unlikely that this capacity has been given attention or nurturance as the child enters the school system. Those adults acting on the child's behalf are likely aware that certain kinds of early experiences in learning can impair the main drivers of reflexivity in later years – experiences that thwart or demean curiosity, exploration, questioning and creating. Or leave the child blind to her or his own strengths and weaknesses as a learner. The earliest signs of self-awareness must be watched for and encouraged. I will say much more about this kind of nurturing and development in a later chapter on being a learner in the Third Schools.

There are a number of stage theories of human development, such as Jean Piaget's and Lawrence Kohlberg's, which may be of use in thinking about the emergence of reflexivity. I will not discuss them here; there are better sources. I am unsure whether reflexivity can or needs to be tied to a specific sequence or schedule of development, particularly one that is age-specific. Perhaps some real life examples will help.

The following are drawn from the life experiences of mature people talking about their youth. They are intended to illustrate the mind-set about learning that the Third Schools will be designed to foster. We will be soon building the foundations of a new system that will develop these capacities in every learner, to the degree possible and as early as possible.

I will start with Wordsworth, which may be puzzling. After all, the famous Romantic poet lived in an era when, although various awakenings of the human spirit were occurring, few life experiences would be described in the kind of language that Walter Truett Anderson uses. Indeed, the search for some sort of divine truth, resident in a deep human connection to nature, still seems to be underway. And Wordsworth is recalling his childhood, with references to the "coarser pleasures of my boyish days" and "thoughtless youth" in *Tintern Abbey*, from the perspective of advanced years. But in *The Prelude*, he reflects on having these thoughts and emotions during some particularly powerful experiences in his early teens where he deliberately leaves the "tumultuous crowd" to hear the voice of Nature, the "thou" whom he addresses here:

> "…thus from my first dawn
>
> Of childhood didst thou intertwine for me
>
> The passions that build up our human soul;
>
> …purifying thus
>
> The elements of feeling and of thought,
>
> And sanctifying, by such discipline,
>
> Both pain and fear, until we recognize

A grandeur in the beatings of the heart."

Book First, lines 405-407, 410-414.

Again, making allowances for the autobiographic accuracy of "emotion recollected in tranquility," Wordsworth is saying that although he may have been unaware of the lessons of the "Wisdom and Spirit of the universe," he was clearly aware of the need to be out on the earth and under the sky with frequent periods of solitude.

Perhaps the most intriguing and evocative examples of self-awareness in one's early years are contained in a book of writings by Arab feminists, *Opening the Gates*, edited by Margot Badran and Miriam Cooke. Here are the thoughts of Aisha Ismat al-Taimuriya, writing in 1887-88 about her early childhood:

> I aged while still young trying to get to the root of the words of those who have gone before. I used to be infatuated with the evening chatter of the elderly women, wanting to listen to the choicest stories. From those anecdotes, I gleaned the marvels of destiny. To the best of my ability and efforts, I pondered all that was repeated to me, both serious matters and those said in jest. From the fruits of those evening chats, I plucked what the vessel of my awareness could hold...

> When my mental faculties were prepared for learning, and my powers of understanding had reached receptivity...Bearing the instruments of embroidery and weaving, [my mother] began to work seriously on my education, striving to instill in me cleverness and comprehension. But I was incapable of learning, and I had no desire or readiness to become refined in the occupations of women. I used to flee her as the prey escapes the net, rushing headlong into the assemblages of writers, with no sense of embarrassment. And I found the screech of pen on paper the most inviting of melodies. I was certain that to become one of this group of people would be the most perfect and complete of blessings.

> I discovered in myself an inclination for poetry...(*Opening the Gates*: *Introduction to The Results of Circumstances in Words and Deeds*, pp. 126-127).

And here, 100 years later in 1988, is Amatalrauf al-Sharki remembering her life as a high school student when she was acting in the theatre, working in a radio station, and teaching in a literacy school. She had a family affairs program on the radio at the time.

> I was trying to reach men, women and children. I was trying to talk to all of them telling them that the family affairs program was not just for women. I was saying that both the man and the woman are responsible for the family. I wonder how I had that consciousness at the time (*Opening the Gates, An Unveiled Voice*, p. 380).

And here is Beryl Markham remembering a morning on her father's farm at Njoro in East Africa as all the daily activities come to life, and she plans to escape her lessons and be elsewhere. Her narrative suggests that she would have been in her early teens when these events took place.

> On ordinary days Buller [her dog] and I were a part of this, but on hunting days we escaped before the bell had struck a note and before the cocks had stretched their wings on the fences. I had lessons to do and therefore lessons to avoid.
>
> I remember one such day.
>
> Together, Buller and I slipped out into the little yard that separated my hut from the dining quarters. There was still no real dawn, but the sun was awake and the sky was changing colour.
>
> ...my father would be out any minute to send his first string of race-horses to their morning work. If he were to see me with my spear, my dog, and the 'bushman's friend' strapped to my waist, he would hardly conclude that my mind was wrapped in ardent thoughts of 'The Fundamentals of English Grammar' or 'Exercises in Practical Arithmetic.' He would conclude, and rightly, that Buller and I were on our way to the nearest Nandi singiri to hunt with the Murani.
>
> But we were adept at our game. We scampered quickly through the cluster of domestic buildings, got behind the foaling boxes, and, when the moment was ripe, we hurried along the twisted path...

> A pack of dogs, half-bred, fawning, some of them snarling, rushed at Buller and me the moment we entered the boma. Buller greeted them as he always did – with arrogant indifference. He knew them too well. In packs they were good hunters; individually they were as cowardly as the hyena. I spoke to them by name to silence their foolish yapping.
>
> We were at the door of the hut of the head Murani, and the beginning of a Nandi hunt, even so small as this would be, did not take place in the midst of noise or too much levity.
>
> I drove the blunt end of my spear into the ground and stood beside it, waiting for the door to open (*West With the Night,* pp. 73, 75, 76).

Beryl Markham goes on to describe an encounter with a lion that does not attack, and a warthog that does, nearly fatally injuring her dog, and which she kills with her spear.

And here, in more contemporary times, is Myrna Kostash describing one of her many interviews with young Canadians in her quest to grasp the outlines of *The Next Canada*.

> When I asked Clarissa Lagartera, Filipina lesbian of Winnipeg, which was the first identity she came to in terms of her political consciousness, her ethnicity or her sexuality, she answered her sexuality, for she had "come out" at the age of twelve. In the familiar ah-ha "click" of self-consciousness first popularized by the women's liberation movement of the 1970s, her awareness arrived all at once.
>
> "I didn't have male friends," she told me, "I thought they were stupid and jerks. My female friends were more intriguing and turned into crushes, but I didn't understand it. I had a crush on a girl in grade one and she found this annoying, so I knew there was something different about me. In grade six we had our first sex education class, spoke of heterosexuality and homosexuality, about men having sex with other men. Everybody giggled. Except me. "What's wrong with that?" I thought. A light bulb went on: "Maybe I'm one of those people? (pp. 142-143).

The tricky part about identifying and describing the capacity for reflexivity in learning is that it isn't just about the kind of curiosity and spontaneity in learning that was lamented as lost by the critiques of the public schools that appeared in the 1960s. Certainly being open to the wonders of the world, seeking new experiences and regarding all life's situations as learning opportunities are very important characteristics. But they are not sufficient. The mind of the learner must be able not only to reflect on experience and make meaning from it but also to deeply understand, intelligently employ, and increasingly take responsibility for the making of the meaning itself.

This quote from Mark Kingwell's book *Better Living: In Pursuit of Happiness from Plato to Prozac* sums up this section very well.

> Given the ability to reflect on the conditions of our own existence, a double-edged gift we apparently enjoy uniquely, humans are both social and contemplative by nature. We form associations and have intentions, not just instincts. We make judgments about the world and ourselves. We possess character, which surrenders its secrets to rational insight. In short, we pursue happiness actively, for it is the end of human actions, that for the sake of which all things are done (*Better Living*, p. 329).

And, we may hope, the pursuit of learning.

From Schooling to Learning

The Club of Rome report referenced above made some very important distinctions that we are just learning to understand and to work through from the standpoint of corporate management and public policy, let alone the public schools.

> Learning, as we shall use the term, has to be understood in a broad sense that goes beyond what conventional terms like education and schooling imply. For us, learning means an approach, both to knowledge and to life that emphasizes human initiative. It encompasses the acquisition and practice of new methodologies, new skills, new attitudes, and new values necessary to live in a world of change. Learning is the process of preparing to deal with new situations. It may occur consciously, or often unconsciously, usually

> from experiencing real-life situations, although simulated or imagined situations can also induce learning. Practically every individual in the world, whether schooled or not, experiences the process of learning – and probably none of us at present are learning at the levels, intensities, and speeds needed to cope with the complexities of modern life (*No Limits To Learning*, p. 9).

This is a remarkably contemporary statement and challenge crossing three decades. Compare it with this plea from a Calvin White, a high school counselor in Salmon Arm, B.C.

> Thinking is not a priority in schools. Compliance is.
>
> Today, we need to teach kids how to learn. We need to immerse teenagers in a school milieu where the paramount expectation is their active involvement and in which we bring them up-to-date on the environmental, political and social realities of their community, country and world.
>
> We need to teach teenagers how to think, question, analyze, imagine, predict and empathize (*The Globe and Mail*, October 10th, 2007).

The Club of Rome report authors go on to say that they will not ignore education "which is a fundamental way and formal means to enhance learning" (p. 9). But they stress the importance of less formal modes and group, organizational, and societal learning. In so many ways, they were anticipating the need for what I am calling the Third Schools, if not predicting their advent. I diverge from their thinking in only one important respect. The authors claim that learning, or "innovative learning" as they call it, "may occur consciously, or often unconsciously." I am suggesting that the need for systems that lead to conscious learning and the capacity to consciously create one's own learning is becoming urgent in Canada. These are paramount outcomes.

Attempts at distinctions between schooling and learning have cut in other, less useful, directions.

Some years ago, the Alberta Government's Department of Education published a list of provincial goals for the education system. They were based substantially on work done in California in the early 1970s, known as the Phi Delta Kappa goal-setting process, designed to be used with parent and community groups. (*Educational Goals and Objectives*, Commission on Educational Planning – Phi Delta Kappa Inc.) The Alberta Government provided two lists headed the Goals of Schooling and the Goals of Education. The Goals of Schooling were, predictably, narrower skill-building and academic goals that the schools were expected to take on as their core work, fully resource, and be accountable for achieving. The Goals of Education were the broader, less academic, socialization and attitudinal outcomes that, it was stated, the schools could not do alone but could achieve in partnership with parents and others. The two lists remained entwined in the busy classrooms of Alberta and the bureaucratic distinction disappeared a few years later.

As Johanna Wyn points out in her paper presented at the April 2000 Annual Conference of the American Educational Research Association:

> The design of education systems in most parts of the industrialized world still reflects the thinking about the relationship between education and society that was current in the immediate post-war era. This was a time of industrial and national reconstruction and the provision of mass education to service new economies. For the most part, school systems have changed little since that time (*Education for the New Adulthood: implications of youth research for education*).

Wyn observes that, "Two elements in particular now seem to be at odds with the ways that young people are shaping their lives in the 1990s… age-based categorization remains a fundamental organizing principle…schooling is premised on the assumption of a linear relationship between school and work." She then warns that, "Young people's life patterns increasingly challenge these linear and categorical assumptions as they make pragmatic choices in balancing and negotiating a range of personal, occupational and educational commitments in their lives."

It is now time to extract the learning baby from the schooling bathwater. The bath of schooling, as we will see, will still be needed, but the bath will probably be a place where learning goes when it needs a certain kind of immersion rather than a long-term home.

The Arrival of our Third Schools

Some signals:

- ➢ The case of a mother who wanted her child to attend school half the time and learn at home the other half may be a straw in the wind.

- ➢ Some schools even open early in the morning: the growing number of breakfast clubs, especially in urban schools, is an encouraging sign. *The Learning Game*, p. 258.

- ➢ Through the down-sizings of the '80s and the boom of the go-go '90s, stockbrokers, PR flacks, dot-com geeks, meeting planners, and many more white-collar folks have broken away from 9-to-5 corporate gigs to have a go at it on their own. These "free agents," as Daniel Pink calls them, now include more than 30 million – one in four – American workers.

- ➢ But the new free agent economy requires a different sort of worker, with different skills and values. And it's already changing the face of American learning.

- ➢ These changes are most evident in three broad education movements: homeschooling, alternatives to high school, and adult education. "Free agency will force the necessary changes," Pink writes, and "these changes will prove [to be] as path-breaking as mass public schooling was a century ago. <u>Utne Reader</u>, Jan/Feb 2002.

- ➢ Roy and her sons are part of a growing community of what they call "unschoolers"; parents and students who feel that the pedantic structures of the public school system are stifling kids by starving them of creativity and passion.

- ➢ Unschooling, also known as "independent learning" or "experience-based learning," differs from conventional homeschooling, where a student will generally follow a set curriculum, which is often based directly on the public school system's program.

➢ Instead, unschooling students are encouraged to find the path that works best for them, and empowers them to choose their own intellectual destinies. *TheTyee.ca*, December 16th, 2005.

➢ …people's expectations are changing. There's a whole new generation of kids who expect I should be able to have control over how I learn, what I learn, and where I learn. I'm not just a consumer, I'm a co-creator and collaborator. I can share/mashup/remix knowledge. *Fastcompany*, February 16th, 2010.

➢ …this year, all 428 sixth-graders at Linwood Middle School in North Brunswick, N.J., are charting their own academic path with personalized student learning plans – electronic portfolios containing information about their learning styles, interests, skills, career goals and extracurricular activities.

➢ These new learning plans will follow each sixth-grader through high school, and are intended to help the students assess their own strengths and weaknesses as well as provide their parents and teachers with a more complete profile beyond grades and test scores. *The New York Times*, February 28th, 2010.

➢ In public schools, private schools and preschools from Roachville, N.B., to Red Deer, AB, and Sooke, B.C., teachers and early childhood educators are rolling out programs where young children spend a big chunk of time exploring the natural world – in some cases, all day, every day, even through the dead of winter. At a time when free play is in a well-documented decline in Canadian kids' lives, these schools represent a new push to see children leave the formal classroom behind.

➢ In the "nature kindergarten" program at Sangster Elementary School in Sooke, four-year-olds spend each morning in the forest or at the beach, mostly engaged in what's called play-based learning; teachers develop lessons around whatever captivates the kids: the clouds, pine cones, the anatomy of worms. No one asks when is it time to go inside, says Frances Krusekopf, a public school principal who spearheaded the program's creation and hired a childhood educator, on a $25,000 salary funded by grants, to help the regular teacher. Amid the heavy downpours of winter, Krusekopf says the kids "notice the puddles, they notice the quantity of worms has gone up.

> Wrapping up year one of a two-year experiment, the program is an example of what are typically called forest schools. *Maclean's*, June 24th, 2013.

So it is time to talk of new places for learning, new meanings of learning, and to make some distinctions and to clean up our language. The signals are becoming stronger and more frequent, suggesting that our Third Schools are beginning to make their appearance.

The signals can be difficult to assess. They contain echoes of the free and alternative schools of the counter-culture '60s. The school as a place of learning has been an important part of our definition of learning, and as change advances, we have tried to make the word school stick, as with home-schooling and virtual and charter schools. We have managed to move the talk, and maybe even the thinking, away from community schools and toward community-based learning. Our language is turning toward non-school and out-of-school learning, suggesting a new openness and new opportunities in the game of creating learning.

Pupils ready to learn outside school

> Studying out of school is becoming more appealing to young people, claims research. A survey from the Department for Education and Skills shows that teenagers are becoming more open to learning outside the formal school day. And to support out-of-school learning the government is promising an extra £75m a year, until 2006. According to the education department, 51% of 11 to 16 year olds say they like learning outside school - an increase from 46% last year. By 2006, the government wants all secondary schools to provide out-of-school clubs, either in the form of breakfast clubs, summer schools or homework clubs. These extra learning opportunities have been claimed as having a significant role in helping to raise achievement (*BBC News*, December 30th, 2002).

Although still caught in the old model, the language is at least beyond "extra-curricular", and the intent is linked to achievement.

Quoting Johanna Wyn's paper again, we see a new form of decision-making emerging:

> ... Raffo and Reeves (1999) found that young people in their U.K. study were making their own decisions about how they relate to their schooling. Not only were the young people in their study making decisions about their levels of participation in the classroom, they were deciding which lessons they would attend. Raffo and Reeves describe young people who are making very active choices about when they would leave school, whether they would take time out from education and which qualifications to study for. Their research provides evidence that young people are developing a perspective on schooling in which education is only one of a number of options which they are managing (*Education for the New Adulthood: implications of youth research for education*).

It seems appropriate to bookend this chapter by closing with another observation from Noddings:

> If we knew and could categorize the full range of human capacities, perhaps we could devise a curriculum that gives reasonable attention to each capacity. Then we could assure parents that their children would all be exposed to, and, we hope, come to value each human capacity, and that they would also be helped to find and develop the one (or more) in which they show special talent (*The Challenge to Care in Schools*, p. 30).

Noddings expresses doubt about the likelihood of finding the one best curriculum that magically contains the keys to unlock each child's unique abilities. Perhaps curriculum must always mean commodifying knowledge and stifling creativity. These are the risks we have been willing to take in using curriculum to ensure a common body of learning for all children. I write in the hope that the power of the ideas of reflexivity, conscious learning, and the qualities of good learning that I have offered will open up new playing fields of learning and make them challenging and inviting.

CHAPTER 5: THE FRONTIER WE ARE IN

Spare Me Some Change

What kind of change are we in? This is a question that haunts our talk about systems and transformation. Decades ago, when I was working with some of the commissions looking at reforms in the Calgary public school system, I would frequently hear the phrase, "that's just change for change's sake!" I have not heard those words for some years. Instead, we began hearing about change as "white water." The image suggests turbulence, complexity and unpredictability. Our current characterizations of change are that it is rapid, deep and profound – history-altering as one colleague has put it. It is also taken for granted.

Are things really changing that much?

A few years ago, I completed a biography of my grandmother, Frances Wilson, tracing her journey from a broken home and orphanage in London, England, to an exploitive boarding house and orphanage in Ottawa, to a caring foster home in the Ottawa Valley, and to a steam train journey across Canada leading to marriage and a happy family life. How would my grandmother react to the florid descriptions of the profound changes of our times? Curiosity mixed with puzzlement, I expect. Kingwell suggests that these themes recur in history and that "every era has at some point produced a feeling of being overwhelmed" (*Better Living*, p. 294).

Well, the nature and degree of the changes we are in is arguable. It depends on how much we value stability and what we regard as a deep or profound change. One person's life-changing experience is another person's makings of an interesting day. It depends on where we look for change and how good we are at reading signals of change, such as those that pointed to the rapid rise of alternative medicines in health care, the emergence of cyber-bullying in schools, the recent economic roller coasters, or, looking further back, the fall of the Berlin Wall and the rise of China.

A number of contemporary observers are convinced that something significant is on its way. Tomorrow may not be just a similar or (if we're lucky) better version of yesterday. Tomorrow may be very different. The reasons given vary.

Many feel that science and technology have put us into a new world where the old rules and assumptions are melting away. Ray Kurzweil is predicting the merging of machine and human intelligence by 2020 – not that far away (*The Age of Spiritual Machines*). Others cite social change and point to new values and views about quality of life. Paul Ray cites research to support the emergence of cultural creatives – people who are bound together by "shared values about ecology, personal relationships, peace and social justice, spirituality, and consistency between word and deed" – people who "tend to be altruistic, optimistic and non-materialistic and they love foreign experiences" (Kier Graff, *Chicago Tribune Magazine*). Others point to the environment and humanity's growing awareness of the critical need to act to save our natural world and with it our delicate enterprise known as human civilization.

Others just talk about change itself – whether change is changing, and if so, how.

> We're headed toward something which is going to happen very soon – in our lifetimes – and which is fundamentally different from anything that's happened in human history before (W. Daniel Hillis, *The Third Culture*, p. 385).

> …the coming integration of IT and biotechnology will have such a profound effect on the way we think and live that "we are standing on the brink of a mind makeover more cataclysmic than anything in our history (Baroness Greenfield, quote from *The Way We Are Going*, in *The Economist* Book Review, October 9th, 2003).

Others reach even deeper and point to the habits of mind we have used to shape and understand the way of the world, the reality we inhabit. I referred to some of these people earlier when I talked about a new kind of learning linked to new uses of the mind. Writers and thinkers such as Walter Truett Anderson, Don Beck, Maxine Greene, Robert Kegan, Ruben Nelson and Margaret Visser are addressing a cultural maturation that has good potential to become a shared global enterprise.

> It is fair to say that, whatever we take our allegedly 'postmodern' or 'transhuman' condition now to be – whether we think, as some people do, that all standards of truth are relative because we can no longer believe in large stories of Progress or Salvation; or believe, with others,

that death can be overcome with technology – we are still coming to grips with the implications, both positive and negative, of this modern, individual-centred world (Mark Kingwell, *Better Living*, p. 27).

Perhaps this preoccupation with change is a way of acknowledging that we need to vacate the twilight of adolescence we have all been living in, grow up some more – it's a continuous process – and take responsibility for the future of our planet and the way we live together. We have the potential to move beyond narrow self-interest and global conflict. But it won't happen by accident. A higher order of consciousness, and new social and organizational designs, commitments and uses of the mind are required. To paraphrase Heilbroner, we need "new social forms into which our primal energies can be poured" (*The Nature and Logic of Capitalism*, p. 22). The reflexive capacity to do conscious learning is central to this renewed taking of mutual responsibility.

The Way Forward

We have, in Canada, a very good chance to bring about convergence of the desires of the human spirit and the drivers of change, be they technological, global, political, environmental, economic or social. How we do learning is just one very important part of this new game we're in. New conversations are required about change, how it can be contemplated and co-created. Our problem is figuring out ways to construct a new version of the commons, a renewed public space, so that we can express our ideas, values and beliefs, and figure out what we need to do for the much more complex "common good." It means recovering and giving new meaning to the idea of participatory citizenship. "Because once we enter fully into a world in which reality is socially created, democracy is all we have left…" is how Walter Truett Anderson puts it (*Reality Isn't What It Used To Be*, p. 183). We know the old narrowly partisan ways won't work. The emerging neural network of global communication is relentlessly moving us toward a global conversation and a more urgent need for sharing and community.

The false boundaries of our lived realities are dissolving, and for some, quite rapidly. We are less willing to divide our lives into the old convenient compartments such as work and family. Our values and our children can come to our workplaces and our pressing career needs for lifelong learning create changes in our homes. "Quality of living" goals are rising in importance to rival consumerism and lifestyle. We want to participate in our children's growing up. We want to slow down time.

As we let the old boundaries and assumptions dissolve, significant connections are emerging. The "music of humanity" is a reminder that, yes, our values and beliefs arise from well-springs deep within each of us, our families, and communities, but also from powerful currents in the amazing diversity in the shared lives of all of us. Taylor, in discussing modernism, speaks of an "awareness of living on a duality or plurality of levels," and of an inward turn. We are on an inward journey that leads to a growing awareness of the depth, "the timeless, the mythic, and the archetypical that…may be transpersonal" (*Sources of The Self*, pp. 480-481). Interestingly, Taylor suggests that inwardness gives rise to reflexivity, "something which intensifies our sense of inwardness and depth."

The inward need not exclude. There is an outward journey in which we connect with humanity and, in our search for new meanings of the good, seek to touch the "ground of being" of some modern theologians. This new awareness expresses itself in a belief in universal values of humanity and common foundations for the good life. This isn't about the ecstasies of eating, praying and loving our way around the planet. We can stay at home. New realities and possibilities now travel well and will seek us out.

The times we are in invite a fuller expression of that central quality of human consciousness discussed earlier – our capacity to see ourselves as actors in our own lives, in the context of the lives of others. They invite us to be reflexive systems thinkers who can have beliefs about our beliefs and relationships with our relationships – a new grammar for a new reality. As a result, we are less inclined to buy into "official" cultural stories such as "rugged individualism," "the march of progress" or "the final triumph of free-market democracy." We seek a personal perspective on reality and change, and the capacity to act, and interact.

Heroic action can still mean virtue, high purpose and passion. But it is now tempered by our growing awareness of our capacity to alter the course of planetary evolution and living systems for all people. We sense that change itself has changed and even though still about speed and complexity, is no longer linear.

All this adds up to an emerging new consciousness in which:

We can see ourselves more clearly as actors in our own lives and, thoughtfully and respectfully, in the lives of others.

We realize that we are now co-creators of reality, from evolution to human systems to the most precious elements of our private lives.

Being of Two Minds

This new consciousness growls and snaps at us when we retreat to what Robert Kegan calls "the bedrooms of our minds," those comfortable assumptions and patterns of our lives we trust and like to take for granted. It disrupts the harmony in the family of our mind – and with good reason. There is a struggle underway as we think together about fundamental questions of values, beliefs and cultural survival. To varying degrees, we are resolving these questions but are not sure how to live in accordance with the answers. So old habits continue in the face of emerging beliefs. Some examples:

- ➢ Reform and industrial institutions – we are no longer believers in the capacity of huge complex industrial era institutions such as school and health systems to deliver services that are central to the quality of our lives, but we keep trying to reform them and make them more accountable in order to save them.

- ➢ Limits to growth and sustainability – we are increasingly aware that the life-giving systems of our planet are being depleted, perhaps more quickly than we care to believe, but we continue to be preoccupied with economic growth, trade, investment, and consumer confidence.

- ➢ Human and machine intelligence – we fret that our youth may not be prepared to be economically productive and to fit into the new technologized organizations and workplaces, while we thrill to the promises of the benefits of advanced robotics and intelligent, perhaps even spiritual, people-replacing machines.

- ➢ Government and social cohesion – we bridle at the intrusions of what some have called the "nanny state" or what one writer is calling the "*Dawn of the Daddy State*" (*The Atlantic Monthly*, June 2004), but worry about our fragmented lives, lack of social cohesion, and the capacity of

> fragile communities to hold us together around shared values and beliefs.

> Wine and warehouses – we look forward to aging like a good vintage wine, productive and in new careers and good health even as we are dismayed by the increasingly dire predictions about the costs and impacts of retiring boomers, longevity, and warehousing and caring for seniors.

> Global village and global theatre – our talk is about one interconnected planet, but in many cases we feel and act like observers who are well informed but unable to change anything. (*Reality Isn't What It Used to Be*, p. 232).

> Authority and creativity – we entrench and entrap power and authority inside our buildings and bureaucracies, as we struggle to enact new forms of leadership and harness the creative energy and sense of possibility in our culture, particularly youth culture.

I sum up these contradictions by referring to them as living in two minds. I have described earlier how similar contradictions are putting stress on the schools. This state of being in two minds can actually be healthy if the tension in a fuller awareness of being pulled in different directions leads to a richer sense of possibility. We come to know more deeply that better is possible and prepare to get down to the work, individually and as a culture, of solving and being solved by the puzzles in the contradictions.

If we can handle the tension, we should get used to dwelling in the state of two minds. We should welcome multiple perspectives, some of them even contradicting others. As Taylor puts it, "Human life is irreducibly multi-leveled" (*Sources of The Self*, p. 480). Or, as Robert Jay Lifton says, "We are becoming fluid and many-sided...this mode of being differs radically from that of the past, and enables us to engage in continuous exploration and personal experiment" (*The Protean Self*, p. 1).

The Shape of the Frontier

I have described the changes we are in as mostly positive. This is not an attempt to be Pollyannaish about it all. There are many people for whom change is anywhere from a vexing to a terrifying and painful experience. I am suggesting that in this focus on public education and learning in our culture, change is mainly a story of possibility and positive challenge. We have much more to lose by not acting than by acting.

To picture the challenges ahead, I like the image of a continental divide marked by a high mountain range. There are no visible passes to give easy access or viewpoints to the other side. There is only one way – up and over, and on a broad front. This continental divide of change that school systems face signifies a clear departure from the last 100 years of schooling. Most schools have explored the flanks and valleys of the divide as they have worked and played with variations and innovations designed to improve teaching and learning. Only a lucky few have had encouragement or opportunity to fully and systematically analyze and draw conclusions about the barriers and opportunities in those rugged foothills and ridges.

The peaks and valleys, the sectors of the divide, are distinct and familiar. They have names: learning, teaching, technology, governance, resources, roles, legislation and so on. But they are intricately linked. Schools have been able to make significant improvements on many of these peaks and have even linked them to whole school improvement. It is highly unlikely, however, that the journey over the great divide to our Third Schools can be made by focusing on only one or a few of these upward climbs. There is ice and snow up there, and scree slopes. One step forward can lead to several steps back.

The continental divide will be crossed soon. It may happen within public education. It may be a courageous and committed school system or partnership of schools. It may be educators who have learned how to map the whole divide as well as the individual peaks and get good at doing unique planning and design work with their students, parents and communities. All would be full partners in the process right from the outset. They would form an ecology of change agents, both supporting each other and encouraging initiative. In response to the question, "Who will provide the leadership to new ways of learning and the next public education?" they will reply, "We choose ourselves."

Or the impetus may come from outside public education. There are increasing signals that people want to leap out of the box we are in.

In any case, once across that cloud-capped divide, new forms of learning and supportive systems and processes that we cannot currently see or predict will become possible. In the last chapters of this book, I will take a look at the many challenges and possibilities. I will offer some scenarios of how this change might unfold – just one way of getting the conversation going. I will suggest some initial steps that might create a beginning and a worthy high-country expedition.

Dee Hock, in the *The Birth of the Chaordic Age*, offers some powerful words of encouragement. He talks about shifting our view from the problems of change being "out there" and needing the intervention of experts who are also "out there." He cautions that the fundamental problem resides in our "collective consciousness," a deeply held view of how the world works and a view we all share (p. 78).

The Three Stages

There are signals that, like messages from the future, can teach us about the journey of cultural change that is already underway. Like most explorations into a new territory, fewer of us are at the leading edge. Most wait comfortably by the fire in the base camps to see how the adventure turns out. Some hope that there will be no need for an adventure. If we just stay where we are, a better future will come to us. The fact is that most of us are caught between the two habits of mind referred to above, the powerful and reassuring one we inherited from our experiences in the latter half of the 20th century and an anxious but insistent one that knows there are better ways of living on the planet and looks for signals of new ways to come. We are in an anxious transition period. The following chart illustrates three stages, conveniently alliteratively, with some examples:

TRADITIONAL	TRANSITIONAL	TRANSFORMATIONAL
consciousness is industrial age – hierarchical command and control systems are accepted as the norm	consciousness is mixed industrial and knowledge age – we seek ways to lighten or get around hierarchy which is viewed as a liability and an impediment to change	consciousness is knowledge age – hierarchy is only an option in an expanding tool kit of ways of living and working together

view of the future is linear – the future is an extension, an improved version, of what we have (1)	view of the future is ecological – the future is shaped by forces and pressures outside the systems we live in (1)	view of the future is transformative – the future is shaped by our changing beliefs, assumptions and consciousness (1)
focus on emulating cultural icons and myths, e.g., the icon of bureaucracy and the myth of material progress (2)	mixed focus on "surface" cultural icons and signals of sub-surface or seismic changes (2)	focus on learning from the signals of sub-surface or seismic change (2)
acceptance of boundaries – borders, silos and turf	resistance to boundaries – building of pacts, partnerships and alliances across boundaries	dissolution of boundaries – open systems creating networks and ecologies of systems
institutions focused on one singular task with a single well-defined method – "methodolatry" (3)	institutions adapt innovations to their narrow focus (3)	institutions open to multiple perspectives and purposes and a variety of means (3)
stability and predictability are valued as systems maintain the "old order" (4)	turmoil and chaos is necessary and seen as a "natural state of evolution" (4)	"dynamic responsive" systems adopt new visions and adapt to new environments (4)

(1) From Ruben Nelson, Three Views of the Future
(2) From Robert Theobald and David Bell, source unknown
(3) From Nel Noddings, The Challenge to Care In Schools, pp. 7-10
(4) From Gene Carter and William G. Cunningham, The American School Superintendent, pp. 157 – 159.

The left column is the safe ground we think wishfully about but, depending on our age, have differing degrees of experience and evidence that it is breaking away from under us. We are venturing into the transitional and trying to learn more about the transformational ways of thinking and behaving. In doing this, we are beginning to learn more deeply about the frontier that we face and are trying to cross. As Sarason points out, referring to change in schools, perhaps the journey must, for good or ill, be both necessary and difficult.

> The hallmark of imprisonment in a long-standing tradition is the inability or unwillingness to consider any truly significant alteration in that tradition, especially if it will require you to think and act in unfamiliar ways. That is not in principle an undesirable reaction. Tradition should not lightly, let alone unreflectively, be changed. But, when in the case of schools that tradition is failing in its purposes and achievements, when efforts to change that tradition have been discernibly unproductive of improvement, when that intractability is puzzling practically to everyone and is seen as a source of and not an antidote to major social problems – when that tradition has these features, the days of tinkering or passive resignation to the status quo should be considered over (*How Schools Might Be Governed and Why*, pp. 131-132).

Sarason is describing the same kind of mental imprisonment Kingwell refers to as "…a set of commonsense assumptions that is so taken for granted that it becomes invisible…." Kingwell goes on to illustrate, using a university classroom as an example of a basic structure that cannot be imagined as working any differently – particularly by students. (*Better Living*, pp. 174-175). We might recall the blunt warning from Jack Welsh I quoted earlier where "the end is in sight." Here is a similar but more elegant warning from Murray Gell-Mann, a Nobel Prize-winning physicist.

> One of the most common reasons, and perhaps the simplest, for the existence of maladaptive schemata is that they were once adaptive but under conditions that no longer prevail. The environment of the complex adaptive system has changed at a faster rate than the evolutionary system can accommodate (*The Quark and the Jaguar*, p. 303).

In other words, even though schools have evolved, often due to the heroic efforts of classroom teachers, they are "maladaptive schemata," systems based on outmoded theories of how the world works. The world is changing faster than the schools are able to evolve and respond.

Some Trail Breakers

We who care about learning are not alone on this journey. Explorers and pioneers have gone before. Luckily for us, they have left tracks and signs and some pieces of a new map. This adventure is part of a larger cultural shift, as the chart above describes with its three stages.

Some examples of frontier-crossing thinking may help to illustrate the three stages in the chart and what it might be like to peer across the continental divide into a transformed world. The following three examples, although presenting different experiences of crossing over into a very different future, have something important in common. They all present ideas that counter conventional wisdom about how the world works – whole societies spiraling upward into higher order behaviours, "chaordic" organizations dancing with complexity and capable of residing on the moving boundary between order and chaos, and "end-to-end" or e2e networks linking the smarts in the human minds at each end while keeping the middle connections "stupid" so that innovation may occur. These writers' explorations have led them to thinking about the world in ways that, for some of us, are difficult or even un-thinkable.

Let us ponder these ideas and allow ourselves to be encouraged and inspired.

Spiral Dynamics

There are signals that we, in North America, backlash aside, are awakening to and tentatively reaching out toward a cultural maturity project. Many of our best minds are coming to grips with the qualities of mind and spirit and the deep reciprocity of relationship required to navigate the challenges of our times. Two writers and practitioners who bring clarity and experience as well as a number of practical approaches to such a fundamental project are Don Beck and Christopher Cowan. In their book, *IU*, having commented on the "Humpty Dumpty effect," in which the "Earth seems to be rocking out of control," they say:

> This book is about the forces inside the human spirals that wind through individual minds, drive organizations to new plateaus, and push societies to evolve through layers of complexity. It is also about a body of knowledge that draws together practically everything that has come before in leadership, management and organizational design. Finally, it is about the next epoch's King's Horses, Men and Women. Arriving in the nick of time... (pp. 20-27).

And, the new repairers of Humpty Dumpty will have their work cut out for them. This is because "The problems that come at us in transition to the 21st century can only be resolved by solutions that they, themselves, create" (*Spiral Dynamics*, p. 27).

The meaning of the spiral image is described in a quotation from Clare W. Graves:

> Briefly, what I am proposing is that the psychology of the mature human being is an unfolding, emergent, oscillating spiral process marked by progressive subordination of older, lower-order behavior systems to newer, higher-order systems as man's existential problems change (*Spiral Dynamics*, p. 28).

Looking ahead, where do Beck and Cowan see these forces taking us? They raise cautions about twisting the *Spiral Dynamics* framework toward a flawed linear concept of progress. They are descriptive and non-judgmental of the relative value of each level. They stress that "older lower-order" may be entirely appropriate given certain life conditions just as "newer higher-order systems" may not emerge automatically but may be the result of tension and struggle. They provide some sample sketches, this one of organizational life:

> The role and scope of the executive function is shifting. Fewer entities are relying on quasi-military chain-of-command structures where power is vested in single persons or elitist groups up and down a power pyramid. Rather, they are now forming task-specific brain syndicates, a new decision-team approach that relies on competency, trust, cooperation, independence, and consensus combined (*Spiral Dynamics*, p. 188).

And, looking globally, they ask, "What choices do we have as global citizens? One option is that we simply let things be, let nature take its course. The fittest on the spiral, or the fittest spiral, will survive." But as we approach the newer higher-order systems, "…we may be developing the knowledge to participate in our own evolutionary history" (*Spiral Dynamics*, p. 313).

What are the implications? It may indeed be that our schools were designed at a time when we resided at a different level on a spiral, or perhaps even on another spiral, one that required "chain-of-command structures." We now need to face the fact that such systems, especially if they are school systems, can block the higher-order thinking that would unlock us from the spiral we are in. It is a very dangerous time to be schooling for compliance and unthinking loyalty to traditional institutions and the values they embody. Those who chafe against the rules of such systems and ask tough questions should not be discouraged or disciplined, as many young teachers have experienced. They are calling us to pay attention to the signals of change. They are telling us not to imagine that we can linger in another time when we might instead "participate in our own evolutionary history."

The Chaordic Organization

In his book, *The Birth of the Chaordic Age*, Dee Hock, the founder and CEO Emeritus of VISA, sets the pace for his argument early in the prologue:

> The Industrial Age, hierarchical, command-and-control institutions that, over the past four hundred years, have grown to dominate our commercial, political, and social lives are increasingly irrelevant in the face of exploding diversity and complexity of society worldwide. They are failing, not only in the sense of collapse, but in the more common and pernicious form – organizations increasingly unable to achieve the purpose for which they were created, yet continuing to expand as they devour resources, decimate the earth, and demean humanity (p. 6).

The kind of organization that Hock goes on to describe is a prototype of the kind of organization that will be required to support the co-creation of unique programs of learning for many people in many different situations. It will be a complex set of thoughtful bargains between learners, parents, systems, communities and governing authorities. It will require an openness and flexibility that current schooling systems cannot provide.

As we have seen, this is a story without villains. The problem of change in our time is our willingness to live with the status quo, the taken-for-granteds that act as a cultural DNA wrapped around various aspects of our lives. Hock goes on to talk about the problem that is " 'in here,' in the consciousness of writer and reader, of you and me." He speaks hopefully with a sense of possibility that resonates with my high expectations for the early days on the other side of the continental divide of change – the work of pioneering new learning systems for a new reality.

> When that consciousness begins to understand and grapple with the false Industrial-age concepts of organization to which it clings; when it is willing to risk loosening the hold of those concepts and embrace new possibilities; when those possibilities engage enough minds, new patterns will emerge and we will find ourselves on the frontier of institutional alternatives ripe with hope and rich with possibilities (p. 78).

I expect so, for the schools especially, this is a change that cannot be imposed or legislated into existence. Once the first steps have been taken, and parents and learners have experienced the new possibilities for learning, the impact of this on learners will create the energy that drives the change forward. It will quickly sweep past the early stages of the Third Schools as I describe them in the following pages.

The implications? Hock is describing the birth of a new view of complex systems, systems that can reside on the moving boundary between order and chaos. This new view will create a revolution that will transform the standard or conventional structures of organizations, as we know them. The pioneering work that he did with VISA is waiting to be reenacted in organizations facing complexity and the need to be continuously adaptive. These will be parallel developments and will provide opportunities for steep learning and creative alliances.

End to End Systems

One of the ways I have characterized the changes I am describing is the emergence of a learning commons – a public space where learning can be co-created in accordance with certain ideals and beliefs held by the community in which the learning occurs. In his book, *The Future of Ideas*, Lawrence Lessig explores the idea of the Internet as an innovation commons. His arguments are convincing, and remind me of Yoneji Masuda's deeply insightful look into the future in his 1980 book, *The Information Society*, which introduced concepts such as information utilities and new voluntary communities. This is still pioneering territory, and Lessig offers us a powerful way of thinking about designs to support learning with his discussion of end-to-end systems.

Lessig introduces the end-to-end or "e2e" concept early on in his discussion of the Internet as an innovation commons. An "e2e" network locates intelligence at the ends of the network but keeps the network "stupid."

> A simple, or, as [David] Isenberg described it, stupid network would facilitate the greatest degree of innovation. A smart, or intelligent, network would perhaps be optimized for certain users, but its own sophistication would inhibit different or new uses not initially understood (p. 38).

When I first read these words, I was shocked at the implications for learning systems – shocked and delighted because of the clarity they created for me regarding the weight of intelligence, frozen intelligence, that sits at the core of schooling systems, in its curricula, methods, rules and regulations. We will need to build wisdom into the new system for learning so that it knows when to be silent and when to offer intelligence. We will need to provide one kind of intelligence for younger children that supports their learning about learning, and gradually invoke a more silent but inviting and responsive learning space as they grow older. But there is more:

> This strategy is an attitude. It says to the world, I don't know what functions this system, or network, will perform. It is based on the idea of uncertainty. When we don't know which way a system will develop, we build the system to allow the broadest range of development (p. 39).

The implications? Placing intelligence at the ends of the learning system and accommodating the idea of uncertainty is very consistent with the idea of a system that supports learning. What is learning if not about intelligence and uncertainty? But we will need to translate and adapt Lawrence Lessig's version of these ideas. He is suggesting that the Internet should not interfere in, moderate or regulate the transactions between users and sources, freeing the innovative space. We will need to carefully and sensitively imbed intelligence in a learning system so that it is there when needed.

And so, three examples that show us that we can spring ourselves out of our own traps. We *can* design the systems we need to support the learning we want. After a brief pause in chapter six, we'll look at some initial sample ideas of how such a change might happen.

CHAPTER 6: INTERMISSION, RECAP, AND ON TO 2025

OK, it is time for a breather. Your coffee cup or wine glass may need refilling (sorry, not included in the price of this book) and your legs may need stretching. But do come back. In this chapter, I will summarize the discussion to this point and sketch some ideas in response to the question, "What might the Third Schools look like?" Then, to prepare the way for the wild and untamed possibilities to follow and in the spirit of creating a scenario, I will take you to 2025 to meet a Third Schooler who is about to graduate. The following chapters are offered in the spirit of this book's invitation to do a new kind of thinking about future public systems of learning by exploring a limited set of interesting possibilities. And so, as a conference agenda might pronounce...

BREAK...and,

RECONVENE...welcome back.

So, let us pause and reflect, then look ahead. I will summarize the logic to this point, and some steps, big steps, that might lie ahead. Many of the proposals to follow are in a very delicate state, and grow out of hints, signals and brave experiments afoot in our society. They need to be grappled with in a way that I will not be able to do and re-shaped into workable strategies and tactics.

The Challenge

It is time for those of us who care about public education as an ideal, rather than an institution, to converge around the following idea: *We cannot continue to tinker with our century-old educational institutions and organizations but must be prepared to rethink them entirely.* Some of the western world's greatest educational thinkers and writers, and best friends of public education too, people like Michael Barber, Larry Cuban, John Goodlad, Maxine Greene, Nel Noddings, Seymour Sarason and David Tyack, have advocated this view. Step outside education and you can add Diane Francis and Richard Florida to the list. We have the opportunity in Canada to create the kind of systems we need for the next era of creating learning in the commons, the public space. I call them our Third Schools. *We have the opportunity to serve the distinctive needs of a knowledge society and elevate and enrich the work of teachers and learners.* As we understand the possibilities more deeply, we will see old barriers and assumptions melt away, and many more of us passionately involved in the "learning game," as Michael Barber has called it.

The Road So Far

I ground this compelling challenge to move from schooling to learning in the following essential features of where we are today and where we may go tomorrow:

1. During the 20th century, schools successfully aligned themselves with commonly held beliefs about schooling and the urgent and evolving needs for learning in Canada. For the first half of that century, our beliefs and needs were predictable and lived easily with each other.

2. Schools have equally successfully responded and adapted to the rapid and complex changes of the last few decades. Teachers, working alone or collaboratively, in the shelter of their classrooms, have initiated many of the more subtle and enduring adaptations such as responsiveness to learning style and integration of information technologies.

3. Schools have responded and adapted to change while honouring and carrying forward familiar cultural expectations and structures from the past. After all, most of us have been to school and "know what a 'real school' is like (*Tinkering Toward Utopia*, p. 9).

4. The heralds of crisis in public education have ignored, misunderstood or, in some cases, misrepresented the context of change and the evidence of success or failure. If the challenge was not to beat Finland or Singapore on test scores, but to evolve neighbourhood schools that were both comfortably familiar and moderately innovative, schools have rather successfully met this challenge.

5. Ironically, public education is trapped more by its success than by its failure. In spite of all the years of reports of crisis and accusations of failure, parents still give their own schools high marks. The problem is this: *The era that schools were designed for is ever more rapidly fading away.*

6. Paraphrasing the 1989 Alberta *Rainbow Report* on health care: *It is no longer good enough to merely learn how to do better what public education already does well* (p. 19). Learning that fosters new and more mature uses of the mind is urgently required. In spite of the heroic efforts of teachers, schools are in danger of becoming places that are toxic to learning.

7. It is dawning on teachers and parents that our next big challenge is to reconstruct the way we as a community create democratic "contexts for productive learning" in the commons, the public space (*How Schools Might Be Governed and Why*, p. 34). New design principles hover just out of touch or sight. They reach right to the foundations of public education.

8. Public education faces a frontier and a continental divide of change that signifies a clear departure from the last century and more of schooling. To my knowledge, no complete and "over the top" maps exist. Fortunately, due to decades of research and experimentation on creating change in schools, some trails and reliable guides exist.

9. Most schools have launched small-scale expeditions into the foothills and steep valleys of the continental divide as they have grappled with prescriptions, innovations and adaptations. Few schools have had the means to fully and systematically analyze and draw conclusions about the barriers and opportunities out in them thar hills.

10. This book is an attempt to provide an initial and more complete map, one that will support some brave expeditions and more detailed mapping.

Keeping in Mind the Purpose

It is important to keep in mind the ultimate purpose and driving force behind these changes. *It is becoming increasingly urgent that young people develop the deep and enduring capacity to take charge of their own learning in a way that leads to more mature, self-aware and socially integrated uses of the mind.* This is the "learning project" for Canada for the 21st century. I call it co-created learning – learning that is developed by the learner and the family in concert with learning designers who create the connections to the disciplines to be mastered and the authorities that must be satisfied. These developments will affect all age groups as we have all been handicapped by old models of commodified and institutionalized learning. The work, as it unfolds itself in front of us, is very exciting. Some of the best and brightest thinkers and writers exploring this level of change are Walter Truett Anderson, Don Beck, Robert Kegan and Ken Wilbur.

The following are examples of new possibilities, tentative new directions that might lead us to the essential features of emerging systems for learning and our "Third Schools." These possibilities and new directions will be developed more fully in the visit to 2025 and the following chapters.

The Path Ahead

1. There are clear signals, such as the pressure for personalization, that new designs and approaches that support and ensure co-created learning will soon emerge. As we will see, these developments take us past the traditional packaging and delivery of commodified schooling. They reveal the intricate connections between the distinct sectors of the continental divide – learning, technology, governance, leadership, roles, and resources. Our growing understanding of these connections leads us to new maps of the future of learning.

2. The continental divide that separates traditional from transformed learning systems will be crossed, possibly quite soon. These journeys will be made by teachers, parents, learners and community supporters who have been inspired by new possibilities for learning, are wrapping their minds around a more integrated map of the learning divide, and have the courage and competence to take on the long-term challenge of the work. A few exceptional organizations will help them. They will invent our Third Schools and will operate them alongside and inside the current system.

3. New legal frameworks will be developed to express our renewed and redirected societal interest in learning. The legal responsibility for a child's learning will be shifted away from the state and toward the parents. Prototype Third Schools will be freed (deregulated) from the constraints of the current system. New linkages and supports, checkpoints and safeguards will follow.

4. Learners and their families will become co-creators of learning, working from a rich portfolio of design options ranging from home-centred learning to community and technology-centred learning to learning centres, some with classrooms. Many of the good bits from the Second Schools will be incorporated into the Third Schools. The more restricted current menus, such as private or charter or alternative schools, will turn into complementary learning systems.

5. Third School learners will advance steadily to their highest conceptual and operational levels of self-governance and co-creation of learning. These capacities will be nurtured and monitored. The nurturance will reside in the learning. Children and youth will be encouraged to take on unique challenges. Additional supports such as coaching and mentoring will be available.

6. Individual learning designs and statements of commitment will be paramount in the process. We will explore how the central concept of the system will shift from a "supply-side" delivery of fixed choices to unique and evolving designs centred on individual learners. This has dramatic implications for current roles and skill sets.

7. Roles will move from traditional top-down leadership to shared governance. The new learning system will require new capacities and professional competencies, and these will emerge through new practice and career preparation. The kind of openness that makes scrutiny both easy and unnecessary will also emerge. The Third Schools will not need school principals or any of the other vestiges of hierarchic school administration.

8. New roles will emerge. Possibilities include a family teacher and learning coach and a learning design specialist. In the scenario to follow, I will suggest that the people in these new careers be called learnists. The family learnists, the prime resource to the learners and their families, will act as learning coaches and mentors. The learning design learnists will extend the already impressive achievements in learner diagnostics and program design. A variety of community learnists and paraprofessionals will work in schools, in the community, in supportive businesses and organizations, and on all the bridges between them.

So welcome to an initial, tentative and almost certainly incomplete map, one version of the new territory that awaits on the far side of the divide. I will describe this unfamiliar world using some of the familiar features of schooling on this side of the divide. In some cases this will not work and I will cautiously introduce some new language and ideas. Maybe I will even be given credit for some new jargon, always a dubious achievement.

To sum up this summary:

- Mature uses of the mind and levels of consciousness are being called forth by the needs of our society and the planet. The need is urgent. It is connected with our future quality of living, if not our survival. As Kegan has put it, "the mental demands of modern life" have given us all a new curriculum.

- Modes of learning are emerging in response to this need that are in fundamental conflict with the old and institutionalized modes of schooling. Nothing less than a new type of public education is required to speed up the emergence of our Third Schools.

This huge and growing gap between the quality of human consciousness and the quality of our educational institutions has grown up through three stages:

Schools are as they should be

In fact, once upon a time, the alternative probably wasn't even a thinkable or discussible thought. Schools were what they were. Rebelling against them would have been like rebelling against brushing your teeth or going to church on Sunday. School days, school days! Once we got out of the places, we managed to wax nostalgic about them. Reading and 'riting and 'rithmatic....

Schools are not necessarily perfect but they are perfectly necessary

The early critiques of schooling raised many questions about the quality of teaching and the intellectual challenges for students, but few about the fundamental problem of warehousing young minds. Even as the critiques began to populate the power structures and ideologies of the public schools, the overriding message beamed out to students was that for all their problems, schools were a necessary part of growing up and preparation for life. As the slogan said, Stay In School! As Sandy Garrett, a U.S. school superintendent once put it, "There's nothing wrong with public education that what's right about it can't fix (*Vital Speeches of the Day*, 1995, vol.61, p. 746).

Schools cannot remain as they are

This is still an emerging point of view struggling to live in tandem with the second-stage view that we can reform what we have got. As the churn and foam of reform continues to engulf the system, parents and students are learning to hive off and adapt parts of it as they create new options. There are increasingly urgent signals from society that a more radical departure is required.

My elementary schooling occurred near the end of the First Schools, in the 1940s. My teaching career, short as it was, took me into the early years of the Second Schools. I am, to my mild surprise and great pleasure, still here to witness the emergence of the Third Schools. Much from those early years, if not exactly 20/20 vision, now makes sense. As we gaze into the future, we are way below 20/20 if indeed we even know where to look. But we are getting better all the time. And we are moving from looking to seeing because of the importance of the challenge and the opportunity.

Our capacity for co-creating learning and the quality of the learning experience must now keep pace with the necessary growth in the quality of our consciousness and mature uses of the mind or we will soon be in big trouble, both socially and economically.

And now, step into your time machine and dial up the years needed to get you to 2025, where you will meet an exceptional Third Schooler, Claire Chappell.

Claire's Graduation – A Third School Story

The mid-morning February sunlight slants in across the kitchen table. Much of Claire Chappell's family life has unfolded around its familiar and well-worn surface. Claire is in a strange mood, dreamy and thoughtful. The unusually warm, gently breezy day adds to her mind's wish to wander.

"It's a nice round number, 2025," Claire thinks. "It's a great year to be graduating – the quarter century mark!"

The significance of the date has been on Claire's mind lately as she begins to focus on work she must do in the next few months to complete her journey as a pioneer Third Schooler. And the celebrations! It is all very exciting and satisfying for a hard-working and exuberant seventeen-year-old.

The work? Claire feels a mixture of anticipation and nervousness. The report and presentation she must create for her Third School graduation requirement is very important. "Sure, all Third Schoolers must do it. But still, I'm one of the first, so there aren't many people I can talk to about how to approach the topic. There isn't a magic fountain of advice out there. Well, it's about me, so I guess I have to be the expert."

"But Sergio, he's been great." She's reflects on her many discussions with her "family teacher," the learning advisor assigned by the Third Schools system, many years ago, to work with her and her family.

"You have some leeway in how you do this assignment," he said a few months ago when they first talked about the presentation. "The core of it must be a written piece that is thorough and thoughtful. We're talking 10 to 15 pages here. But beyond that, you can add visuals like images and graphics, music, and art work. For example, how about quoting a few strips from that cartoon autobiography you did a few years ago?"

Claire sighs. "Fine, but what about the topic, the content? I'm struggling with this assignment. My life as a learner has been filled with projects and presentations. But this one really matters and I want to do it well."

She has talked with her Mom, who sat in on one or two of the meetings with Sergio. "It's about you as a learner, Claire, and what you have learned in a dozen years of carefully assuming a great deal of responsibility for your own learning. You're right. This is an important assignment because it sits right at the heart of the Third Schools, their main reason for being. What do you know about yourself as a learner. How do you, like a gourmet chef, go about creating good food for your mind – good learning for yourself? Tell that story clearly and honestly and you'll do just fine."

Claire sighs again. "Clearly? Honestly? Agreed!" She goes to the counter and refills her coffee. Her mood lifts as her thoughts turn to the coming weekend gathering.

Mmmm yes! The celebration! This coming weekend, her family and friends will gather to celebrate the completion of a year-long series of graduation projects.

These projects, progressively more challenging as the year moved on, were designed by Claire and her family, with advice, ideas, and a very helpful bit of reading suggested by the Third School staff. She remembers her rising excitement when she read, many months ago now, the piece from *The Cultural Creatives* by Paul Ray and Sherry Anderson, describing just such a year of challenges. It was called "Preventing Ophelia." It was inspiring and Claire was moved to imitate some of the projects that a girl named Laure took on a few decades ago in the 1990s. Claire's own projects moved from a room redesign and redecorating project to some research and writing of family history to the culminating activity – doing the planning and most of the arrangements for a hike, with some favourite cousins, along the West Coast Trail on Vancouver Island.

"Whooee – more than I bargained for." She smiles as she remembers. "But what a rush, the scenery, the evenings by the fire and…finishing the hike. I never thought the end of a trail could look so good. And what a year. I did major learning about some worthwhile things," words she knows her family teacher would love to hear. Claire has created a presentation, using her own photographs from the West Coast Trail, for a biology project. Her material will be kept on file for other Third Schoolers to use.

Some of her West Coast Trail mates will be at the celebration. She can't wait to see them and talk about it all over again.

Claire's thoughts drift back to the presentation she's trying to get started. Possibilities begin to float into her head. "It's time to get some of these ideas down and head for the keyboard." Claire pulls a piece of paper toward her and begins making a list.

1. Looking back – the story of my learning to be a learner.

2. Who and what I am as a learner.

3. The mistakes I've made; the insights I've gained.

4. Relationships and how my approaches to learning engage me with my family, friends and community.

5. How I think about the strategies I will use to create learning.

6. The possibilities I see ahead for me as a learner – my interests, passions and possible vocations.

7. There's more – keep thinking.

"I could divide it into sections. I could write about my early years, how my life as a learner began, then about the years I hit my stride and felt I was succeeding more than failing to take charge of my own learning, and then about maturing as a learner and feeling that I understood why I was making certain choices and decisions."

"Actually, my story will also be a story of the creation of the Third Schools! I should include something about the struggle of the new system to come to life as well as my struggles as a learner."

Claire's mind wanders to some conversations she remembers having with her parents about how they made the decision that their children would be Third Schoolers. Claire was curious back then because as a child she knew that she was not "going to school" like many of the other kids were. She wanted to know why, and she asked. Her Dad wasn't around very much. He was constantly travelling and working in various countries, work that has now taken him more or less out of the lives of his family. But she remembers the few conversations they had had in her early teen years because he had spoken openly and forcefully about his initial doubts about the Third Schools.

"Your Mom saw the possibilities more quickly than I did."

"Yeah well, she knew us better too." Claire remembers being surprised at how quickly that sad and angry unspoken thought sped through her mind.

"And, we were both worried about the existing schools, about whether you and Scott would get what we, back then, thought of as a good well-rounded education."

"Why?"

"We had heard stories from other parents with kids in school. It seemed like a great struggle was going on. There were constant issues and crises over things like grades and testing, budget cuts and fundraising, staff turnover and sensitive topics like evolution. It seemed like some of the most important things to us, like who your teacher would be and whether you could develop your own unique approaches to learning, had big question marks around them – like whether we would be even be involved."

"So we talked to some ordinary schools as well as lots of other parents. I didn't like the picture we got. To only be around in case you needed help with homework and to do some fundraising – it just didn't seem good enough for us. So we talked to some people who were organizing a support group for something they called the Third Schools. At first, I couldn't take it seriously. But your Mom kept talking me into going to 'just one more meeting.' I had to get past the idea that we couldn't simply turn you and Scotty over to a good school system, that they couldn't take it all over and offer us the kind of involvement we really wanted."

"Then they started talking about the development of good minds, maturing minds that could cope with the challenges of the 21st century. That's when I really started listening. They talked about a particular kind of self-directed learner, a learner that would be both independent and connected to their family, community and good learning in very significant ways. It was music to my ears, Claire. They used a term I've always liked – co-created learning. And while these folks didn't seem to have anything against the ordinary schools back then, they were quite clear that the kind of learning they were talking about would not and could not happen in the school system as it was. Sure, there would still be some classrooms and some classroom teaching. They knew that some kids, like your brother, would need that at times. So the Third Schools said that some bits of traditional schools would be part of the mix. But the deciding and the doing, what we called the design and delivery of learning, that had to be centred in the home and on the learner. I could only guess what would follow!"

Claire remembers one of her last long conversations with her Dad where he paused and gave her a very direct look.

"You know, Claire, I was more involved in your learning at first, in those early years. I wanted that. I was away so much and, well, it brought me closer to you and Scott when I was in on designing learning with you kids, your Mom and our family teachers. And then, to see you two, in your own ways, wrap your minds around the challenges of understanding your own learning was very satisfying…exciting too. Knowing what I need to learn and how to get on with my own learning has been very important to my work. I wanted you kids to be able to do that too."

Claire is grateful for this memory of some significant conversations, so fully recalled. She feels a surge of gratitude for her Dad, whom she thought she hardly knew at all. Well, they obviously had had a few great conversations. Maybe her report could be based on her memories and those of her parents as pioneers of the Third Schools. She could interview her Mom, who could also help recall past conversations with herself and her Dad. And what about her brother Scotty? So smart, but so serious about his projects and his schedules. Yes, she would talk to him too, about his memories and experiences, his unique path through the experience of the Third Schools.

In the meantime, a nice sunny day beckons and a visit to the gym sounds good. Claire asks her Mom for the car, grabs her phone and begins calling some friends.

The next day, Claire digs out some old family binders and file folders. Her memories of her early years of learning are vague and disconnected. She wants to put some real events in place to give her memories a place to land. She opens the learning logbook, the binder that contains her family's learning history. She goes to the fourteen-year-old page where her parents and their very first family teacher, Meg Owens, recorded their thoughts on why learning was important to the Chappell family and what the outcomes of learning might be for Claire and for them all. It was called the Statement of Commitment, a required part of any family's choice to enroll in the Third Schools.

"Wow," Claire thinks as she reads. "My parents sure gave this new system a tall order."

In a preamble on what matters about learning, her parents had written that learning both opens and disciplines the mind. The mind is constantly opened by new experiences and opens to new and challenging ideas. The mind is disciplined because it is willing to do the hard work required to understand something fully and it is able to make the connections between new and past learning.

"Pretty serious stuff," thinks Claire, "but then, look at this!"

Her eyes scan down to the section on the first year of Third Schooling. Her parents titled it "Learning to Play; Playing to Learn." Her parents wrote that they would like to be part of a "learning system that studies their child" more than a situation where "their child is learning to study for the system." There are signs that a great deal of help was given by the family teacher. For example, there are specifics about how the play environment should have fewer toys and more open-ended materials – chunks of wood and cardboard, armloads of fabrics, and paints, crayons and glues so that games and play spaces could be invented. The outdoors played an important role too; more important than her faint memories of excursions, camping and hiking with family, friends and other Third Schoolers would have led her to believe.

Claire recalls hearing about the great toys and computer games some of her cousins' pre-schools had. But this was not "pre"-school and the usual manufactured toys and games didn't fit the plan. This was her playful entry into the serious game of learning. Her parents, again, no doubt with help from their family teacher, went on to emphasize that they expected assistance with creating such an early learning environment and, more significantly, assistance with methods they could use to observe and note the emerging patterns in their daughter's learning.

Later, Claire talks to her Mom.

"Was I at home all the time?"

"No. Fortunately we were able to join a group of Third Schooling parents and we took turns hosting the play/learning centres. It helped to have other parents observing and commenting in that learning logbook we kept. We found a progressive early-learning centre nearby and they were willing to take Third Schoolers in part-time. They were very good at getting you kids involved in a variety of activities, some of them early skill building, but mainly designed to see how well you could do things like cooperate with other kids, organize your play and games, and sustain your own activities. They gave us lots of good information."

"But how did you and Dad find the time? How could you go to work?"

"Your Dad travelled a lot and worked seven days a week when he was off doing mediation and conciliation work. But when he got home, he would take several days off. He said that helping you kids helped him wind down. I worked part-time at home and could go in to the office whenever, even in off-hours if I liked. It wasn't easy, but I guess we became believers in this new system and were willing to take the time. And remember, you were learning at your own pace, so we weren't doing this for a fixed 10 months a year. We travelled and that was part of your learning plan."

"Yes, the learning plan." Claire had not thought to include it. But of course she would. It contained some of the most important pieces of the puzzle. She remembers how, as she got older, she became more and more involved with the design of her own learning plan. She worked with Meg and then Sergio when he took over. They worried over the priorities, the essentials of the government-mandated curriculum, the many short-term studies and projects she did with her family, other learners and community volunteers, and the long-term deep themes she pursued around ecology, family history and caregiving. At certain points, the learning design people in the local Third Schools learning design centre took over and re-created the annual plan and the updates.

"I'll come back to that," thinks Claire. Some of the most important information in the learning plans was in response to her family's and then her own growing mastery of her learning and how to co-create it with the Third School system. "These were the key steps in my growth as a capable (I hope) self-directed learner and I need to find those bits of personal history and build my report on them."

Claire takes a few days off from her graduation project. She attends a youth conference on building democratic processes around the role of the citizen – a full day which she thoroughly enjoys, even the long bus ride, thanks to the bright sunlight and the feel of an early spring. While at the downtown conference centre, she attends a briefing on becoming a Third Schools junior learning assistant. Claire will graduate early, and one of the options available to her is to stay in the Third Schools and work with families and the other learning specialists – the learnists. Her salary would come from the provincial per-pupil grant that would have been paid for one more year of learning. Not that this new assignment won't mean tons of learning. Claire finds out that, while she is being a learning assistant, she can also take an advanced history course she has been interested in. It's offered to senior Third Schoolers by the local college, thankfully a decent bike or bus ride away. It involves lots of reading and independent study, but importantly for Claire, it also involves talking to and documenting the lives of women and men who were leaders in the successful transition on the prairies from large-scale food production to smaller-scale and more diversified farming, driven, in part, by climate change. This is a passion of Claire's which grew out of one of her learning plan themes around sustainability.

When Claire gets back to her graduation report, she begins to think about her mid-childhood years. Like her early childhood learning, memories are faint. She decides that for this section of her report, she will spend time with Sergio and ask him for some help with her binders of learning plans.

"After all, he picked up my learning file when I was seven or eight years old. He ought to remember some bits I can use, and he certainly should have some ideas about the changes in my learning plan. But first, it's time for a chat with 'little' brother Scott."

Scott's learning plans have always specified more time in the local learning centres. He likes to spend time with small groups of learners and the instructors, learning coaches and subject mentors that make up the rather diversified team of learnists. So Claire knows she must wait until early afternoon when Scott usually gets home, brews a cup of tea, and heads for their shared work space they call the "brain drain." She waits for him there.

"Hey Scotty, how goes your day?"

"Oh, s'alright, I guess. What's up?"

"I'm doing my graduation project. Y'know, me as learner. I need to talk to you. I'm doing a bit of a history of me as a Third Schooler. You've done some things differently and I want to know your thoughts on the route you took compared to me."

Scott looks at Claire over the rim of his cup. There is a brief silence.

"Sure, why not. It's just that, like, you were there watching it all happen. What'll I add?"

"Quite a bit. Sure, I can go scrounging in the binder through your learning plans, but I want to know how you remember the choices being made that are in the plans. I think it would help me make my story clearer if I could kind of compare it with yours."

Another pause.

"Well, OK. So when?"

Claire knows that Scott would rather schedule their chat so that he can think about it a bit, plus he probably has plans for the rest of his day. But Claire doesn't want to wait too long.

"Sooner the better for me."

"Well, I can't get into the graphic design studio tomorrow morning. Let's see…" and here Scott pauses.

Claire jumps in, a habit she has when her brother hesitates.

"Tell you what. I'll meet you at the learning centre in the morning and I'll buy us coffees in the café by the main office."

"Sounds good," says Scott as he turns to his waiting work.

When Claire goes upstairs, she is pleased to see that her Mom has taken a break from her office, is in the kitchen and has just put the kettle on. Claire gathers up some questions on her mind about a topic that currently intrigues her: "How was it possible that I was given so much freedom to pursue learning?" Claire knows that Third Schoolers have the freedom to move around in the community, connect with knowledgeable and interesting people, and with a lot of help from the learnists, create a huge variety of learning situations, few of which would bring to mind a traditional classroom. True, transportation was a challenge, especially in the early years, but parents learned to carpool, walk with their children, and create safe ways for them to travel by foot and bike. As climate change and energy shortages loomed larger, many more people became self-propelled and public transit systems responded, especially when the Third Schools were able to provide assurances that young learners with bus passes would avoid peak ridership hours.

It all seems quite normal to Claire, but she knows that the kind of liberated learning she takes for granted doesn't work for everyone and, only a few decades ago, was permitted for almost no-one. She thinks, "Without the freedom to make contacts, talk to people, arrange meetings, go places…just lay out the work, the Third Schools would not be possible. Once upon a time, this freedom to design your own learning wasn't approved or allowed for anyone except some home schoolers. What happened?"

"Hey Mom," she says, sliding into a chair at the kitchen table.

"Oh, hi Claire. Would you like some tea? A biscuit?"

"No thanks. Not thirsty; not hungry…for a change."

Her Mom pours the hot water into a teapot and looks at Claire through the small cloud of steam. "What's up? You look kind of preoccupied."

"Well, I am, I guess. I'm trying to remember something you told me years ago about kids being either at school or at home with their parents and, you know, safety and security and what a huge deal it all used to be. And here I am, running around, a free spirit doing my learning thing. Oh, and who was the world's worst Mom?"

"I think it was America's worst mom, actually. Let me think. I recall a news story from around 2010 about a Mom in New York who got criticized by other parents for letting her young son ride the subway on his own (*The Globe and Mail*, April 21st, 2009). She started a web site. It had a neat name – Free Range Kids, I think. Yes, I remember that story because, at about that time, a backlash started against what was called helicopter parenting – overly protective parents hovering over their kids' lives. And hovering was something your Dad and I definitely did not want to do. And yes, it was all part of a huge issue around safety and security, how to keep trouble away from our kids and our kids out of trouble."

"Why was it such a big deal?"

"Well, things were quite different then, back around when you were born. Some schools actually promoted themselves to parents by promising no recesses or field trips – almost like they were saying, 'Once your child gets to our school, your child is kept in the school.'"

"Recess," interrupts Claire. "Was that when kids were allowed to go outside and run around and play games?"

"Yes, but with lots of supervision – even surveillance in some schools. But recess was being reduced and restricted, not just for safety, but because of the pressure on staff time and schools wanting to do more physical activities and sports in class time. Anyway, moms and dads walked or drove their kids to school and were there, or made sure someone was there to pick them up at the end of the day. If no-one came, the schools had to keep the kids there, have a teacher drive them home, or start making phone calls. Kids were kept close to home, even mostly indoors in some neighbourhoods. The schools, they had to be very cautious and account for every kid all of the time – and fair enough, it's what parents wanted and expected."

"Was it that dangerous, really?" asks Claire.

"Well, yes and no…mostly no. The world hadn't suddenly gone hostile to kids. Yes, there were some terrible incidents, assaults and abductions, and missing kids, some runaways. But there was a growing feeling that parents were overreacting. The mom, "America's Worst Mom," went on to talk and write about her "free range kids" who had the freedom to roam, play, meet friends and run around that their parents had when they were kids. I think that we, your Dad and I, were likely influenced by her views."

"So to be Third School Parents, you had to ignore the fears and kind of just trust the system?"

"Well, other things happened. For example, people stopped moving as much. Biking and walking became much more common. Neighbours whom we knew could keep an eye on the streets and the neighbour kids whom they knew. Neighbourhood policing got better. Technology helped too, like your MeHear, the little GPS transmitter and instant communication necklace you wear. Sure, years ago kids carried little phones around, but now you just press a button and you've got us or someone on line…well, you know how it works and it has been very reassuring that you and Scott can wear something like that all the time. And then, there's the kind of scheduling and key contacts we've been able to have. I know where you are or should be, and who you are working with, all the time. That's why we always stressed: Call us if anything changes. Of course, when you were younger, the Third Schools meant working in supervised groups. When you weren't learning at home, that is. Sure, there were some missed connections, but I don't think you were ever at risk. A motto of the Third Schools could be: 'Let the kids back into the world.' "

"Really," thinks Claire, staring out the window as her Mom sips the last bit of her tea. "I can't imagine what the last 10 or 11 years might have been like. How small my world could have been, bouncing between home and a big, red brick building with, yes, lots of people, but…those bells and schedules. And having to be driven, escorted everywhere. Wow."

Claire wrestles with her thoughts. "Ok, fine, I wouldn't have liked it, but how does this puzzle piece fit into my report? Is it about how I used my freedom to learn?"

Claire's Mom puts her cup by the sink and, seeing Claire deep in thought, slips out of the kitchen and down the hall to her office.

"It's not just about my freedom. It's about all those details in my daily plan; where I was, who I was with, the work I was doing, the study segment, project or learning outcome I was moving ahead on; details that used to bug me so much at times, but now I see how they made up a structure for my learning and a web of support and security for me and my parents. The processes of my Third Schooling helped create…hmmm, what should I call it…liberated learning. Well, it fits in my report somehow. And now I'm even more curious about how Scotty dealt with all this."

The next morning Claire, in a mood to jog, arrives early at the learning centre. She knows the building well. Her meetings with Sergio have been here for many years. The learning design studio, mostly computers now, takes up most of a wing. As she wanders down the gleaming lino hallways, she remembers how it used to look.

"Hard to believe this used to be a junior high with real live classroom teachers. I wonder if they all became learnists or moved on to a traditional junior high somewhere else. I'm glad that some stayed here and became learning specialists, many of them in subject areas. It's been especially good for Scott, who likes to work with other people, especially specialists in the areas of math and science. And then there are his study focus groups…I'll hear more about them in a few minutes."

Up until a few years ago, the sprawling old, red brick building still operated a few classrooms of traditional, fully scheduled schooling. The enrolment was already low and sinking back when Claire started out as a Third Schooler. In a bid to keep the traditional junior high operating, the new Third Schools learning centre was located there. Claire can remember the hallways still echoing with the voices of teachers and large groups of students as she and her parents, and then later, she on her own, went to the frequent meetings with her family teacher and the annual meetings to review the updates to her learning plan. But the junior high started losing even more students, teachers and programs as the Third School enrolment grew. Then, in 2022, after the costs had become too high and the programming too scant, the old public school was closed.

Claire sees the changes to the building as she slowly makes her way to the café. As she passes the learning design centre, she can see the screens glowing as the learning design specialists work on learning plans for a host of learners. In the distance, at the back of the centre, she sees the small meeting rooms where learners and their families meet with staff and go over learning plans, review progress on the plans and new resource needs, and schedule diagnostic tests as well as the few remaining provincial exams. Claire thinks about the time spent by staff, not to mention parents, in following up these meetings with the search for resources to support the many individual learning activities, resources such as software and online text and media, books and other print material, expertise in the community and in the partner companies and organizations, and the many gems of learning housed not just in libraries and museums but in professional associations linked to engineering, medicine, law, architecture, the arts…the list goes on and on.

Claire passes a door marked Learning Archive, and she knows that back there are shelves containing the learning plans of other Third Schoolers, slowly being edited and put online. She has worked back there as a volunteer sorting materials, removing personal information, and applying key words such as "independent," "online," "learning group," "self-study," community-based" and so on. This enables the learning design staff to access and use previous learning designs and plans to create new ones for learners with similar needs.

"I sure hope they get the funding soon to finally get this all online," Claire muses. "I've been very lucky with the time and attention so many people gave me for my learning plans. I guess copies of some of my learning plans are, or will be, in there somewhere. Hopefully they'll be of use to other Third Schoolers."

She retraces her steps so she can loop through the learning-activity wing. She'll soon be a part of offering learning assistance in these rooms so her interest is more heightened than usual.

"It's always fun to see who's in and which small groups they're working with. The groups are such a neat mixture of learnist briefings, the mini-modules of instruction (I'll be doing some of them), kids helping kids, computers, media.... Sometimes I wonder what it would have been like if I had put more group work into my learning plans. Oh well, it just wasn't me, my way of learning, and figuring that out has been a lot of fun and should be a part of this report I'm working on. I'll bet Scott's in his math group. I'd better be careful. He might think I'm snooping. Ah, little brothers."

A constant buzz of conversation, more distant voices from the e-learning world, presentations and even music float out of the small rooms that used to be larger classrooms. Some spaces are set up as small labs and workshops, many of them multi-purpose so that an array of materials and many kinds of learning activities can occur in them. There are no classrooms in this building. Now, learners with learning plans calling for more structure and scheduled classroom time ride a bus to another learning centre equipped to offer varied modules of traditional instruction.

"I'm glad I can still be a part of this next year. The doors of the big university lecture halls will close on me soon enough. Then we'll see how well I can adapt to a more traditional kind of learning."

Claire rounds the last corner into the large common room and building lobby that once was a small gymnasium. Behind an island of potted plants is the café. She can smell the coffee and fresh baking from the centre's own kitchen and…there's Scott. He has arrived ahead of Claire. His head is bowed over a bottle of juice and an e-book. Claire grabs two coffees and joins him.

"Hey Scotty, how's it going?"

"OK. And you?"

"Oh great. I just had a stroll around the learning centre. It brought back some memories. I'm looking everywhere for inspiration so I can write my grad report. So, thanks for doing this."

Scott nods. He waits for Claire to take the lead.

"Were you in one of your study focus groups this morning?"

"Yeah, the math gang."

"How's that going?"

"Good. It's working, and I'm glad."

"You sound, I don't know, relieved I guess. Why?"

"Well, it's really helped." Scott hesitates. "At one point early last year, Sergio thought I might have to request some classroom time over at the instruction centre. But as it turns out, I didn't."

"You're kidding," Claire says, surprise in her voice. "That's for kids who really need structure."

"I know. I thought I might be one of them, but I guess not."

"The study focus groups, they were your idea, weren't they?"

"Well, sort of. I talked with my friend Anthony and to a couple of kids I met in the math learning-activity rooms. We all agreed that we needed to be more focused on, y'know, results and deadlines. Problem is, we all like math, but we tend to get distracted. We learn something and then we all want to play around and apply it in different ways. Sergio asked me what I thought would work. I said that we all needed some regularly scheduled times to meet, share our work, help each other with the rough spots, get a lesson or two if need be, y'know, nail some things down, skills, key ideas, but then move on. Sergio suggested the name, math study focus group. It worked for us and we've stuck with it. We have study focus groups now in science. We were slowing down, especially in physics. We wanted to just explore stuff, like the huge upgrade to that monster particle accelerator in Europe that they got fired up a few years ago."

This is more than Claire is used to hearing from her brother. "It is *so* Third Schools," she thinks. "He knew what he needed *and* figured out what to do." She is intrigued, and presses on.

"Scott, if you don't mind my asking, when did you know that you needed this, um, special kind of approach. I don't want to just say structure, except it is, only it's your own."

"Yeah, I guess so. Even back in years five, six and seven — I remember those years because I used to get so frustrated. When Dad was around…well, we talked about it. I felt like whenever I learned something, all it meant was, like, time to move on. I guess I picked things up pretty quickly, but that didn't mean I was always ready to gobble up more. He helped me explain it to Sergio when he was first assigned to us."

"Ah, so that's when you started getting into those special projects. I remember you and your pals walking around with tape measures. Doing a survey project. You were barely out of basic arithmetic and you were keen to measure things and make maps. That was a neat map you came up with of the shopping centre down on 58th Avenue. It was a group of dads, wasn't it, that kept taking you over there and talking to the store owners?"

"Yeah. Mom was interested, but I think she worried about me not getting on with my learning plan." Then, hesitantly, "I…I think that Mom maybe wanted me to be more like you. Independent and just getting on with it all. Happy just learning and forging ahead on your own."

He waits for Claire's reaction. She thinks for a minute about how Scott must miss his Dad more than he has shared with his sister or his mother.

"Mmm, maybe. I think she worried that she just wasn't doing enough to help you figure out your own approach to learning. I'm older, so I had to go through this Third School stuff first. Maybe I was just a handy source of examples."

"Yeah, maybe."

"Scott, if you don't mind me asking, do you feel like you have a better handle on how you like to do learning now? What was the biggest problem you had to solve in figuring this learning thing all out?"

Scott seems relaxed, leaning back, legs crossed, but Claire watches as Scott's right foot begins to twitch back and forth, an old signal of nervous energy. Maybe she has pushed too far.

"It isn't all figured out; not the way you mean. At least, I hope it isn't. There are other ways to play this learning game that I haven't figured out yet. I'm not through learning about stuff and I'm not through learning about how I might learn. About where I jump off from how I like to learn now to how I might learn in different ways. Even if there's risks. But then, as Mom and Dad always said, the scores aren't everything."

"Another thing…my pals and I call it 'learning by not doing.' We've always liked to do things with what we've learned. Almost right away. Like, science is great, but can it help me get that old electric car of Dad's going again. Mom wants it out of the back yard anyway. But sometimes things just need to be thought about. And fitted in to the next chunk of learning that is always waiting. How do I get better at that, better at making my learning flow."

"Have you talked to Sergio?"

"Yeah, I have. He listens and is sympathetic. But he knows I'm doing OK and maybe doesn't want to upset the apple cart. But, hey, that's all right for now. I haven't pressed him and it could be I'm not quite ready. When I am ready, I'll know, and Sergio and I will have to talk. Maybe I'll recruit Mom too and get a review of my learning plan."

Claire doesn't really hear Scott's last sentence or two before he trails off, staring at her wide-eyed expression. She thinks, "Wow. Our two paths. Scott's is learning *about* in order to get to *why* and *how to*. Mine is learning *how to* and *why*, with other people, in order to figure out what it's all *about*, to work back into the ideas and theories. Hmmm, maybe I'm oversimplifying, but I'll work on it, and it's got to go into my report somehow!"

She sees Scott staring at her, his eyebrows raised. Before he can resist, she leans over and hugs him and says, "Scotty, thanks. That was great. Really helpful."

"Really?" he says, pleased. "Well, OK. I guess I should go and see when I can get at the graphic design system, and then finish this book. See you later."

"Yes," says Claire. "And really, thank you."

Later, at home, Claire captures her chat with Scott in some notes, notes she hopes will become part of her report. She is having trouble summing up all the ideas she has gathered together in her notes. "How do I make sense of and communicate all this?" she worries. She knows that she is getting closer to having information to answer the questions that she listed several days ago. She can describe herself as a learner and dissect her learning strategies. But it all seems so abstract, bloodless almost.

"What if I did a typical day?" she wonders on a sudden impulse. "Could I pull it all together to describe a day of learning in the Third Schools? I would re-create a day in my life as a learner in my more senior years, when I was, say, fourteen or fifteen years old. That way I could demonstrate some of the skills I had developed – I hope. It might be too hard to crowd it all into one day."

Claire begins to sketch it out, tapping rapidly on the small e-sistant she always has with her. It turns out to be a difficult assignment.

"There really wasn't a typical day," she admits as she plays with the possibilities. "Not like getting up and going to a structured learning centre with a set timetable. But maybe I can fit in some of the usual activities and also show some of the many options I had to choose from. Even though each day seemed unique, there were some rhythms to them. It's worth a try."

Claire worries that talking about a typical day could be confusing to other Third Schoolers and misleading to non-Third Schoolers. But in spite of her nagging doubts, Claire begins pulling together some activities that would be typical of an "average" day, circa 2022. She pretends she is still fifteen. Some explanatory notes are necessary.

- ➤ Wake up, shower, and then a quick breakfast, often with Mom, sometimes with sleepyhead Scott.
    - o This is often a good time to talk about my day. Mom is always willing to help or at least hear me out with any questions or issues I have before she vanishes into her home office.
- ➤ Go for a run or play handball or badminton with Lycia.
    - o I like doing physical things so I might also take a break during the day to go hiking or cycling.

- Fire up my computer.
- If it's Monday, check my learning plan to see what deadlines and major assignments in my learning plan are coming up. Block in times for this week as needed. If necessary, call Sergio.
    - Yep. I have a big say now in creating or adapting assignments and setting deadlines, but I've learned (the hard way) not to mess with them.
    - It's usually not necessary to bother Sergio; our monthly meetings are enough.
- Make or confirm any appointments for the week, e.g., the local high school to use their science labs, my community mentors, and any volunteer commitments.
    - My (our) agreement with the school lets me use certain facilities when they have room, often with other Third Schoolers and always with an instructor or learning assistant.
- Lay out my workplan for the day.
- Grab my bike and head out to the local library or hop the bus and go downtown to museums and galleries to do any research related to projects such as history or art.
    - This may involve writing, so my e-sistant goes with me.
    - There is often more than one of us, but when I was younger, almost all our learning activities had to be done in groups. I like getting out on my own!
- I like to do math in the late morning when my concentration seems the best.
    - I'm doing my math on-line from a local learning centre that also works with adult self-directed learners.
    - Not my favorite way to learn. I like lots of people contact, but I get to see my e-learning advisor almost whenever I need to.

- And…they like working with Third Schoolers.

➢ By now it's probably noon, so take an exercise break.

- OR a group of us often gathers at a local community centre, church or private home for cooking, music or book club.
- I like to do a lot of my creative writing and reading in the evenings, but the monthly noon book club helps ensure we're all reading the novels and sharing our ideas about them. I like it when learnists and adult learners drop in because they're always interested in our book and they push our discussion into new areas. It makes my reports so much more fun.
- Cheryl, our community learnist sets this kind of stuff up. She's great. (And she'll bug us if we don't turn up!)

➢ Early afternoon is language time.

- It's great going down to Chinatown three times a week.
- My Chinese language coaches are volunteers, and they are very good.
- (Now I am also learning French at home using DVDs and a computer program.)

➢ Mid afternoon. No time to be dreamy or drowsy.

- This is the time I set aside for my long-term theme projects.
- My favorite projects are in the Caring theme, which ties in to my other fave, Living Sustainably, where I learn and get to apply a whole bunch of natural science.
- This time of day is good for the steady, focused reading and writing involved. (Still is, especially in winter.)
- (It was also a good time to make the contacts I needed with people such as the climate-change experts in the government, the gardening and horticulture folks on the city staff, and so

many others. (I had to catch them when they were in the city – if only by phone. Sometimes it felt like I lived on city transit.)

➢ In the late afternoon head over to Westland Park, the Senior's centre.

- o I am learning quilting from Amy Lafferty.
- o I also help her with her email.
- o (What a great connection. She looked so severe she scared me at first, but she is so wise and kind and we have become good friends. I miss it, but my two years of grad projects have filled up my extra time. I still get over to see Amy once in a while. She'll be at my celebration – yay!)

Claire scans the list. "Well, I do jump back and forward a bit," she thinks, "but not a bad start given the problems with that word "typical." Some of my most memorable days were the most untypical – the field trips, seminars and hands-on cooking and crafts workshops with community volunteers. I seem to have been interested in picking people's brains as far back as I can remember. And I always seemed to be saying "explain that to me" or "give me an example" rather than just letting them tell me about it. Some of my real enduring interests could not have been fitted in to a typical day. But I think it helps to tell my story."

The winter light has faded, and Claire realizes she is staring at a bright computer screen in a darkened room. It's getting late in the day and…it's Friday. She decides to have a quick bite of dinner, phone some friends and head off to a movie.

Monday morning arrives and her meeting with Sergio. Claire goes over the questions she wants to ask him. Conversations with Sergio are always good, even intense, but they can wander. Then there's that bit of nagging nervousness over the draft outline and some bits of text she has sent him. What will he say? And suggest? The walk to the learning centre calms her nerves and clears her mind.

Sergio looks up as Claire comes into his office. "No, his studio," Claire thinks. "That's what he likes to call it, his learning studio."

"Claire, good to see you. I've been reading over your outline and notes for your graduation report and, so far, it's looking very good."

"Thanks Sergio, but I need your help with all my old learning plans. There's just so much in them…"

"I know Claire, but we can hit some of the high points for that part of your learning story. I can help you with some background on things like the old subject areas – basic knowledge and skills in math, science and history – how all that worked. This is your story, but you can decide what you would like to include. You know, we were very fortunate, you and I, that your parents and your first family teacher…"

"Meg Owens," supplies Claire.

"Yes, Meg. They and you did a great job in your early years before I arrived on the scene. They began, and your initial learning plans show this, a process that elementary school teachers many decades ago called expanding horizons – family to neighbourhood to community to city – except that unlike those many years ago, you learned *in* those places rather than *about* those places with real people helping you to do many different activities. Do you remember the cooking and crafts with your Mom and other Third School parents?"

Claire nods, but there is a faraway look in her eyes.

"I thought you would. But do you remember the arithmetic of weighing and measuring? The geography of the ingredients you all used? And early on, you were only in year two or three, you and your Dad started collecting bugs in your yard, your garden. Just some identifying and describing, very elementary biology. And then, you got hooked on leaves; they became beautiful and fascinating to you. There are entries in your learning log about how you suddenly wanted to know everything about how leaves worked. You took pictures of leaves, pictures of pictures of leaves in magazines and books, surfed the web, and your Dad helped you draw a 3D cutaway of the interior world of a leaf.

"So, here's an idea about how your learning plans evolved. The engine of your learning was your curiosity. But very skillfully, Meg and the other learnists did not miss a chance to connect your interests with some critical skills and understandings, whether in science, math or history. It was some of the best learning design work I've seen since I got into this game of being a learnist. And some of the little booklets and reports you did back then, work that's in the learning portfolios from your early years, are very good."

Claire knows that Sergio is a great fan of the Third Schools and one of the most enthusiastic promoters. She loves to hear him tell stories and give examples of good learning design, but she jumps in and asks, "Thanks Sergio, but how do I do the big picture? I want to include some of these examples, but what's the big picture, as you see it, that emerges from all these years of learning plans…my learning plans?

"Well OK," says Sergio, "Good question. I think the big picture for you in the early years was about growing your own world of learning. This is not unusual for young Third Schoolers who are ready to launch. But you were especially eager to dive into all the activities that were offered to you. And, you were very good at doing the focused learning when it was added to your learning plan. So, the learning logs describe how talking to and writing about your neighbours and their families led you into some world history and geography. Very simplified, of course, but you wanted to know where everyone's families came from, and especially for the faraway ones, what it was like to live in their villages and cities. You drew maps and illustrated them. The food stories led you to try some of their interesting-sounding recipes, with help from your parents, and your learning plan responded with some arithmetic for making recipes work. You were very young and so were the Third Schools, so as we learnists like to say, we low-level helicoptered your learning, which brings us to the next phase."

"But wait," says Claire, "I want to capture an image here. I like it. I expanded, or grew, as you say, my learning world much in the same way that elementary kids years ago had their horizons expanded for them. Except, with a lot of help, I was able to use my interests to drive the growing and the learning."

"Yes, you just need a good graphic image here and the right words Claire, and you can sum up your early years for your report."

As Sergio pulls out another binder and opens another screen on his computer, Claire imagines strange combinations of images; layers like an onion and vanishing points. "The curved lines of an onion and the straight lines of perspective…hmmm. I might have something here," thinks Claire. "Yes, I remember something from my painting workshop about a famous illusion created by the Italian artist who built the monstrous domed roof over the Duomo in Florence. It was a painting with a hole where the lines of perspective met, a hole that you looked through from behind the painting and into a mirror. You felt like you were looking at the real building.... Oh, I'm not sure how this will work, but maybe I could use that image. The hole, or the window in the vanishing point, could somehow become my entry point to my expanding horizons of learning...."

Claire realizes that Sergio is staring at her with a look of fond amusement. "Sorry," she says, "I was thinking about that idea of an image you mentioned. My head was into layers of horizons and lines of perspective. Now I'm back."

"Not a problem," says Sergio. "I think that when you get lost in thought like that, you must be visiting some interesting places."

"How about Renaissance Florence," Claire replies, "but please, say more about doing an image. Hey, maybe I could call it...*the matrix*!!" Claire says the last two words dramatically to tease Sergio. But he doesn't react; he's off again.

"OK, it isn't really this simple, but think of a grid. There are intersecting rows and columns, or sets of parallel pathways that cross each other at right angles. It's really just lines, but let's say that the spaces between these intersecting lines are actually pathways that meet and cross each other to create...OK...your learning matrix. You, Claire, are standing at one of the four sides of the matrix, let's say the bottom or south side. The pathways that you are looking out at, indeed travelling along toward the north side, are the pathways to achieving many of your learning plan's core purposes and learning outcomes and, very important, to responding to your interests and passions that have emerged and matured over the years. These pathways are, if you like, paved with your many assignments and projects, your solo studies and group work, and your long-term themes with all their activities designed by you, us, your parents and all the others in the community and elsewhere with whom you've done your learning. From where you stand, the pathways are like long mosaic strands. Each mosaic tile is a shorter or longer commitment to a specific chunk of learning. Most are months long and some years. They are...."

"OK, I think I get it," Claire breaks in, "but what about the other pathways that cut across my learning paths? They must be about what we've come to call the 'stuff,' or sometimes the 'requireds' of the learning."

"Exactly," says Sergio. "You'll remember the many times we talked about content opportunities and filling content gaps. Those right-angle, west-to-east pathways contain what we used to call subjects, each with their own knowledge, skills and understandings. Once upon a time, before the Third Schools, those were the paths a child, a young student stood facing, west to east. Taken together, these eastbound paths were the curriculum, and teachers hoped it would intersect with students' interests often enough that getting through 'the program' wouldn't be too much of a grind. Legions of talented teachers became very good at softening a system with ideas about learning reaching back into 19th century Prussia."

"Ah…the kind of system that Albert Einstein ran smack into and escaped from?"

"You got it," says Sergio. "Now, in the 20th century, those legions of dedicated teachers became very good at finding opportunities to swing their students down to the south side of this matrix and use their questions and interests to fire up some real learning. They called it motivation, student engagement. But then, technology started to take that motivation elsewhere."

"Wow," says Claire. "It's almost like the Third Schools took the traditional landscape of schooling, turned it on its side, and turned it into a landscape of learning. Maybe that's the image we're talking about, my landscape of learning. Could that be my title?"

"Why not? I like it better than… *the matrix*." Sergio grins at Claire and checks his watch. "But there's a bit more to add here to answer your questions about how the learning plans worked. We learnists are pretty good at capitalizing on the high energy coming from your interests and your thoughtfulness about the deep maps and unifying themes that, from your perspective down there on the south side of the matrix, are the core of your learning plan. So, gazing at your progress sideways, from over here on the east side, when you and we review and revise your learning plan, we wily learnists drop chunks of content across your path. Sometimes big chunks of it. You are in on it, of course, and we use fancier names for it. But that's what we're doing. An example. Some years ago, you had pushed your drawing and sketching to the point where you were very interested in the composition of a painting – everything from subject matter to technique. You were taking your art work very seriously. You were excited and committed to pushing your skills and understanding further. So, when we were discussing some revisions to your learning plan, I suggested that you spend some time studying the Renaissance. We didn't need to call it history or social studies. We just needed to be sure that it served two purposes: addressing the provincial learning design requirements and enhancing your learning plan. For you, it was an expansion of learning to *do* painting, your interest in art, not to mention a rather nice virtual tour of 15th century Florence."

"No wonder I like to go there in my head," thinks Claire.

"Over the years," continues Sergio, "in other projects, you had developed a pretty solid outline of world history, so I felt that dropping you into the busy world of 14th and 15th century Italy wouldn't get you lost. And it was a great complement to your art studies."

"But, isn't that just a piece, one mosaic tile, and not a whole path?" Claire protests.

"Yes, you're right." Sergio taps on his computer screen. "From your perspective, the path you were on had different names. Earlier on, we agreed to call it Understanding the Human Struggle through the Arts. Later, you wanted to change it to The Arts and Reshaping my Reality. Looking at it sideways, we learnists just called it a module of history which we could modify to meet your needs. Those labels didn't matter to you, so we didn't use them…well, unless we called them 'requireds' and turned your attention to some pieces we'd missed. If you had the time, and it would take a while, and could read through all the years of your learning plans and our documentation, you would see how, by design, your learning paths were crossed by the content paths many times. You grew in your understanding of the human journey as it became part of Claire's journey. In fact, remember last year when you got interested in the Axial Age, we decided to reach back to your work on art and the Renaissance, using a theme of rebirth, and compare the flowering of human understanding that occurred in the Axial Age with the Renaissance."

"I remember," says Claire. "Yeah, I was on a path, as we're calling it, of looking at belief systems, not art this time, and was focused on what I came to call 'mind prisons.' I tried to bridge over 1,500 years of humanity and look at what was similar about the struggles. It was a lot of reading. And work. But, the subject specialist that evaluated my final essay seemed to like what I'd done."

Sergio nods. "One of the best-written assessments I've seen."

They pause as Claire struggles to fit this all together. "OK, you're saying that the matrix took my interests in learning, like ecology, family history, care-giving and so on, and connected them with things like, um, marine biology, the science around alternative energy, the history of poverty and aging, and…yeah, I think I see it. My learning paths didn't lead me into math the way Scott's did, so I guess that's why I spent so much time on those e-learning modules."

"That's right Claire. But don't forget that the learning pathways aren't as clean and tidy as we're talking about them here. Sometimes the edges were blurred, or they converged and overlapped, or even raised new learning challenges. So we squeezed a bit of math in that way too. Actually, most of the time, we didn't need to be formal about it, like 'OK Claire, time for some content, some real learning.' Most of the knowledge and skills just resided in your learning pathways, powered by your learning interests." Sergio grins. "Although…we weren't above trying to nudge your learning interests into new pathways. If we needed to, we would have laid on some content to fill those gaps and avoid roadblocks. Let's face it, there were those provincial GQE's, your Graduation Qualification exams."

"Right," says Claire. "However, they really weren't such a big deal."

"No," Sergio agrees. "But then, not everyone is as natural a Third Schooler as you are. Some learners need more time in on-line tutorials and assigned units."

"I guess so. Hmmm, I'd love to see Scott's graduation report. We're different. But I think that in his own way, he's a pretty effective Third Schooler too." Claire pauses. "I'm curious. As we've talked here, you've often referred to 'we' as though there's more than my Mom, you and me in on my learning plans. I know there are a lot of learning specialists in the Third Schools, but in my case, who's the 'we'?"

"Well Claire, in your case, the answer is simple. Some Third Schoolers present us with some challenging learning design problems, and that's good, we thrive on it. In those cases, a lot of specialists, usually learning design specialists, need to be brought in by the family learnist, folks like me. Some need more complex designs to steer them through serious learning difficulties such as late readers or social and teamwork issues, all the time keeping them on track to becoming self-aware and self-directed. So, the 'we,' aside from you and your Mom, was a learning design learnist named Sarah Baker. Sarah seemed to have a sixth sense about how I could advise you, and of course your Mom, about where to go next to enrich, expand and take the next steps in your learning plan and where the appropriate resources might be."

"Sarah, of course. I remember that name from some of our learning design sessions. Wow Sergio, what a great chat this has been. I owe you and Sarah a lot!"

"Hey," laughs Sergio, "this is what I do, and I love it."

"Well…." Claire pauses here. "You've shared a lot with me Sergio, more than I expected. Is there a reason for all the time and detail you've shared with me today?"

Sergio responds quickly with warmth in his voice. "Two reasons, Claire. You are among the first wave of Third Schoolers to graduate. You have pioneered this new way of learning with us and I think that you're going to write a great graduation report that we'll all learn from. Secondly, you'll be joining us next year as a junior learning assistant. I've spilled some beans that might both help you with your report and your work next year. Be warned, we'd love to hook you on this learning design business and see you go on to becoming a learnist yourself. You would be a natural."

"Thanks Sergio, thanks so much." Claire gathers up her notes, turns at the door to say a quick "see you soon," and leaves, her head spinning with information and images of her own learning landscape and the rich possibilities for her graduation report.

Good Luck Claire…and Congratulations

We wish Claire good luck in completing her graduation assignment. She has good ideas and material to work with and does come up with a very interesting history and thoughtful summation of her qualities and future as a learner. We must leave her now or Claire's story could become a small book of its own.

As I said at the outset, Claire is an exceptionally engaged and self-managing Third Schooler. I chose a character like Claire, and added her brother Scott, so that I could explore the theme of co-created and self-directed learning more fully. It is important to keep in mind that Claire's is but one of many stories of learning that might be possible in the scenario of public learning I'm calling the Third Schools. Claire's story contains suggestions that other Third Schoolers may require more structure, supervision and even direct provision of learning. These would be equally interesting to explore. The purpose of looking at a possible future like the Third Schools is not to rule structure out, or to cast cold water on classroom and large group learning. It is only to show that the route to a more structured learning design can and should include co-creating learning, the larger context of self-directed conscious learning, and include the learner and the family in the decision making.

Claire obviously resides in a larger city with many resources. What about other contexts?

Again, it would be interesting to go to a contrasting example and take a remote northern community as the setting for our scenario. Obviously, the learning designs would have to consider very different circumstances. Many remote communities are First Nations, Métis and Inuit (FNMI). It is important and perhaps a bit ironic to note that aboriginal communities once had in place many of the processes for family- and community-based learning that you will encounter in the next few chapters; learning from the lore-keepers, the elders, the stores of knowledge and know-how in the community, the many wise and capable leaders, and the inherent discipline imposed by some activities such as hunting, finding edible plants, and winter survival. Some of these traditions could be and are being revived. The many learning requirements of the modern world could be addressed through a mixture of local coaching and mentoring, online learning, and learning packages of print, media and self-assessment materials.

The availability of the key resource people, particularly the learnists, would likely be a mixture of resident, on-call, and scheduled visits. Progress on learning plans might need to be tracked more closely so that learning assistance would be available with the least delay and resources such as reading materials and media, not as easy to lay a hand on, could be brought into the community in a timely and effective manner. Learners might not be able to spend as much time in a home learning centre as Claire and Scott do. If the community has a school building, and many of them do, its classrooms, other than those needed for structured learning, could be converted to varied learning spaces for all age groups in the community. Social, health, and other community services might fit more comfortably into this kind of active and flowing human space where young people especially feel more empowered and in charge of their own destinies.

Maybe, but indulging in light speculation at this point is unfair to the many possibilities for good Third Schools learning in rural or remote communities, FNMI, farming, ranching, resource extraction or otherwise. It is unwise and impractical to imagine other Claires and Scotts and attempt to create more stories. It takes us away from the purpose of this book, which, as I have stressed, is to offer possibilities, not solutions, and to give examples of the kind of thinking we need to do together as a society to move us toward a whole new model of public learning, built on and incorporating the many successes of its predecessor, public education.

Oh, as for Claire and Scott, Claire does get hooked, goes into a post-secondary program uniquely designed for preparing learnists, and becomes a family learnist and eventually a Learning Design Specialist Team Leader. Scott plans to become a physicist and do research into the now mainstream string theory of particle physics. He gets diverted, and ends up as a skilled and valued technician assembling components for a new class of orbital vehicles operated by the bravely named Lunearth Transit Corporation.

And so, it is time to flesh out the Third Schools scenario a bit more.

CHAPTER 7: BECOMING A THIRD SCHOOLER

On Making an Entrance

On a golden warm Regina day in September 1944, Irene Winnitoy took me by the hand and walked me from the Franklin Apartments along Dewdney Avenue and Robinson Street to Albert School. I had reached the legal age, and so it was time for me to enter kindergarten. Accordingly, I was escorted into a red brick, high-ceilinged, echoey building filled with strangers who were mostly sitting in straight rows or standing in lines. After a while, my Mom, who had other things to do, left me on my own in one of the many big rooms. It had a lot of people in it, mostly my size, and one big person who I knew was the teacher. We were all given things to do. After a while, we were escorted outside to play. I assumed that the people in this mysterious building were finished with me and so I walked home. My rather surprised Mom again took me by the hand and walked me right back to Albert School, a walk that no doubt included an emphatic explanation of recess, safety, rules and the importance of listening to teachers. It turned out that I had another 13 years to go, give or take.

Was I ready to start school? I was certainly a bit slow at picking up on the recess thing, not to mention staying put until given permission to leave. On the other hand, I was clearly capable of initiative, even if my timing was off. I was bookish and picking up on reading very quickly. Thanks to my railroad engineer Grandfather, who was very proud of his big pocket watch, I could already tell time. But what would a readiness assessment have revealed?

Fast forward 63 years. According to the *BBC News*, five-year-olds in England are assessed on 'early learning goals' in areas such as:

- ➢ personal social and emotional development
- ➢ communication, language and literacy
- ➢ mathematical development
- ➢ physical development
- ➢ creative development

> knowledge and understanding of the world

They are expected to "recognize and say words like 'red' and 'dog' or 'pen' ". They should be able to "say the letters of the alphabet" and write "shopping lists, stories or letters" (November 10th, 2007). Well, I'm certain I could have done all that…I think…and if not, what were the implications for my success in the prairie public schools of the mid-1940s?

Was I ready to make my entrance? What is readiness? It is an especially interesting question as we contemplate a new system of learning.

I use 'making an entrance' to contrast with the old words such as 'registration' or 'admission.' When I was young, being accused of 'making an entrance' meant that you were drawing attention to yourself. There was often a tone of teasing or even mild disapproval for your exaggerated sense of self-importance. I will be suggesting how learners could 'make an entrance,' *with* new kinds of attention and much approval.

The old 'readiness' and 'school admission' language suggests a process by which the learner is not granted entrance as much as injected into a finely tuned and well-oiled machine. The schooling system takes most of the responsibility for packaging the learning and delivering the programs and services to the learner. The earliest admission, perhaps a junior kindergarten, places the learner on the lowest rung of a system fully designed and detailed to move the average student smoothly up the rungs. From then on, everyone, the teachers especially, work very hard at adapting schooling and delivering education to a range of learners in ways described in previous chapters.

Instead of making your entrance as a unique character stepping into a somewhat improvisational drama of learning, an age-specific slot in the machine opens and you pop through.

In the Third Schools, the new system design supports the co-creation of learning by the learner, the family and the teacher. Entrance to the system is a process of mutual agreement around a purpose, a plan and a design for learning.

As I move into the last section of this book, I will try to describe the core processes of the Third Schools, starting with making an entrance, in a more or less logical sequence. This means that at times I will be referring to possible system features or processes that I may have illustrated through Claire's story but likely haven't yet explained or defined. Bear with me. We are edging onto a new map.

Growing Good Learners

This extended scenario about our next public eduction system, with my sense that the arrival of our Third Schools is a real and imminent possibility, is focused on the elementary and high school years and adult learning. There are significant forces and pressures that will be acting on families and children as they prepare for entrance to the Third Schools. A quick look at early childhood is in order.

The early years are a very critical period in the development of the child. Successes and failures during this stage of development can have huge implications for youth and adulthood. Years of research into early-childhood keep piling up evidence that these early experiences in mapping out the self and building relationships will be telling in future years. Most children grow up in caring and supportive homes. But even severe stress and trauma need not hold a child back. A *Calgary Herald* article describing the work of early-childhood researchers Fraser Mustard and Stuart Shanker reports the following:

> Shanker says one of the biggest breakthroughs that has occurred in the field since 2000 has been in understanding the role emotions play in what he calls 'the healthy wiring' of the brain. It turns out emotions are critically involved in everything from memory to how a child solves problems. Children who are raised in stressful homes, like those suffering from poverty or abuse, can experience actual structural changes in the brain "that can affect their immune system and make them vulnerable to everything from coronary disease to depression later in life", he says. But there is good news, says Shanker, if we can reach those children early enough in life, we can get a child with a potential disorder back on to a healthy brain development trajectory.(December 3rd, 2006).

Paul Tough has written about the damaging and long-lasting impact of high ACE scores, the number and severity of adverse childhood experiences that could lead to enduring childhood trauma. Again, there is good news:

> We now know that early stress and adversity can literally get under a child's skin, where it can cause damage that lasts a lifetime. But there is also some positive news in this research. It turns out that there is a particularly effective antidote to the ill-effects of early stress, and it comes not from pharmaceutical companies or early-childhood educators but from parents. Parents and other caregivers who are able to form close, nurturing relationships with their children can foster resilience in them that protects them from many of the worst effects of a harsh early environment (*How Children Succeed*, pp. 27-28).

Complicating the process is the still growing trend for both parents to work. Two parents working is no longer an option designed to bring more luxury items into the home or make exotic holidays possible. For most Canadian families, the loss of the second income has very serious consequences and in some cases means the difference between comfortable living and just scraping by. Even for wealthier families, the loss of one income may mean a drastic change in lifestyle, including a change in communities and the break-up of a precious circle of close friends. This reality colours some of the debates in our culture about stay-at-home moms or dads and access to affordable and effective day care. There is the pressure of the sandwich generation where elder-care can occur side-by-side with the peak years of work life and parenting. There is career change and financial uncertainty.

Another complication is the enormous pressure on parents to ensure that their children will do well in school. Since post-secondary schooling is now the basic credential for most jobs, success in the elementary and secondary systems is of critical importance. A really successful career and the best opportunities arise from getting 'blue-chip' credentials such as science and engineering or the more familiar law and medicine degrees from the elite universities. The result is that the two-income families I described above are struggling to ensure that their children get the best preparation for the fiercely competitive race to follow. After all, does not 'curriculum' mean 'race course' in Latin?

> The term 'school readiness,' once denoting a child's ability to separate from her parents for a few hours without too much fuss and to go to

the bathroom by herself, now refers to her mastery of early numeracy and literacy skills. What's more, well-meaning remarks about potential developmental delays, such as lisps or mispronunciations like 'persghetti' can send parents scurrying to find doctors and therapists to 'fix' a 'problem' that might otherwise disappear on its own over time (*Maclean's*, November, 22nd, 2004).

Children who start kindergarten with a basic grasp of numbers and the written word are the most likely to shine through elementary school, regardless of whether they start out with behavioural problems, says a new international study. The study is believed to be the first major endeavor of its kind to show it's what you know, not how you act, that determines success in the early grades. The study found that mastering informal math concepts…matter[s] the most in predicting later success in school (*Calgary Herald*, November 13th, 2007).

And so there is enormous stress on parents and children as they get ready for readiness. These pressures are probably unnecessary in any case, but especially so in the case of entrance to the gentle and personalized continuum of co-created and family-based learning in the Third Schools. Time for curiosity and creativity-driven play in an intimate setting with parents and other familiar adults may be much more effective.

Consider the implications for the emerging outlines of the Third Schools as I am describing them and the following two samples of research into childcare in the early years. The first is from an article in *Maclean's* summarizing findings from the National Longitudinal Survey of Children and Youth.

> The statistics divide the children into seven groups, based on how they were cared for before entering school, ranging from at home with mom, to full-time day-care. The categories include blends of different types of preschool experience, taking into account the reality that many Canadian children attend part-time early educational programs. These include activities such as organized moms-and-tots groups or a few hours at preschool every week. The data suggests those stimulating extras are crucial. The top three categories, for both 'learning skills' and 'communication skills,' are filled by kids who got the benefit of those other educational programs, whether they were at

home with a parent or in daycare the rest of the time (*Maclean's*, September 27th, 2004).

These findings challenge the idea that children do not do as well when cared for by their parents as when cared for in an early childhood program, a daycare centre or by a paid care worker. I suspect that the parental care included more than babysitting and that many moms and dads helped with the skills. The Third Schools will widen the variety of learning experiences in the early years, with many 'stimulating extras.' The findings suggest that the home can effectively nurture and support personalized learning.

This next bit of research is from Stanley Greenspan in his very thorough and sobering look at human development and the ways we are putting deeper reflective intelligence at risk in some of our child-rearing and institutional practices. He stresses the central role of emotionally mature and caring adults and the need for continuity of this caring in a child's life. Most families are able to provide this love and continuity, but traditional schooling seriously fragments a child's contact with caring and familiar adults. He describes the 'seven irreducible needs of childhood' and the second is of importance here.

Second, consistent, nurturing relationships with the same caregivers, including the primary one, early in life and throughout childhood are the cornerstones of both emotional and intellectual competence, allowing a child to form a deep connectedness that grows into a sense of shared humanity and, ultimately, empathy and compassion. Relationships with both parents and daycare staff must have this stability and consistency. If these ties are cut off at arbitrary points, such as the end of fiscal years or semesters or when a child has reached a specific age, new losses are inflicted on youngsters who may already have been scarred by loss and upheaval (*The Growth of the Mind*, p. 265).

Some of the key features of the Third Schools speak to these needs, specifically, the central role of the parents and family, the continuity of the family teacher or learnist and the rich contribution of the neighbourhood and the community. So how to prepare the young child? A good first step would be to follow the research findings of people like Stanley Greenspan, and many parents do seek out the best advice from meetings, books, family counselors and friends. It is important that some of the central features of the new system be implemented, such as a cohesive family approach to the child development and early learning, participation in creating a varied and healthy menu of preschool experiences, and some thought about the home space as a centre for play and learning.

The rest of this book should provide more than enough ideas for parental participation in enriching and enlivening these critical early years – hopefully without blowing the safety valve off the family pressure cooker.

Readiness Or Not...

All the tension and expectations around readiness probably serve to make school entry into too big an issue, more an anxious rite of passage than a celebration. Five years old seems to be the magic age, with some recent debate about whether boys ought to start at six. I expect that five years is the most likely age at which parents and children will present themselves, or be required to present themselves at the Third Schools, hopefully with some arriving earlier.

> ...one expert on school readiness said that children who enroll in kindergarten or even attend an early-childhood program around the age of 5 tend to adjust better to the school environment. Magdalena Janus, an assistant professor in psychiatry and behavioural neuroscience at McMaster University, said those children know how to follow rules and are exposed to working with others in their age group. 'Five years old is a little bit of a magic age in terms of child development,' Prof. Janus said. 'Around that age, children become more independent, and in many cultures across the world, take on most responsibility' (*The Globe and Mail*, November 28th, 2006).

Whether five-years-old or not, these questions remain: how does a child make an entrance into a system that may seem, as we try to imagine it, ill-defined and even a bit alien in comparison with what we have now? What level of independence and self-control is required to enter a system that is designed to create conscious learning and self-management? What about the very young who can play only a small role in shaping the learning they are about to encounter?

We may not be giving the very young enough credit:

> Simona Ghetti, a psychology professor at the University of California, Davis, has found that an element of introspective thinking called

uncertainty monitoring occurs in children as young as three. Uncertainty monitoring is the thought process that occurs when a person thinks about saying or doing the wrong thing. It has generally been believed that this ability doesn't develop until age four or five. But Dr. Ghetti, who has tested 55 children to date, found that this is not the case. Dr. Ghetti won't go as far as characterizing them as mini-Descartes pondering big issues of the day, but she argues that finding the early stages of a 'mental metric…suggests there is something meta about their thinking.' In other words, they can think about thinking (*The Globe and Mail*, September 11th, 2007).

So let us reduce the tension and, if not the strangeness, at least some of the uncertainty around readiness and making an entry into the Third Schools.

At the outset, the Third Schools will embody and take very seriously a belief statement expressed by many schools over the years: 'All children can learn.' This provides the initial focus and challenge: if all children can learn, what are the most fundamental attributes they should bring to the process of learning as they enter this new system? As in the past, parents and others will nurture their innate desire to explore, express their curiosity and creativity, figure things out and solve problems, be part of family life by caring and contributing, and engage with others in games and competitions.

Greenspan gives a very helpful list of what might be called the basic basics. He stresses that these 'are not innate characteristics but proficiencies that can be taught.'

> First, a child must be able to regulate his attention. Whether he learns this easily or with difficulty depends, of course, on the particular endowment he arrived with as well as the early nurturing he received. Second, he must be able to relate to others with warmth and trust. Those who lack adequate nurturing may not have learned to engage fully with other human beings. No teacher can then marshal this basic sense of connectedness. The child will not be motivated to please her, and ultimately himself, by doing well at schoolwork. Finally, he must be able to communicate through both gestures and symbols, to handle complex ideas, and to make connections among them. Those who have not mastered these early levels obviously cannot succeed at more advanced ones. The real ABCs come down to attention, strong

relationships, and communication, all of which children must learn through interaction with adults (*The Growth of the Mind*, p. 220).

The importance of high-quality nurturing and care in the pre-school years cannot be emphasized too much. I first encountered the data and findings from the High/Scope Perry Preschool Study over three decades ago thanks to the early-childhood specialists at the Calgary Board of Education. The results were convincing then and even more so over time. As the study approached its 50th birthday, *The Christian Science Monitor* reported:

> While many studies have shown preschool's short-term academic effects, this one offers a rare glimpse into how far-reaching the gains can be. Although it tracked just 123 students – at-risk African-Americans from Ypsilanti Mich. – the half that were randomly assigned to a high-quality preschool program graduated high school at a higher rate and have had significantly better incomes and more stable personal lives than the half that had no preschool education (November 23rd, 2004).

There is controversy, however. The key words in the above quote are "high-quality." Many children are in preschools of much lesser quality than the Perry children, and there is fear that if universal programs are implemented, there will be pressure to cut costs. As one person quoted in the *Monitor* article put it, …some children who have 'a rich source of cognitive and linguistic achievement at home' might actually lose ground in a preschool setting. The Canadian findings noted above reinforce this observation. Whether at home or in preschool, play school or care, parents need to be closely involved in co-creating good developmental experiences for their children with the program leaders and specialists.

If Greenspan's advice about early-learning and development is heeded, and the advice of many others who have studied childhood carefully, there should be little problem. Some attention needs to be paid, as noted above, to the quality of the early years of home play and care experiences. Almost all of the children, almost all of the time, will arrive ready to take on the challenges of the Third Schools. This new system is emerging, in fact, because it resonates more closely not just with the historic opportunities and challenges of Canada but also with the way minds seeking learning actually work.

And so, given a decent chance at some good early-childhood experiences, most learners will be ready to enter the Third School system if they meet the usual criteria of age and residency. The Third Schools will still need funding, and learners will be admitted if they are eligible to be funded by the governing authorities. There may be a downward extension of funding into the pre-school years.

The usual process consists of determining whether the children can be registered and included in a school's enrollment count. Very often, maps are published telling learners where their attendance-area boundaries are and the school they are expected to attend. Deadlines are given. Telephone numbers and web sites are listed to help with information. Some schools advertise separately. However, it is important to remember that the Third Schools will probably not overtake and replace the traditional schools but will operate in a parallel system, or perhaps as an optional program. The usual processes of registering may not apply.

It is at about this point that a telephone call or a visit to someone's office will be made – and the 'usual' begins to change. This is where my story about a possible future of learning, my 'extended scenario' as I have called it, needs to get a bit more detailed.

Hello, I'm Your Family Teacher

The moment a family with a young learner contacts the Third Schools, a learning advisor who is a trained specialist will be assigned. For families, the learning advisor role will parallel the traditional role of a family doctor, in this case a family learning advisor or general learning practitioner. As you will remember from Claire's story, this is Meg, and then Sergio, their family learnists, and the role is critical.

The first and most vital assignment of the learning advisor is to develop with the family and the child a statement of the central purposes and outcomes of learning, looking as far ahead as they are able. Specifically for the young learner and more generally for the family, it is to answer the questions, "Why are we seeking to create a learning partnership with the Third Schools?" "What do we hope and expect will result from the years of learning together that lie ahead?"

The learning advisor will offer processes that move the thinking forward and coaching assistance to help with the decision-making. To the extent that the parents wish to and are able, they will, with the child in the loop as much as possible, surface and clarify their reasons for wanting to take on the challenge of co-creating learning and to work in partnership with a unique learning support system I am calling the Third Schools. If other family members will be closely involved in the child's learning, they should attend at least some of the sessions.

This will not be the first time, very likely, that families and learners have thought about or bumped up against the familiar issues associated with these questions. It *will* be the first time, also very likely, that there is expert assistance available to address these questions. The answer will become a statement of commitment describing the family's purposes in learning, their expected roles and the learning outcomes they seek. The learning outcomes will drive the learning design work that is to follow. The learning advisor will ensure that the family and the learner revisit these outcomes regularly in the years to follow, with the learner playing an increasingly significant role. The processes that will be used to develop the statement of commitment will be at least as thorough as those used by professional financial advisors and planners.

The statement of commitment is essentially the core contractual agreement the family makes with the Third School system. It will outline the ways the family will participate in the design and implementation of the learning plan, support the child's learning and their learning together as a family, and help the system monitor the child's progress toward specific outcomes. As well, all statements of commitment will include a specific reference to the core purpose of the Third Schools.

There will always be a stated commitment, no matter how much altered to suit that particular family and learner, of the fundamental outcome of a reflexively conscious learner who becomes capable of taking over, at least in part, the design of her or his own learning.

In the past, learning outcomes were largely assumed and unwritten or stated very generally as goals. I gave some examples, like the PDK goals, in a previous chapter. The desire to express learning outcomes that relate specifically to a learner and a family is emerging, currently as "personalization," and will become a powerful pressure in the next few years. As we have seen, the 'taken-for-granteds' of the system and of the individual school do not apply to every learner and are not acceptable to all parents and learners. Year after year, the competing interests and voices in our society swing the spotlight around from job preparation to citizenship to personal financial management and other priorities. And schools swing between improving test scores and creating caring and inclusive communities. And those that try to do it all are often the most stressed and beleaguered.

Initially, many families will stay with familiar and more conventional goals, such as 'master the basics' or 'develop a love of learning.' Later on, we will look at how they might move beyond the safe and predictable into outcomes unique to their own learning needs and life story.

This means that a central role of the learning advisor is to truly act as a 'family teacher' and to be an interpreter and an advocate for the carefully thought out and earnestly sought outcomes of that family and learner as they approach the learning system of the Third Schools and the design challenges that lie ahead.

At the outset, the learning advisor will be assigned to the family and learner, but from the first time they meet, the relationship will be voluntary. A new learning advisor can be requested at any time. The intention is that they will develop a close and ongoing relationship with families and learners and will develop a long-term knowledge and understanding of their needs and experiences. Most important, the learning advisor will act as an interpreter and advocate as the learners encounter a system filled with choices and possibilities. For reasons that will become evident, the Third Schools will leave room for much more negotiation with and by the learners than current schools can allow. There will be limits of course, but it will be essential to have a system guide or navigator who is readily accessible.

Is it a stretch to imagine that, given the proper resources, a wide range of families might state their intentions around learning? Some years ago, in the spring of 2001, our local *Rocky View Adult Education* catalogue offered a course entitled *Strengthening the Family and Developing a Family Mission Statement*. The course outline declared that "A rich, family culture cannot be fully enjoyed without the family coming together to focus on what they hope to achieve as a family" (*Rocky View Adult Education*, Spring 2001 Catalogue). Our local monthly *High Country News*, in an article on investment strategies, presented a detailed outline on the preparation of a family mission statement. (Spring 2005) Some people must have been listening. *Maclean's* reports that "a growing number of upper-crust Canadians" have family mission statements that "help to ensure that the legacies of the wealthy are secure."

> In most cases, mission statements focus on a family's commitment to charity, community, business, one another and, in many cases, God. Commonly used words include 'legacy,' 'excellence' and 'stewardship' (*Maclean's*, November 19th, 2007).

So there may be some sketches, at least, of this part of the new map!

Meet You At The Studio

The learning advisor and the family will likely need to have just a few meetings before a very important next step occurs. The next step is to meet with a learning design specialist who works in a learning design studio, probably located in a school building, hopefully nearby. Eventually, learning design studios will be available throughout a school district so that they are accessible for families and learners and, very importantly, their learning designs can be linked to the regions and communities where families live and work.

The work of the learning design studio is at the core of the Third Schools. The studios and their specialists ensure that a unique design for learning is created by the parents for their young learners and, as they grow older, by the learners themselves. Each unique design is based on the core purposes and learning outcomes as stated by the family and the learner. At this point, the strategies and tactics are put in place.

A unique and critical balancing act now comes into play. The learning design will wrap itself around the needs of the family and the learner such as, family structure, resources, work and family life integration, parent careers and changes in required skills and knowledge, and views of learning. It will probe at and respond to the preferred modes and styles of learning for that family and learner such as, 'free range' versus more institutionalized, the balance of 'high tech/high touch,' as John Naisbitt once put it in a book title, the use of technology for direct instruction versus class time, reading and research, personal mobility and community-based learning, interest in collaborating with other parents, and degree of independence in decision-making. It will reach into a massive resource of design possibilities and provide individual designs that are suited to that learner that are tested and practical. But it will also begin the process of gently pushing that learner toward the central goal of the Third Schools, the development of reflexive self-understanding and co-creative design skills that will enable the learner to take increasing responsibility for creating their own learning for the rest of their lives. And importantly, the design must ensure that amidst the many options and choices, there is what Carl D. Glickman has called 'pedagogically valid work.' He adds, "Students need to make choices, accept responsibility, and become self-directed." (*Renewing America's Schools*, p. 25). The Third Schools will provide a new framework for meeting these basic, if rather traditionally, worded objectives.

This means that the learning design specialist will support the close partnership that is being created between the family and the learner and the family's learning advisor. The role of the parents in supporting the primary goal of conscious learning will be very important. This role of the family will be spelled out in a contractual agreement between the family and the school system. The contract will ensure that everyone in the family understands their responsibilities and, individually, is willing to meet them. The resources of the family may be stretched by the unique learning designs, as we explored with Claire, and there must be clarity around what will work and what to do if the process is not working. More detail will be provided later, but the design process will also address the home as a learning centre and the meshing of school-aged and adult learning requirements in the home.

And if, as I suspect it will, compulsory school attendance, the obsession about regulating 'seat-time,' fades away, the role of the family will move toward legal accountability for implementing the learning design. Monitoring and support, primarily through the family teacher or learning advisor, will be essential.

Co-creating Learning

The learning design studio is the critical crossroads where the family and the learner meet the Third Schools system. Some will be larger, like the one Claire and Scott had coffee in, with many specialists and resources. In rural or remote communities, it may be one or two people in a portable classroom or who travel and use more online resources. It will be a place where the rich learning resources of the Third Schools system, the community and the family are drawn together and set down in a way that gives the family and the learner a clear learning map.

There will be a mixture of preferences and requirements. The design will have to include all elements that satisfy the legal requirements of curriculum and assessment, although I hope that by the time the Third Schools emerge, more thought will have been given to the impact of heavy loads of required content and testing. Even though we all know that 'you can't fatten a goat by weighing it', school systems are constantly under pressure to test frequently and repeatedly (Greenspan, p. 213). These schooling rigidities may, we can hope, eventually yield place to learning. Be that as it may, the learner and the family must know that no matter how unique the design, the state still has an interest in the education of the child, and its requirements must be understood and part of the design. This will create a challenge for adapting 'cookie-cutter' processes to the emergence of thousands of unique learning designs.

The local learning design specialist will be supported by gifted and experienced learning designers at the whole-system level. They will have at hand a vast repertoire or resource bank of learning possibilities. The design process will initially take the form of probes or questions that the family and learner, with the assistance of the advisor, respond to. Some examples of learning design options were given above. There will be specific questions about the time, energy and support the family is able and willing to provide. For example, how much home education are they interested in providing? Learning modes will be explored. How much learning would the family like delivered by technology, and how will the social needs of the learner be met? The family may have access to special settings for learning, such as a magnet or workplace school, and these will be drawn in to the design process. An important but potentially tricky area, due to new concerns about safety and security, will be the community-based learning, most of which will be created in real time with community learning specialists, community volunteers and organizations, and families and learners, likely working in coalitions or groups. And of course, the option of directed group learning (the classroom) will still be there.

It is important to note here that these unique designs for learning are not the usual bits and pieces, fragments of schooling such as social studies units, math modules or field trips, stitched together. They are sets of specifications for one person's learning that call into play complex sets of resources and patterns of delivery. For example, learning in the community will not mean a greater emphasis on traditional field trips. It will mean determining the substantial learning outcomes that will be met by learning in and with the community, perhaps over extended periods of time, potentially requiring the creation of a unique support system in the community for that learner. Other learning modes, such as traditional classroom work, will already have a support system. A huge challenge for the classroom mode will be to respond flexibly to each learner as learning designs are developed and adjusted in an ongoing way.

There is a range of possibilities. Some learners may have a learning program that is primarily supported in the home, with some community- and learning-centre staff involvement. Technology may play a lesser or greater role, depending on learning-style preferences and the desired outcomes. Others may base their learning on group learning and learning centre-supported experiences, but again, with variation in the amount of whole group and individual experience and technology support and delivery.

Families, communities, businesses and not-for-profit organizations represent significant untapped potential for offering specific, ongoing, perhaps even unique and vital learning experiences. They are, as Claire referenced, important puzzle pieces in the assembly of a learning design.

A Plan for Learning

So let us assume the commitment has been made and the design work has been done with care and thoroughness. The end result is a personal map of learning with substance and utility. We might call it a family learning plan, but in most cases, it will be an individual learning plan, particularly for adult learners. If properly done, learning plans will guide the learner, the family, and all who will support that learning through the various stages of achieving the outcomes. There will be some who choose a more traditional pathway into the Third Schools. Their first steps might involve home learning using standard curriculum resources at the appropriate grade level with some mixture of kindergarten or grade one classroom time. Others will choose a more intensely co-creative approach. Their first step might be a meeting with other parents who have chosen similar learning outcomes. They could begin by setting out strategies to provide learning experiences collaboratively for all the children as well as to support individual families working in their own home. Or they might meet with agencies or non-profit groups in the community who have resources or can provide the experiences that fit with the first stages of the learning plan, such as an emphasis on the arts or the environment. In any case, all these steps will be described in the learning plan.

The design work will build the learning plans using a template or set of protocols, yet to be developed, that provide an assurance to the partners in the learning process and the local or provincial educational authorities that productive learning will occur. I will continue to go out on this very long limb of my Third Schools scenario and suggest that probable elements of a learning plan will include:

The Statement of Commitment
As described above, this will contain the learning purposes and outcomes that the family seeks, not just for their children, but also for the adults. Some parents, for example, may want to include their own learning about child growth and development, technology or specific content areas such as science. The statement of commitment will provide the basic specifications for the learning design work to follow. It will describe the role that the adults will play, from intensely participative to the traditionally more distant partnership, with a school. It will describe the preferred learning modes for the children, such as home, virtual, traditional, blended or other kinds of learning. The learning design work will continue into the following elements of the plan.

Learning Activities
This will be, of course, a central element of the plan – how the child will set about doing learning. For the initial few weeks and months of learning, some specific activities and engagements need to be clearly described. Longer-term strategies that connect the learning activities with the purposes and outcomes need to be made clear as well. Since much needs to be said here about things like play spaces, learning with family, use of technology and games, and early experiences in the community and with other learners, I will go into far greater detail in the next chapter.

Learning Partnership
In the Third Schools there will be a number of partners that will be involved in the family learning plan. The plan will make an initial statement about the roles they will play. Certainly the parents will play an active and participative role in providing portions of the child's learning. The specifics of their role will be described. Other partners may include the extended family, family friends, a local or regional school, a community-based learning resource or service such as Guides or Junior Forest Wardens, other parents, a business, and a volunteer

group such as a seniors association. Their involvement and connections with the learning plan will also be described

Resources

This section will describe the resources that are needed to support the learning plan. In most cases the family will provide resources such as a home computer, a home learning centre and the purchase/loan of books and other learning materials. The work at the learning design studio will determine the additional resources required to fulfill the learning plan and how these will be made available. Some resources, from books to hands-on learning materials to online modules, such as Dr. F. David Peat's *Basic Books in Science* (http://www.paricenter.com), will be available to parents from the Third Schools system. The other partners in the process will help to locate and create additional resources needed by the learner.

Information and Communication Technologies

There is no question that technologies such as computers and wireless devices will play a major role in learning in the Third Schools. There is clear evidence that while the older generation (that would be me) regards an electronic gizmo as a tool or appliance that is external to them, the young generation is blurring the boundary between their smart machines and their intelligent selves. The learning plan will recognize that growing trend and will spell out how much technology and for what purposes. Some families are worried, and understandably, about the implications for physical health and richness of experience when great periods of time are spent communing with a screen or keypad. The learning plan will incorporate the enormous power of these technologies and networks to go beyond expanding a universe of information toward providing access to the building blocks of knowledge.

Scheduling, Space, Transportation and Safety

One or both parents will be scheduled into frequent, perhaps daily, learning sessions with their own child. When they are not, they will want to know exactly where their child is and who is responsible. Procedures will be required for monitoring and communication. The learning spaces may be in the home, a school or learning centre, the community, or in a special location farther away. Walking, cycling, public transit and car-pooling will be primary ways of getting around, with occasional charter busing. The safety and security of the learner must be paramount at all times. This section of the learning plan will set out these arrangements with procedures to ensure that any and all changes, no matter how minor, occur only with the knowledge and consent of the parents.

Monitoring and Assessment

Another important piece of the learning plan is to describe the milestones leading to the outcomes in the learning plan and to have a process for assessing and judging progress. Some families will want a heavier diet of formal 'paper-and-pencil' assessments. Others will want less formal but ongoing verbal and written feedback to the learner and family so that constant adjustments to the learning activities can be made. In addition, the approving and regulating authorities must be kept informed of the learner's progress through the curriculum. There will be testing schedules that must be met, even if the learner's progress does not correspond to the traditional grade levels. In the traditional schools, the struggle was to keep the parents adequately informed. Now parents will be on top of the process, and it will be important to respond to the information needs of the Third Schools system and other levels of governance.

Portfolios

The portfolios will offer a shortcut to a learning plan, one that may be necessary for many families, especially at first as the learning design systems gear up. Portfolios will be pre-packaged or will be generic learning plans that can be modified to fit different family and learner situations. The simpler portfolios will offer a mixed à la carte menu of programs in traditional public, private, charter, and other specialized schools as well as plug'n'play modules for use in home schooling, in the learning centres, and from online learning systems. The learning design studio will keep an up-to-date catalogue of available programs and services. The specialists will make inquiries, do research and match the blend of schools and services to each statement of commitment rather than leaving parents to look around and assemble them on their own. More complex portfolios will offer defined blends of content and learning process that can be designed and refined ahead of the arrival of the family and the learner in the learning design studio. These can be selected as appropriate and modified to the extent necessary. As the years go by, the variety and specifications of the portfolios will increase, and many will be courtesy of those who have gone before and will be built on successful family and individual learning plans.

All this is just a tantalizing preview. More will be said about the learning plans in the next chapter, particularly about growth towards reflexive learning and the deep maps and unifying themes or projects that give the learning energy and continuity.

Support Systems

In many school systems, the system is not viewed as a support; it is viewed as a weight. According to the cynics, when the system says, "Hey, I'm just here to help," it's gonna hurt. So I take a risk when I introduce the language of a support system into a discussion of the Third Schools.

The likelihood is that the kind of conscious learning I am describing here cannot work unless a new kind of system emerges to effectively scaffold and encourage the co-creation of learning by the family, the learner and the staff. Much must happen. The change will be evolutionary rather than revolutionary and discontinuous. Some of the best elements of the Second Schools, the schools of the last half of the 20th century, such as fostering community, adapting technology to different learning environments and modifying instruction to meet special needs, will be adapted and retained.

The burden on some families could be enormous. Many will not be able to engage with the Third Schools right away. Their interest in the current system must be protected, so the Second and Third Schools will operate in parallel even as some elements of the older are being incorporated into the newer. As parents and learners experience and observe the benefits of conscious learning and the impact of participatory creation of learning on the minds of the learners, many more will want to get involved. The shift will be experimental and adaptive as it responds to the needs of families struggling to balance and integrate work and living and the sandwich generation trying to raise children and care for parents.

But many parents will make the shift simply because they want their children to develop uses of the mind that are aligned with the challenges of the 21st century. They will understand that their children must engage with the problems and opportunities of their time in history, an imperative from which no one is exempt. Put simply, people will see the difference between the two ways of learning, and it will be convincing. And if done right and supported effectively, the Third Schools will do much to enrich and integrate family life and community life and undo the damage of the old industrial-era institutions.

This Third Schools extended scenario can provide only brief glimpses into a new order of learning. More is needed. Let us go on to see how some of these core elements will work and what it might take to put a supportive system in place.

CHAPTER 8: THE LEARNER AND THE LEARNING

We now move closer to the heart of the matter. This means thinking about the processes of co-creating learning in the family in concert with the Third Schools support system and the community.

The prime commitment and legal responsibility for creating and implementing a plan for learning will now reside with the family and the learner. The Third Schools system with its learnists, specialists and design centres will be the most critical support system, with the community a close second. This new system will create a learning plan that is intimately related and responsive to the unique characteristics and commitments of the learner and the family.

How do we construct a myriad of activities that are both pedagogically valid and ensure the increasing role of the learner in enacting learning based on growing self-knowledge and capacities for self-direction?

In this chapter, I will consider what it will mean to be a learner in the Third Schools. Please keep in mind that the Third Schools is one of many possible scenarios of a very different future, an initial and possibly inaccurate map of new territory. I will look at the challenge of designing for growth toward conscious and reflexive learning, the reality of some operational questions, and the need for deep maps and unifying themes or fundamental projects. I will take an initial look at the role of the family as the new home ground for learning, the home as a learning centre, and learning in and from the community and the importance of this ingredient in a learning plan.

Learning My Knowing, Knowing My Learning

The growth toward conscious and reflexive learning can start, as some of my earlier examples of precocious people suggested, at a very young age. Although these were usually cases of self-awareness recollected in maturity, as Wordsworth might be anxious to point out, there are many who believe that even very young children can begin taking ownership of one of life's greatest adventures – responsibility for their own development and maturity. The following suggestions should be tempered with the reality that I am not an expert in child development. Thanks to the work of others, some of these ideas may be close to the mark and offer us a starting point.

Following Greenspan's ideas, work with younger learners should begin with careful monitoring of the child's conversations. Parents and others working with the children will keep track of reactions and feelings about early experiences as a learner and record them in the family's learning logbook. More information will flow from similar conversations about play and being a helper in the kitchen and around the house. Statements about liking or not liking certain experiences need not always lead to responses such as, 'let's try something else' without some conversation and exploration about what is liked or not liked about those experiences. For example, Ken Low's Action Studies Institute research reveals that children who are experiencing frustration with a task are often not aware of how much progress they've made or how well they are doing. They need constant feedback that is more than just encouragement. They need to learn to attend to clues in their efforts that would give them feedback they themselves could work with.

The following suggestion is a wee bit dishonest in that I am not a journal writer and jotted in a long-abandoned diary on only a few brief occasions. But I am a firm believer in the usefulness of keeping a learning journal of some sort, even if it is more of a scrapbook than a written narrative. The entries will need to be gently structured or guided in some way. The learner should be prompted to capture important elements of the learning experience as well as many other precious moments and brief sketches of significant people and times in their lives. The learning journal will become an increasingly powerful resource as the years roll by (as they do, even in youth) and the learner and others see the patterns, styles and consciousness of learning emerging. The journal will probably be used, along with the family's learning logbook, as part of the discussions and reviews with the family teacher and the annual visit to the learning design centre.

The learning journal will be a key resource for a unique and significant challenge to all Third Schoolers. You will recall Claire's struggle to create a culminating declaration to her dozen or more years of steady focus on her own capacities as a learner. Let us look again at this significant piece of work that I am calling a graduation requirement. It will be a written report on topics like 'the nature of my learning' and 'my hopes and dreams for the future.' It may be, like Claire's, more of a reflective and introspective piece, but it might also be a succinct declaration or manifesto about the young person's commitment to learning in the future, the form that it will take, the kinds of learning experiences that will be sought and avoided, and the responsibilities of the writer to ensure that the learning journey continues. Regardless of approach, there will be key topics such as 'when I reflect on my career as a learner so far, here's what stands out as significant,' and 'there are essential lessons for me from my experiences as a learner, and they are…' and 'there are challenges that I know I will enjoy in the future and here's how I'll reach out for them,' and 'if learning were like gourmet cooking and I were the chef, here are some ingredients I would always use,' and 'the next steps for me as a learner are…' and so on. The learning journal will be a valuable resource for assembling the ideas for this culminating effort at reflexivity. There could be annual statements, summaries or essays that begin well before the senior year, perhaps right back to year one. The ongoing theme might be 'What am I learning about my learning?' and again, the learning journal will be an essential personal record and resource.

Michael Barber talks about completions of courses and qualifications as floors, not ceilings. It should always be the beginning of the next course and qualification, never just the end. While his view of curriculum is very contemporary, it is more grounded in state prescriptions of what should be taught than will be the case in the Third Schools. The spirit of the Third Schools is more fully captured when he says:

> If the notion of lifetime learning is to become a reality, then education should have a beginning and a middle, but no end: less a good story and more an unfinished symphony (*The Learning Game*, p. 205).

Well said! I predict that if a system like the Third Schools unfolds, the floors will be constructed and the passages of the unfinished symphony will be composed by a remarkable and evolving cohort of young learners. More importantly, these learners will be able, by graduation time, to write and reflect about their own unique ways of constructing and composing their learning. Twelve years of discussing, reflecting and writing, slowly revealing the combination to unlock one's own unique ways of learning, will make all learners into adept players in their learning game far faster than we now believe is possible.

Surface Issues

The issues I am about to describe are not surface in the sense of being trivial. They are surface in the sense of being prominent on our current mental and policy landscapes of learning. These issues will need to be addressed early on in the process of creating the learning plan. They will be front and centre in the minds of even the most dedicated and emancipated Third Schooling family. These surface issues include curriculum requirements, specialized programs and testing. Even though the Third Schools will be distinctly different in their approaches to constructing learning, parents for their peace of mind, and system leaders and specialists mindful of the public interest, will want to ensure that the minimum basic requirements are being met in the learning plans.

Curriculum requirements reside in thickets of regulations and online publications dealing with content to be learned and materials and resources to be used in teaching to specified results. Curricula still retain a strong flavour of the 1970's preoccupation with measurable objectives and behavioural characterizations of changes in students. But compared to the requirements that existed when I began teaching, teachers are now given significant discretion in their choice of resources and modes of learning. Indeed, the most serious constraints on teachers are the numbers of students they have in their classrooms, the range of needs, and the number of high-stakes tests they must prepare students to write, factors that nudge teaching toward methods that work efficiently with traditional classrooms. Teaching has become less prescriptive. Particularly in the early years, initial approaches to core learning such as reading and numbers emphasize capturing the child's interest and self-confidence so that positive engagement with learning can occur.

This means that effective learning plans for very young students will ensure that adequate blocks of time are allocated to critical learning tasks, what we used to call 'time on task,' and that there is balance in the design so that there is room for healthy activity, creativity and group activities. The learning design studios will need to be well staffed and prepared to ensure that learning plans are educationally sound and that no critical elements are being ignored. Unless there are highly prescriptive and unusually onerous testing programs for young children, there will be room for the pace of learning to vary and be driven by the priorities and the family and the emerging interests of the child. Third School parents especially will resist falling into the 'normal schedule' trap where they attempt to achieve the co-creative aspects of the Third Schools while insisting that their children achieve certain outcomes according to a mythic normal schedule.

The learning plan will need to address 'building block' or 'threshold' concepts and understandings so that learning is not delayed or frustrated because there is no order or priority to mastery. Most traditional curriculum is a massive form of 'crystallized consciousness,' where the ordering and separation of instructional outcomes, things to be known and shown, is greatly overdone. But even in a system as integrated and fluid as the Third Schools, it would be irresponsible not to create milestones of mastery and then assess to ensure they have been achieved in a manner consistent with that particular learning plan. As Dewy said, in a different context many decades ago, Just because traditional education was a matter of routine in which the plans and programs were handed down from the past, it does not follow that progressive education is a matter of planless improvisation (*Experience and Education*, p. 28).

For older learners moving through upper elementary into secondary curriculum, content requirements may be such that blocks of time for Third Schoolers must be set aside or negotiated with a nearby neighbourhood or community school for access to science labs and other specialized spaces or instruction, perhaps in the evenings. The pace of change in technology is drawing us nearer to the day when specialized spaces can be virtual and still provide the challenge and richness in the learning for individual or groups of learners. The learning design centres will alert learners and parents about specific hurdles they must prepare for and therefore require special attention and a deadline in the learning plan. These requirements may shift the locus of learning into more traditional methods and subject matter from time to time, especially if a particular learning plan is intensively home and community based.

Some learners will require the assistance of a specialist, such as a psychologist or resource teacher, from time to time or even continuously throughout the life of the learning plan. Specialists may be available only in a school or a centre that provides such services to a traditional school system. Contacts such as this will need to be reflected in the details of the learning plan so that blocks of time, resources and people are drawn together. These needs will require a specific place in the plan and a commitment to and from others to participate in the same way as appointments and gatherings for art, music, sports and many projects.

Time will be a different variable in the Third Schools where, depending on the wishes of the parents and the preferences of the learner, learning can occur seven days a week and at many different hours a day. Many children and young people are over-committed and victims of unhealthy levels of stress. The big issue will be to ensure that there is ample time for play, alone and with friends, family leisure activities and just plain time out with electronic games, family outings, visits from friends – anything that ensures that stress is under control and there is time to dream, reflect and enjoy being a child and a young adult.

Tests and assessments of various kinds are required by provincial and local authorities to provide information to those who make decisions about student progress and program effectiveness in the Second Schools. It is unlikely that Third Schoolers will be exempt from these, and even though there is a risk that, for some, tests will discourage and subvert the goal of conscious and reflexive learning, any responsible and mature approach to designing for learning will include a schedule of assessments and incorporate testing schedules. The learning design centre will know how to ensure that the child's or young person's name is entered into the role of test-takers and details such as place and time.

Deep Maps and Unifying Themes

Now, to some of the really exciting and enticing core elements of the Third Schools' learning design process: the next two sections will address more design possibilities for an individual learning plan by exploring the concepts of deep maps and unifying themes or fundamental projects. Deep maps and unifying themes are ways of creating pathways of learning that act both as a propellant and a magnet so that the learner feels firmly pushed and constantly attracted through many years of learning. These longer-term commitments to learning will make the relationship between the family teacher, the family and the learner richer and more meaningful. They will tie the learning together in ways that illuminate the deeper significance of the learner's growing store of knowledge and skills. They will reflect the qualities of good learning as set out in chapter four, all of which should be in play in a thoughtful and challenging Third Schools learning plan. The deep maps and unifying themes are one of the most important ways that reflexive learning and the capacity to reflect on the uses of one's own mind will emerge.

First to the deep maps. The initial creation and most basic deepening of the map of learning would involve gradually increasing the child's, then the young person's capacity to extract learning interactively from their immediate environments. Starting with the very young child, it might involve asking the question, "What if my family were my school?" and working the implications out for and with the child. We know that families are a huge source of informal learning. There is much 'teaching and learning,' some not always welcome, exchanged between family members. And there is the child's relentless curiosity and endless questions about their lives together and all that is mysterious or hidden, such as where Mom or Dad go every day and what they do there. There is more silence during the teen years, but the questions and curiosity don't go away. They just get more complicated and emotionally charged. This stage of deepening the map would explore all the family has to offer to learning and committing to some longer projects, such as a family history or 'story line' or a cookbook or a series of photographs and collages that communicate what it means to be in "my" family. The resources of the family, both immediate and extended, would be catalogued in some informal way and linked to the outcomes in the learning plan.

The next stages would be an expansion of the 'what if…' proposition outlined above. What if my community or my city or region were my school? The learner would be taught strategies such as digging out sources, conducting interviews, designing activities, and enlisting partners in specific areas of learning. While the family will always provide a primary and foundational source of learning, sometimes for a lifetime, the community, city or region will be deepened as sources of learning through deliberate actions that can be taught. The place to start is in the family with the horizons being widened as the learner matures and can safely venture out to activities outside the home. The result will be a learner that is situated in a context that is more than geographical, that is relational and reciprocal in a way formal learning rarely is. The products can be everything from normal assignments, such as paragraphs and essays, or solutions to problems in math and science, perhaps arising from the community context, to more complex expressions of learning, such as histories, murals, maps of parks and playgrounds and group projects.

Community resources can be catalogued and shared with other learners. More will be said about this in Chapter 10, which looks at learning in the family and the community. Significant human connections will be created and there will be outcomes and 'gifts' that benefit the community. These will be recorded and become part of the evaluation and the record of learning. The bonds created in the family and the community will be part of an intensely personal journey to be captured in the learning journal kept by all Third Schoolers.

Unifying Themes
Deepening and extending the pathways of learning will also involve unifying themes. A unifying theme is a long-term, perhaps several-year commitment to major growth in knowledge and personal capacity for action around a challenging and non-trivial topic. It is learning that is representative of a large chunk of real life on the planet and requires the active participation of the learner. The unifying theme will draw on a mixture of traditional subject areas and will both build on and lead the learner into an increasingly rich array of knowledge, skills and understandings. Ideally, two or three unifying themes will operate together for long but perhaps different periods of time, wrap up, and perhaps evolve into new themes that touch on each other. The whole family can be involved, but the unifying themes will usually place increasing responsibility on the learner to reach out to good sources, knowledgeable people and other learners. Again, it is likely that the characteristics of good learning will all be addressed in well-designed themes. The unifying themes will be integrated into and explicitly defined by the learning plan.

A few possibilities are explored here and are meant only as initial examples. The creative minds to follow will swamp these offerings with new and exciting unifying-theme ideas.

Citizenship and Community
A unifying theme might be constructed around the meaning of citizenship and community. This theme could address the challenge of creating forms of citizenship and community-building that are directed toward a common good that we intentionally construct with one another. This theme could also address contemporary concerns about lives disconnected from community, loss of civility and violence.

Children become curious about their neighbourhood and groups and group life at a very young age. They initiate connections and are open to discussions about having friends and doing things together, such as making a play space or having a club. They learn early about having opinions and taking stands, supporting friends and opposing bullying, for example. They learn early about the difficulty of having a well-thought-out point of view while being open to changing that view based on the ideas and beliefs expressed by others. They struggle to hold on to a sense of the self during the teen years when peer pressure is the most powerful. They gradually encounter the central features of an inclusive and civil society, the ability of citizens to encounter, as Hanna Arendt puts it, "the reality of the public realm that relies on the simultaneous presence of innumerable perspectives and aspects in which the common world presents itself." And another key feature, "Being seen and being heard by others derive their significance from the fact that everybody sees and hears from a different position. This is the meaning of public life…" (*The Portable Hanna Arendt*, p. 204). When young people yearn for their schools to be safer and more civil, they are not just seeking to get on with their social lives – or even their studies. They are searching for safe and inviting spaces for the sharing and debate of ideas and issues central to their lives and to their futures.

This theme could explore a number of areas. What are the changes, the forces and factors that could have a great impact on our community? What are the issues that are raised by the impacts of change? How do we distinguish the significant issues from the trivial ones so that a more robust public debate might occur? What is the history and heritage of our community, the key events and people that made it the way it is? Can we discern the values they were expressing? What can we learn from our past as we look into the future? What sorts of public spaces invite us or repulse us as we look for opportunities to express our views as citizens? There are many interesting angles to explore in a theme such as this.

And then there are the many ways that young people can enrich their communities. There are great opportunities here for parents to model behaviour for young learners as they volunteer in the community, perhaps helping seniors, the ill, or the disabled to get through parts of their days. As learners mature, they may want to express this theme in a more specific commitment to care for homeless animals, to bring a certain kind of art or music to their community, to create a conversation café, or to help at a local long-term care centre. The central focus will be on the growth of an awareness of reciprocity, of give and take, in being a citizen and part of a community.

Caring

Noddings suggests, "…caring is the very bedrock of all successful education and…contemporary schooling can be revitalized in its light" (*The Challenge to Care in Schools*, p. 27). She also cautions:

> But we must keep in mind that the basic caring relation is an encounter. My description of a caring relation does not entail that carer and cared-for are permanent labels for individuals. Mature relations are characterized by mutuality. They are made up of strings of encounters in which the parties exchange places; both members are carers and cared-fors as opportunities arise (pp. 16-17).

Just as in growth in citizenship, where the learner develops a sense of the importance of respecting the views of others and being open to a change of mind, the learner as community builder can be open to being nurtured and cared for by those who might otherwise have been viewed only as the objects of care. In learning to be a citizen and in learning to be a caregiver, humility will play a major part as young people learn to open their minds and their hearts to the ideas, feelings and emotional contact of others.

Noddings believes that education could be organized around the theme of care and the domains it contains:

> Care, as we have seen, can be developed in a variety of domains and take many objects. We will want to consider care for self, care for intimate others, care for associates and distant others, for nonhuman life, for the human-made environment of objects and instruments, and for ideas (*The Challenge to Care in Schools*, p. 47).

Nodding's thoughts offer us powerful ways of providing a unifying theme around caring in a learning plan. Such a theme is quite consistent with the approach to learning embodied in the Third Schools. Learners' efforts to become more reflective about the uses of the mind and conscious of the emerging capacity for self-managed learning require intense contact with and feedback from other people, people who are trusted. The many kinds of caring relationships described by Noddings provide a rich and inviting array of possibilities for this kind of learning, even when the objects of care are 'non-human.'

Living Sustainably

When I read David Orr's eloquent call for a new kind of education in his book *Earth in Mind*, I thought immediately of the possibilities for a Third School learning plan. Orr's call is a great inspiration for a long-term unifying theme. Orr's message is most relevant to post-secondary students, but his challenge translates easily into a unifying theme for all learners.

> We should worry a good bit less about whether our progeny will be able to compete as a "world-class workforce" and a great deal more about whether they will know how to live sustainably on the earth *(Earth in Mind*, p. 148).

> The world…needs…hundreds of thousands of young people equipped with the vision, moral stamina, and intellectual depth necessary to rebuild neighborhoods, towns, and communities around the planet. The kind of education presently available will not help them much. They will need to be students of their places and competent to become, in Wes Jackson's words, 'native to their places.' They will need to know a great deal about new fields of knowledge, such as restoration ecology, conservation biology, ecological engineering, and sustainable forestry and agriculture. They will need a more honest economics that enables them to account for all of the costs of economic-ecological transactions. They will need to master the skills necessary to make the transition to a solar-powered economy. Who will teach them these things? *(Earth in Mind*, p. 164).

Here is an example of a unifying theme that can expand from simply connecting children with nature to, over the years, reaching into the kinds of knowledge and skills that Orr's quote above touches on. Certainly the kinds of learnings that lead to the qualities of character and competencies Orr describes can start at a very young age. It is easy to see how this kind of theme, housed in a good learning design, connects with the family and community learning described above. With very young children, the basics can begin with curiosity about 'critters' and the many places and ways they live with us on the planet. Or questions about where our food comes from and what sustains our ability to eat so many good things whenever we want to. For city children, maps can tell stories about the small amounts of food that can be produced in our own communities and the distances foods of various kinds must travel.

In the more mature years of learning, this theme unites many of the traditional subject areas or disciplines. It gives them a richer meaning and demonstrates how knowledge can translate into action in one's own life and in one's community. It also deepens understanding of many of the issues of the day around the environment and, in the long run, may produce more of the good minds Orr is looking for.

As I have suggested, there will likely be more than one unifying theme in a learning plan, and the themes will be integrated with one another and the elements of the learning plan that address core knowledge, skills and understandings.

The culmination of these themes might be a series of challenges that are designed into the senior or final year of the learning plan. You will recall Claire's pleasure and satisfaction in recalling her year of challenges. I drew that idea from a section in Paul Ray's and Sherry Anderson's book *The Cultural Creatives* entitled *Preventing Ophelia*. This is their introduction to that section:

> The story we turn to now is about a very rare experience in our time: a young woman's guided rite of passage. In this story, the guides were not the traditional elders but parents determined to reverse the effects of modern culture. How they did this and worked with their extended family and friends to create a year-long adventure seems to us to be an example of culture-making at its most creative (*The Cultural Creatives*, p. 280).

Ray and Anderson go on to describe how Laure Katz and her parents worked together to create a "year of challenges" based on a "menu of possibilities," (p. 282) 20 of them, from which Laurie chose 12. The challenges gave the parents an opportunity to pass on knowledge, arts and skills that were part of the family's and Jewish traditions. Some were "quite arduous and others just interesting and new" (p. 283). They involved carpentry, hiking, cooking, meditation and community service. In one instance, roles were reversed as Laure taught her mother how to read the Torah in Hebrew in order to accompany Laure at her bat mitzvah, the culmination of the year of challenges.

> By the time we had heard the story of the whole year, we began to understand how thoughtfully it had been arranged. The "challenges"

clearly had a cumulative effect, becoming more demanding as Laure's confidence and independence developed (*The Cultural Creatives*, p. 284).

On a smaller scale, but no less significant, one family near Sidney, B.C. created an evening rite of passage for their son as an initiation into manhood. Involving about a dozen men, "they were asked to share some personal experiences and insights about what it means to be a man." The parents carefully selected men that they "admired and respected" who talked to their son about "the necessity of doing the right thing, as hard as that may be, staying true to yourself and not following the crowd, finding something important outside of yourself and contributing to it" (*The Globe and Mail*, May 27th, 2006). Such a rite of passage could be an important culminating event in the senior years of a learning plan, or at key points during the learning plan.

The above are just a few examples of the rich possibilities for unifying themes. Other examples are:

> ➤ A theme might capture innovation and entrepreneurship, where learners are encouraged to be inventive, look for good ideas that might be expressed as products and services, and develop small local enterprises. Martin Lindstrom tells us that today's youth are avid entrepreneurs. Writing for Fast Company, he says, "A quick visit to Facebook will show you just how many teens have begun selling products on their pages" (*Fastcompany*, November 16th, 2011).

> ➤ A theme could be designed around the creative arts and gifts to the community where learners, both singly or in groups, develop a set of creative and artistic skills and provide gifts of visual and performing arts to their local community. Some of these projects may become resident companies of writers, artists or performers who hone their skills through the years and make many connections to other parts of their learning plans.

> ➤ A theme responding to an interest in science and technology might lead to a multi-year focus on a branch of science, from astronomy to microorganisms. Over the years, much learning in the elementary grades has been ignited through an interest in dinosaurs. In the current era, when creationism vies with Darwin, and public understanding of science as a way of knowing is flawed, a theme around the fossil

record and paleontology or the emergence of life forms around the planet could be very timely and offer connections with geography and history. Research on Charles Darwin could potentially lead to history, geography, oceanography, economics and religion.

Well, no need to go overboard here. There are, no doubt, many more examples of how unifying themes offer endless opportunities to "defrag" learning and connect the learner-driven and the content-driven elements of the learning plan together.

New Cradles of Learning
The kind of continuity, the gradual building of commitment and deep understanding that these deep maps and unifying themes suggest, cannot be achieved in a conventional-schooling situation with the year-by-year turnover of students and teachers and the fragmented approach to content and instruction that many experience. It will take many years of nurturing, encouragement, mentoring and coaching to see even a very committed learner through the various unifying themes and strands of content to the outcomes envisioned in the family's statement of commitment. The critical importance of the learning specialists and the Third Schools support system, the family and its home-based learning, and the community as school becomes clear. The ongoing updates with the family teacher and the annual review of the learning plan at the learning design studio become elements that must be carried through with commitment and professionalism in order to ensure that our nascent self-managing learners thrive and succeed.

But…are these maps, themes and plans just a different version of subject areas; light or trivial treatments of what could have been rigorous areas of study in a conventional classroom?

First of all, the learning plans will be constantly assessed for their design quality, pedagogical validity, degree of challenge, age- and stage-appropriateness, learner responsiveness and fidelity to the learning plan outcomes. There are various ways this can happen. In *The Challenge to Care in Schools*, Noddings gives examples of frameworks that could be used to assist in the design of a learning plan and also to assess the richness, balance and diversity of the elements of a learning plan. In her discussion of "An Alternative Vision," she mentions multiple intelligences, human activities and "a scheme that speaks to the existential heart of life – one that draws attention to our passions, attitudes, connections, concerns, and experienced responsibilities," all arising out of her commitment to caring in schools (pp. 46-47). Other ways will be devised to test the capacity of a learning plan to deliver on the promises made in the statement of commitment. The frameworks described by Noddings would be a good start.

Secondly, there will be safety nets. For example, while keeping the overall purpose of the Third Schools in mind, it's important to remember that certain parents and their family teacher may agree that the family's learning plan will be based, partly or wholly, on traditional and conventional group learning or classroom instruction. In some cases traditional teaching and intellectual rigour may be identified as having similar priority as growth toward reflexivity in learning. The family teacher's job is, in part, to ensure that a familiar and traditional mode of learning is not a convenient default position that revokes the learner's chances for ongoing participation in learning design and full development as a self-managing learner. For some families, enrolment in a more traditional school, at least for the early years, may be recommended.

The fact is that in the early years of the Third Schools, the system will itself be learning how to be responsive to an array of design preferences, needs and requirements. The learning design specialists will be figuring out how to design customized learning plans as well as how to fit learners into group learning opportunities, hopefully drawn together around individual assessments of desired knowledge, skills and outcomes rather than reverting to traditional units of instruction in age and grade groupings.

Many non-traditional statements of commitment and design requirements will be driving the development of learning plans. I cannot imagine a situation where there would be a shortage of opportunities to enrich core elements of the learning plan and make links to the requirements of the official curriculum and testing programs. Hopefully most learning plans will be highly personalized and feature a uniquely diverse mixture of home, community, technology and learning centre-based group learning. In all cases, the milestone competencies, the essential en route learnings and the requirements for external assessments and tests will be flagged and annotated in ways that show their connections to specific portions of the most varied banquet of learning activities. That is, after all, what the Third Schools will be for.

Who will do all of this? Let us go on to the next chapter to find out.

CHAPTER 9: TEACHING AS KNOWLEDGE WORK – THE LEARNIST

Enter the Learnist

"All our schools are good (or excellent)."

"All our teachers are good (or excellent)."

The above statements are the automatic responses we school board employees were instructed to deliver when parents asked, "Where are the best schools in our part of the city?" or "Does that school have good teachers?" Parents were often just curious, but mostly they asked because they were new to the city or were exploring the option to send their children to an out-of-boundary school of choice or on a bus to a special program, such as French bilingual. So the question would come up, and we would dutifully assert that our schools were all good, that our teachers were all good, and that there were many examples of excellence in both. Parents usually seemed satisfied with our confident declarations about the goodness of our system, but I'm sure that many were quietly unconvinced.

We all remember teachers, and we know that they are not all the same. The word "average" gets applied to students often, but, it seems, to teachers rarely. On any simplistic scale of effectiveness, some are bound to be a bit better or worse than others. And of course, there are the exceptional teachers. They are the ones parents hope their children get in the next grade, mostly because of the parental grapevine's songs of praise. They are the ones that are sought after by senior and adult students, most of whom are disappointed because of limits on class size or enrolment quotas. They are the ones that principals bargain for in the annual staffing battles as they try to roll the ineffective teachers out the exits and onward to their next schools. They are the ones, the remarkable minority, who live in the memories of their students over time and are sought out at reunions for brief but gratifying conversations. Interestingly (and cautionary regarding simplistic scales of effectiveness), some students remember and revere teachers who just didn't make much of a connection with the rest of their classmates. A unique teacher/student bond was somehow created.

It is one of the abiding peculiarities of the teaching profession that almost all of the teacher/student connections that will be made in schools will be made through a kind of lottery. Very rarely will teachers and students be able to just seek each other out. Some would argue that it is just as well, for the stand-out teachers would be overwhelmed, and many under-appreciated others would never be given a chance to make that unique connection with a group of students. The sunlit quadrangle, somewhere in old Europe, where the beloved master is surrounded by admiring seekers of enlightenment may be a quaintly nostalgic image but can never be part of the reality of the public schools. There is a curious fact at work here.

It does not matter how exceptional a teacher is. She or he has little or no authority over how decisions get made about the critical factors that surround her or his professional duties in the classroom.

As far as determining who arrives in their classrooms, what is to be taught and tested and on what schedule, or the kind and quality of supporting infrastructure and services that surrounds their work on a daily basis, teachers have a varied and often limited role, a role that is determined by others. Yes, they are responsible for the most important things of all – the quality of teaching and learning and the human relationships that occur in their classrooms, but these are pursued in the face of the many constraints. We see signals that we must step outside these constraints. The press has lauded efforts such as an Ontario 'student success teacher' who "works his magic on teenagers who are struggling" (*The Globe and Mail,* November 12th, 2005) and "parenting coaches who don't preach from the safety of an office. They come right into the trenches… (*Maclean's*, March 13th, 2006).

I am not suggesting that there are only a few truly remarkable teachers and that in some kind of caricature of a free market; they should be able to set their price and recruit those students they want. I am suggesting that it is unfortunate that the synergies that occur between teachers and students are mostly the result of, and at times in spite of, the luck of the draw. There is no opportunity for the teaching styles of teachers and the learning styles of students to be deliberately matched in what researchers David Hunt and Bruce Joyce have called "student push" and "teacher pull." This refers to the creative tension in many classrooms where teachers pull students toward them with a particular teaching style and students push the teacher toward their own individual learning style. In the traditional classroom, the results tend toward an average of what is most effective most of the time.

What is very clear is that in the Third Schools this kind of lottery system will not work. It is inconsistent with the reflexivity and co-creativity that is at the core of conscious learning and the quest for choice and learning design possibilities. A new category of teaching professionals will emerge and will work under very different conditions to those described above. I call them learnists.

From Knowledge Worker to Knowledge Professional

Public school teachers, as I interpret Peter Drucker's thinking in *Post-Capitalist Society*, have always been knowledge workers. All the tools of the trade from subject area content to psychology to the craft of engaging and motivating could be carried about in their heads. Knowledge was applied to work in the real world, the work of delivering lessons to students. Knowledge created new knowledge through site-based research and the capturing of good practice. Like most knowledge workers, teachers needed an organization to make their work practical and effective on a large scale. But that word organization leads us to a few twists in the tale.

Teachers got more than they might have bargained for. They needed an organization, but they got an institution. That institution, the public schools, endured some relentless pressures during the last century, pressures I referenced earlier in my two stories of reform. In the shadow of the assembly line, the teachers' role as knowledge worker was constrained and routinized as school systems succumbed to the dominance of the industrial era. Teachers, still expected to be exemplary role models, were increasingly viewed as production workers moving children through subjects and through grades.

Under the influence of industrial-era consciousness, schools were called "school plants" and were high on gleaming fluorescent-lit work spaces and low on lamp-lit reading corners and cushioned conversation centres. The schools, we might say, playing with the language of economists, were the "means of instruction." Too expensive and technically demanding to be owned by the workers (that is, teachers) anyway, schools became "public works" or infrastructure. The "raw materials," such as official curriculum and authorized texts, were funded in the public domain, were governed by lawmakers and were part of the core legal framework of the public education system. The children, often characterized as raw material, as in "shaping young minds" or "producing good workers," were also required by law to be present. Teachers were not seen as semi-autonomous professionals but as government workers delivering instruction in classrooms efficiently and cost-effectively. Lesson plans were expected to conform to a template which was reinforced by principals and checked by school inspectors. One well-known academic offered a seven-step lesson planning guide. Teachers were allowed to put their limited stamp on the product, which was valid and effective instruction that faithfully adhered to the government-approved curriculum.

That is a drab and somewhat caricatured picture I have just painted. So here is a bright contrast. The knowledge of teachers, knowledge about teaching as a learner-centred process, about childhood, about motivation and discipline, and about a growing personal repertoire of tacit skills and classroom strategies, operated quietly in parallel with the industrial model, sometimes even covertly. Unique teaching styles flourished and shone out behind the classroom doors, more openly in recent years. One book even characterized teaching as a "subversive activity." Good teaching could not simply be legislated. It could not be canned or commodified and transmitted through training to others. Masterful teaching could be observed and absorbed, perhaps imitated, though rarely very effectively. It could, by taking the best bits, be adapted into one's own unique teaching style.

As I have argued elsewhere, that era is ending with effects that are similar for knowledge workers everywhere. Creating opportunities to learn is less and less dependent on a specific person in a specific place and space called the school classroom at a specific time on a timetable. New uses of knowledge, the strategies and tactics of fostering conscious learning, are increasingly on the minds of teachers, sometimes in the guise of thinking skills and greater personalization and self-direction. Traditional structure and organization are increasingly seen as a deterrent to effectiveness. Like other knowledge workers, teachers cannot do their work without some kind of organization. But now, their work is evolving toward new roles which will require non-traditional structures. Consider the emergence of many variations on and substitutes for the word teacher – learning facilitator, guide, mentor, skills coach and so on. Consider the growing concern of teachers about the warping effects of testing on learning. These are symptoms of the coming changes. We will need a new word to capture the unique roles that learning designers and advisors and deliverers will play in the Third Schools. I call this new breed of professionals "learnists" to distinguish them from all that has gone before. They are being liberated from the old system designs and will come into their own as knowledge professionals in the field of learning.

In *Post-Capitalist Society*, Drucker discusses the emergence of the knowledge worker. His discussion has implications for the work, and indeed, the role of the teacher.

> The leading social groups of the knowledge society will be "knowledge workers" – knowledge executives who know how to allocate knowledge to productive use. ... The *economic* challenge of the post-capitalist society will, therefore, be the productivity of knowledge work and the knowledge worker (p. 8, italics in original).

> That knowledge has become *the* resource, rather than *a* resource, is what makes our society "post-capitalist." This fact changes – fundamentally – the structure of society. It creates new social and economic dynamics. It creates new politics (p. 45, italics in original).

But instead of "knowledge executives," how about learnists as knowledge professionals who will engage with Drucker's new dynamics and grasp the new opportunities to design effective systems to support co-created learning. We can begin seriously developing the organizational capacity to match the learner's own goals and desired outcomes with unique approaches to engaging the learner in customized learning activities.

> The knowledge we now consider knowledge proves itself in action. What we now mean by knowledge is information effective in action, information focused on results. These results are seen *outside* the person – in society and economy, or in the advancement of knowledge itself (p. 46, italics in original).

Learnists will apply knowledge to designing and implementing the processes by which individual learners are able to grow toward self-mastery in learning. They will apply knowledge that creates personalized knowledge, knowledge that learners use consciously and reflexively to construct good learning. They will be in the mainstream of knowledge work, and here is the kicker, which is all about attracting and keeping the talented:

> [Loyalty] will have to be earned by proving to knowledge employees that the organization which presently employs them can offer them exceptional opportunities to be effective (p. 66).

The learnist will keep some elements of the traditional roles of teacher, counselor, nurturer and community developer, but as a knowledge professional, will step up to a place alongside engineers, physicians, researchers and academics, perhaps even scotch tasters and app builders. But how will this new work be constructed?

Variations of the Learnist

Is a learnist really still a teacher, just one who has been let out of the institutional bottle? Will the new role be so different that a new label is called for? Can we imagine the next destination of a shift from delivering instruction (yesterday) to creating good teaching/learning environments (today) to designing processes for learners to co-create their own learning (the day after tomorrow)?

It is tricky to foresee how specific roles and functions will develop this far ahead of the actual events, even though I have limited myself to one scenario, the Third Schools. But having edged this far out on the Third Schools limb, why stop now?

Consistent with all that has been said so far, I think that something like the following roles and careers will emerge at the outset or will evolve as the Third Schools are established. I will offer some general descriptions that may put more flesh on these new professional roles. I will touch on some other foreseeable roles, such as leadership and governance, in the concluding chapter.

But first, let us allow these new professionals to speak for themselves.

"I am a *family learnist*. I work closely with the learner and the family, perhaps over many years, help them state as clearly as they can what they want out of their years of learning and what their commitment is to help learning to happen, and then work with a learning design specialist to ensure that an appropriate and effective personal learning plan is put in place and amended and revised as needed. (P.S., you met one of my colleagues, Sergio, in a previous chapter.)"

"I am a learning design specialist or *design learnist*. I take the learner's and the family's goals, desired results, and commitment to learning as thought out and expressed with the family learnist, sift through the many options available in the learning design centre, and design the personal learning plan that is a unique and evolving learning map for that learner and her or his family."

"I am a learning development specialist or *development learnist*. I take the many different approaches to learning almost anything that might appear in a learning plan and develop the specific learning modules, activity sequences, avenues of inquiry, delivery "gateways" such as mini-courses or seminars, ways of getting and using sources and resources; the building blocks of learning that are housed in the learning design studios and used to develop a variety of learning plans."

"I am a group-learning specialist or *group learnist*. Most learning plans include large, medium and small group-learning sessions, and learners request them too, so I assess all those needs, apply the best participative group learning process for each situation, often act as a presenter or group leader, and ensure that, whether it is a small discussion, reading or math skill strategy clinics, or a presentation on a major topic, there is staff, space and a time slot available in a learning centre."

"I am a *community learnist*. Some portions of many learning plans call for learning to be delivered in and by the community, so I review those parts of the learning plans, research the resources and the "funds of knowledge" that are available in communities, create social maps, recruit volunteers, organize and coordinate the community learning engagements, and take steps to ensure the safety and security of the learners."

"I am a *technology learnist*. Most learning plans call for a variety of information technologies to support and deliver learning, so I respond to each learning design with a complementary info-tech design that identifies software systems and online sources unique to that learner's resources and capabilities that runs the gamut from games and social media to advanced simulation and modeling and helps each learner create a distinctive learning partnership with intelligent machines."

For people who do not exist, they speak rather well for themselves. A few more observations may help.

Family Learnist

This will be the most critical role in the Third Schools system. This learnist will be the crucial link between the learner's and the family's desired goals and outcomes and the Third Schools system. For the learner and the family, the family learnist will be the face of the system, its inviting spirit and its guiding intelligence over many years. This role will include coaching and mentoring the learning, not just of the children, but also of the whole family. This role will include an activist version of advocacy, which means more than speaking on behalf of. It means acting to create opportunities, access, resources and partnerships to and for learning where none may exist.

Much time will be spent in visits with families, learning design and development specialists, community people, and partners and staff at learning sites. Some families will need the occasional telephone consultation; others will need frequent face-to-face meetings at the learning centre or in the home. It will be the professional responsibility of the family learnist to balance this all out.

In the early years, these crucial learnists will be required in significant numbers. There will be no option – their roles will initially have to include some of the design and development work of the other learnists. The Third Schools system staff resources will be built on the redeployment of the many staff in classrooms and in supervision that were required to make sure that traditional schools operated well. My expectation is that as fewer traditional classroom teachers are required, the professional staff needed to provide the family learnists will be freed up. Without the family learnist role, there cannot be an effective support system for the co-creation of reflexive, self-managed learning.

Design Learnist

This will be the key role within the local learning design studio, the learning design facility that is central to the co-creation of learning by the learner, the family and the learnists. As mentioned earlier, a learning design studio will be readily accessible to every family in the Third Schools system. The learning design specialist will coordinate the design process for their assigned learning plans and will be accountable for their quality.

The design learnist will be a translator and bridge-builder. This learnist will be able to interpret the specifics of the family statement of commitment so that they become the drivers for the design of the individual learning plans. Then a bridge can be built into the myriad of learning design elements or building blocks housed at the studio and a personalized learning plan can be developed. The design learnist will stay in close touch with the family learnists and will respond to any significant changes in the learner's and family's goals and statement of commitment. The more customized learning designs will tend to locate the learning in a variety of places from community facilities to computer screens to home-learning centres. Sometimes the work will be simpler, where the goals and needs of the family can be matched to an "off-the-shelf" portfolio of commonly used elements or design features of learning plans. Such portfolio designs will likely include more group-learning. As the era of the Third Schools moves forward and more processes and resources are assembled, it looks like the design work will become more complex and challenging.

Standard processes and templates that can drive the learning plan design work will emerge over time. Eventually each learning plan will not have to be a unique challenge. The design learnists will adapt and modify these recurring processes and templates as necessary. In all cases, they will apply the evaluative criteria to ensure that a sound and challenging plan has been developed. For continuity, they will remain at the same studio for as many years as possible so they get to know the family learnists, and indirectly, the learners, families and community as thoroughly as possible.

Development Learnist

The development learnists will create the components and building blocks that are used in the design studios to develop the unique pathways of learning in each learning plan. They will apply the most up-to-date knowledge of learning theory, developmental psychology, and program-design principles to the work. Their knowledge and skills will be universal to the learning-development challenge, that is, they will be qualified to develop a learning system for a post-secondary school, a business, a corporation or a not-for-profit organization.

These learning-development specialists will specify the activities, processes, content to be covered, possible resources, knowledge and skills to be acquired and expected outcomes for each topic, major objective, program segment or module of learning. They will suggest ways these fundamental elements of learning could or should be assembled or hooked together. They will anticipate a range of outcomes involving a variety of content, learner interests and resources. They will also assess current learning media and materials that are rapidly appearing in a growing market. Just to make things really interesting, curriculum and assessment requirements will still exist. The development specialists will provide the tools and techniques that will assist the design learnists to create personal and unique learning pathways, navigate through the curriculum and assessment requirements, and yet add additional challenges that are of significant importance to the learner and the family. The development learnists will work in centralized learning development centres, and their work will be disseminated to all the learning design studios.

This role will reshape and restore what we used to "affectionately" refer to as "downtown" staff, curriculum or program development departments and teams, many of which have been budget-cut out of existence as school systems ran out of ways to fund or camouflage the work and turned program issues back to the teachers. Since a profound and extensive knowledge of the theory and practice of personalized learning development and design will be central to the work, the training and preparation may need to reach outside of the academy where traditional methods may still play a dominant role. More on the training and preparation of learnists shortly.

Group Learnist

Some elements of an individual learner's learning plan will be delivered under the roof of a community or regional school. It may, at long last, be appropriate to begin calling these buildings learning centres! Group learnists will provide a range of instructional and participative learning services to a variety of groupings of students. They may provide content to large- (30+) and medium- (15 to 30) sized groups. They may manage a learning process in a small group that operates like a seminar or discussion group. They may act as a learning coach or mentor to students addressing outcomes in a specific subject or content area.

The group learnist will encounter many different groupings for instruction. The Third Schools will likely use age-grade groups only as necessary, perhaps for bundling curriculum or assessment and measuring progress in order to account to a public authority. Some groups will operate on a drop-in basis, such as a reading skills clinic where the learner is diagnosed, receives some one-on-one coaching, but practices the skills as part of a larger group focused on reading. Some groups will exist for only a short time. Their learning plan might call for direct instruction on a critical or keystone concept, perhaps in math or science, or an introductory session to a concept in social studies or a writer or genre in literature. Other groups will offer storytelling and volunteer presenters who are travelers, from local galleries or the zoo, or photographers and filmmakers. Some of these will be family events.

Some instructional engagements will be predictable as they arise out of a number of learning plans that call for longer-term group instruction in a school setting. Many will be less predictable, perhaps learner-driven (remember Scotty), and will be added to the necessary and protected open time slots in the learnists calendar. Due to this need for responsiveness and flexibility, some learnists will be full-time; others will be part-time and will be contracted in as necessary. Their expertise will be primarily in content or skill areas, but they will also have a background in participative or collaborative process design and individualized learning design theory.

Community Learnist

The people in this role live most of their work lives in the community, either working directly with learners or developing the community's "funds of knowledge", a concept that will be explored further in the next chapter. They will organize and coordinate the learning that is delivered in the community. In addition to the training of a learnist, they will likely have a strong background in community development. They will be encouraged to develop skills and interests of their own, such as the arts, crafts, carpentry, mechanics, electronics, languages, local and family history… the list is likely endless, and may provide group learning in their areas of expertise. They will create a "social map" of the community and lead the "funds of knowledge" and community resources cataloguing projects. This work will require what Luis Moll, citing educational anthropologists, calls an "anthropological imagination" or "state of mind" and may require formal training in anthropology and ethnographic research techniques (*National Center for Research on Cultural Diversity and Second Language Learning, Educational Practice Report 6,* 1993).

The community learnist will be responsible for ensuring that the community partners and volunteers have been screened in accordance with normal duty-of-care standards and can deliver the learning processes and supports that have been identified in the community resource catalogue. Standards and procedures, such as parent sign-offs and supervision, or policies, such as a requirement that all community learning to be done in groups with no solos or one-on-ones, will be needed, and it will be the community learnist who monitors and enforces these. The community learnist will be primarily responsible for interpreting the learning plans and ensuring that the learning linkages in the community are valid and will contribute to the outcomes.

Technology Learnist

Learning through technology will be one of the pillars of the Third Schools and one of the major portfolios of basic learning plans used by the learning design studio. Some learners and parents, in their learning plans, may call for a high level of technology-based learning. The family learnist and the learning design studio may simply recommend a virtual school to fulfill most, if not all, of the outcomes. Other learning plans may limit contact with IT to the acquisition of basic computer and network skills with very little actual learning occurring online. I suspect that most learning plans will call for a mixture of various levels and kinds of technology support and delivery of learning.

There will be two kinds of technology learnists or e-learnists, designers and learning process managers. The technology learnist designers will be able to acquire, adapt and apply the power of information technology to the design of quality learning experiences in various domains. Although quality is improving rapidly, there are still problems with weak instructional techniques such as rote memorization or "drill and practice" finding their way into these advanced learning technologies. Much research is being done on this issue of quality. Some cutting-edge work was done at the National Research Council of Canada's Institute for Information Technology (www.iit.nrc.ca). Their learning and collaborative technologies web page stated that:

> Learning and collaboration are two facets of the same activity where individuals and organizations acquire, share, and apply knowledge:

knowledge cannot be acquired without it having been shared; and it cannot be shared without it having been acquired. Each is necessary to support the other. The objectives of NRC-IIT's Learning and Collaborative Technologies (LCT) research program are to use tools and processes to increase the abilities of both individuals and organizations to acquire, share, and apply knowledge.

One of the NRC's projects had advanced violin students in centres across Canada working with Pinchas Zukerman, former music director of the National Arts Centre Orchestra in Ottawa.

The technology learnist process managers, now sometimes called virtual teachers, will manage a learning process on behalf of students, using the technology as a powerful learning engine. Similar to the learnists described above, they will be responsible for interpreting the learning plans and ensuring that the technology-based learning processes are valid and will contribute to the outcomes.

Well, there are some confidently stated but nonetheless wild guesses, with accompanying confidently wild detail, about what the staffing of the Third Schools might look like. There are many implications here for career transitions, re-training and new forms of para-professionals (para-learnists) and volunteers. In fact, I suspect that as the Third Schools evolve, we will see a greater development of what educational researchers, years ago, called staff differentiation – the advent of many different skill levels and roles. There will be room for student or apprentice learnists, para-learnists and even licensed practical community and school learnists (LPLs) in these positions, to freely borrow from law and medicine. And there will be opportunities for new forms of professional associations that will hopefully be more inclusive of diverse roles and skill levels than in the current teaching professions.

This probably sounds like a lot of people and roles, which may be potentially inefficient and confusing. This is a good place for some wise words from Jane Jacobs commenting on the alternatives to education as efficient processing.

> Nurturing and instructing human beings in a complex culture demands redundancy of mentors and examples. Redundancy is expensive but indispensable. Perhaps this is merely to point out that life is expensive. Just to keep it going, life makes demands on energy, supplied from

inside and outside a human being that are voracious compared with the undemanding thriftiness of death and decay. A culture, just to keep it going, makes voracious demands on the energies of many people for hands-on mentoring (*Dark Age Ahead*, p. 159).

The Learning of a Learnist

The traditional university or college education may not turn out to be the place for a learnist's professional preparation. As Orr says, "…we have organized education like mailbox pigeonholes, by disciplines that are abstractions organized for intellectual convenience."

> There is… a good bit of grumping about academic specialization, intellectual narrowness, and pigeonhole thinking. But despite decades of talk about "interdisciplinary courses" or "transdisciplinary learning," there is a strong belief that such talk is just talk. Those thought to be sober, or at least judiciously dull, mostly presume that real scholarship means getting on with the advance of knowledge organized exclusively by disciplines and sub disciplines. It does not seem to matter that some knowledge may not contribute to an intelligible whole, that some of it is utterly trivial, that parts of it are contradictory, or that significant and life-enhancing things are omitted.
>
> We educate lots of in-the-box thinkers who perform within their various specialties rather like a dog kept in the yard by an electronic barrier (*Earth In Mind*, pp. 94 – 95).

Tough language! I think Orr is aiming his frustration at the academy in general, but especially at the liberal arts faculties where he might say they ought to know better. Schools of education in the universities and colleges have taken major steps to ensure that the preparation of teachers reflects changes in learning theory and views of knowledge and effective practice. Various approaches, including one-on-one coaching and mentoring, pairing of more and less experienced teachers, and collaborative group work, are used. Some post-secondary learning organizations are taking serious steps to involve learners more fully in the design of their own learning.

Those who will be working, participatively, with parents and learners and designing learning plans for individual learners aimed at creating conscious, reflexive and self-managing learners will seek to get to their professional qualification by a similar route. They will want to be designers and developers of their own learning plans that will lead them to professional certification as a learnist. For practical reasons, this will likely require including a mixture of traditional courses and credits, perhaps grounded in learning theory, psychology and sociology; some new off-campus programs-in-action studies, such as the very remarkable work done in Calgary by Ken Low at the Action Studies Institute; and some learner-initiated inquiries and action learning, particularly in the areas of technology and community development, all with the guidance of an academic mentor and a practicing learnist.

In other words, inevitably, the learning of a learnist will come to mirror, as much as possible, the learning to be co-created by the learnist. This will be an intriguing challenge as there are not many guides available.

One possibility for the learnist in training is to join a community of scholarly learners, perhaps associated with a particular design studio and the community of parents and learners served by it. Their professional learning plans could then be designed to emphasize practical or apprenticeship-style learning. This will be particularly useful in the early years of the Third Schools. As the Third Schools emerge and begin to jostle the assumptions and practices of existing schools, those making the transition from teacher to learnist will need the scholarly "scaffolding," the insight and support that their colleagues and others making the transition can offer. Those pioneers who have made the transition can become the community of practitioners that coach and advise the learnists to follow.

Learnists may result from teachers who make problems…well, make certain things problematic. Research conducted by Marilyn Cochrane-Smith and Susan L. Lytle, reported in the 1999 *Review of Research in Education* in a chapter entitled "Relationships of Knowledge and Practice: Teacher Learning in Communities", is particularly helpful here. They analyze three conceptions of teacher learning: knowledge-*for*-practice, knowledge-*in*-practice, and knowledge-*of*-practice. The third conception, where, "… teachers across the professional life span – from very new to very experienced – make problematic their own knowledge and practice as well as the knowledge and practice of others and thus stand in a different relationship to knowledge" is most relevant (p. 273).

> The knowledge-*of*-practice conception turns on the assumption that the knowledge teachers need to teach well emanates from systematic inquiries about teaching, learners and learning, subject matter and curriculum, and schools and schooling. This knowledge is constructed collectively within local and broader communities (p. 274).
>
> [This conception]… entails collaboratively reconsidering what is taken for granted, challenging school and classroom structures, deliberating about what it means to know and what is regarded as expert knowledge, rethinking educational categories, constructing and reconstructing interpretive frameworks, and attempting to uncover the values and interests served and not served by the arrangements of schooling (p 279).

These knowledge practitioners and challengers of the "taken for granted" may become our Third School pioneers. Cochrane-Smith's and Lytle's chapter uses phrases like "transformed and expanded view," "transform classrooms, schools, and societies," and "linked to larger change efforts," that resonate with my sense of the fundamental transformation our school systems are about to be invited to take on (pp. 276, 278, 281). The insights of their knowledge-*of*-practice conception of teacher learning will be a valuable resource as the early explorations of the brave few begin. Learnists learning in this mode or "conception" will be in a powerful position to understand and interpret the forces of change acting on the schools and the nature of the opportunity I am describing.

In the Third Schools, collaborative inquiry won't be preferred or optimal; it will be central and critical to the success of learners and learnists especially, but also parents and community partners.

Other Modest Possibilities

As the Third Schools develop more fully, they will become "mature coalitions" of people: learners, parents, learnists, volunteers, partners and others, who are dedicated to the co-creation of good learning and to growth toward a more conscious and reflexive understanding of self and learning. The old titles and fixed patterns that distinguished teachers, students and administrators will melt away. There will be clear roles, expectations and accountabilities, all related to the intense effort to put energy and quality into the fulfillment of a myriad of learning plans bringing people together in various kinds of focused learning engagements. And there will be the shared commitment to the long-term view of learning and continuity of relationship between the family learnist and the families of learners in their learning community.

Walking into a Third School learning situation, it should be difficult, and unnecessary, to see the positions or hierarchies of the people involved. This will be chaotic at times, but like any complex system harnessing human intelligence to deep purpose, some meaningful and practical patterns should begin to settle out. Many new and exciting possibilities will emerge. Let me briefly discuss just one example.

Because of the non-graded structure of the Third Schools, students will move along at their own best pace and will incorporate many life-enriching experiences into their program. Many learners will be ready around the age of 16 to take on a greater challenge than working at a fast-food outlet. However, once they stop earning credits, the Third Schools system will stop receiving grants. But what if some of these bright and capable young people were willing to work as apprentices or learner-learnists in the Third Schools? It would be a case of "let's make a deal" with the authorities, but what a deal. The province or state would continue the annual per-pupil or foundation grant either as a stipend to the learner-learnist or deposit it to an account to be used for post-secondary education. The Third Schools would get an additional resource, the learner would get a new challenge, and the learnist preparation programs might get new candidates and entries to the profession. You will recall Claire's plan to take part in just such an opportunity.

Well, there are probably variations on the above idea, and many more possibilities to come. But it is an example of just how far we can move away from the days when some Calgary senior high school students were counseled to stretch their programs out from three to four or even five years. In some cases, a program extension met real learning needs. For others it was just warehousing, good for the school-based budget, staff allocations, range of programs, and yes, even the football team, but a rather curious way to keep the original Latin meaning of *educare*, to lead out, in education.

CHAPTER 10: LEARNING IN THE FAMILY AND THE COMMUNITY

To Family A Learner

By now you undoubtedly are thinking about the central role of the family in the Third Schools and wondering how that role can possibly be fulfilled in contemporary society. One frequently mentioned feature of our allegedly postmodern world is the rise of the non-traditional family. We also hear much about neglected and latchkey kids, children whose families either can't or choose not to be fully present in their young lives. And what about the pressing need to have two incomes in most Canadian families, incomes that all too frequently must be earned and maintained through long hours, shift work and retraining for new careers?

Non-traditional may not be all that new.

> While today's census families are characterized by diversity, this was also the case for families in the first half of the 20th century, but often for different reasons.
>
> Widowhood and remarriage following the death of a spouse were more common in the early decades of the 1900s, when there was higher maternal mortality and higher mortality rates overall for infants, children and adults. There were also many deaths which occurred during the two world wars and the Korean War. In 1921, for example, nearly one in 10 children aged 14 and under (8.8%) had experienced the death of at least one parent. As a result, lone-parent families were relatively prevalent in the early decades of the 20th century. These families represented 12.2% of all census families in 1941; a level that was higher than in 1961 (8.4%), near the height of the baby boom, and that was not surpassed again until 1986 (http://www12.statcan.gc.ca/census-recensement/2011/as-sa/98-312-x/98-312-x2011003_1-eng.cfm).

There have been other instances in our history of unusual family patterns. The huge war efforts of the 20th century are a good example. There were families without fathers, with mothers working, like Rosie the Riveter, in factories.

Parents working the evening and night shifts in the service industry have always needed to arrange for family and neighbours to provide care.

However, looking at the past few decades, the diversity of families does seem to be ramping up. In July 1991, the City of Calgary's Standing Policy Committee on Community Services considered a report proposing a new definition of "family." The report noted that there were increasing numbers of single-parent, extended and non-traditional families in Calgary. The older 1987 definition of a family as a household consisting of one or two adults responsible for children under age 18 was now too restrictive for matters like the sales of annual passes for swimming pools and recreational facilities. A planning staffer at the Calgary Board of Education jotted a note on the report; "We used to know what a family was – times have changed." And the times continued to change.

> Today, with so many more visible forms of family – from single-parent and blended to same-sex and even no-sex – characterizing society's basic unit is a much thornier proposition at a time when just four in 10 families fit the traditional nuclear mould (*The Globe and Mail*, November 29th, 2004).

Numbers can be treacherous when thinking about human systems. Nonetheless, the statistics do give us a fairly clear picture of the changing Canadian family. A *Maclean's* article entitled *How We Live* reports data from Statistics Canada and the 2001 census. Of the families with kids at home, 65 % are married, 25 % are single parent, and 10 % are common law including same-sex couples. (*Maclean's*, November 4th, 2002) And a story in *The Globe and Mail*, again citing Statistics Canada, tells us that over half of grandparents live in multigenerational families and that 56,700 or one percent are raising their grandchildren on their own. (December 10th, 2003) Moving forward to the 2006 census data, *The Globe and Mail* reports:

> Canada is a place where married couples are in the minority, grown children cling to the family nest, grandparents are moving in and there are more childless couples than ones with youngsters...Statistics Canada's 2006 census data reveal the dramatically shifting nature of Canadian society, with profound changes in the notion of a so-called traditional family. And the numbers starkly illustrate the inherent

stresses of the sandwich generation – middle-aged people housing their offspring and elderly parents under the same roof.

The census data on Canada's 8.9 million families reveal that just nine percent of them have five or more people in a household, and 26 percent of households have just one person. Five decades ago, those numbers were reversed (September 13th, 2007).

The big stories in the 2011 census data are about common-law and same-sex couples. Statistics Canada reports that between 2006 and 2011, "the number of common-law couples rose 13.9%, more than four times the 3.1% increase for married couples" and "the number of same-sex married couples nearly tripled...reflecting the first five-year period for which same-sex marriage has been legal across the country." (*Statistics Canada*, http://www12.statcan.gc.ca/census-recensement/2011/as-sa/98-312-x/98-312-x2011001-eng.cfm)

It may be good news for the Third Schools that increasing numbers of families are multigenerational. In the years ahead, it will be critical that someone in a care-giving role steps forward and provides the support that the co-creation of learning will require. Like the current school system, but perhaps even more urgently and competently, the Third Schools will have to provide appropriate safeguards around care and support. We are currently having trouble keeping our promises to the disadvantaged and aboriginal children of Canada. If the family or a caregiver cannot fulfill the role, then the family learnist will have to act as an advocate for the learner and for the younger children in particular. If there still is such a thing as an average family, we will likely find that it lives in a city, has one child and possibly a live-in grandparent, and needs two incomes. It is a family dealing with serious time stress.

The planning that occurs in the learning design centre, while trying primarily to address the family's values and goals in learning, will also have to take lifestyle into account. Full-scale home schooling, except in cases of wealthy families, requires a considerable sacrifice of income foregone and a long-term commitment of time and energy. Most home-schooling parents will say that the outcomes are well worth the sacrifices. But in many cases, practicality will require that the Third School's learning plans have a carefully balanced blend of home, carefully supervised community, and formal group learning.

Stanley Greenspan offers a compromise solution. He calls it the "four-thirds solution," in which each of two parents work, two-thirds in order to provide care to their children two-thirds of the week. He suggests that his plan "does require sacrifices in early career achievement, not to mention the reeducation of employers, but it can pay extraordinarily rich benefits in family life and child development" (*The Growth of the Mind,* p. 313). There will be various ways in which the needs of the family and the opportunities offered by the Third Schools can be reconciled with each other. Part of the reason for having a statement of commitment is to ensure that families decide the role that they will play in co-creating and supporting learning in the family and make plans to fulfill their commitment. We should keep in mind that families are having children later, in part so that careers may be launched first, so early career achievement may not be as threatened as in the past, and parents may be in a better position to negotiate some flexibility in their work lives.

Here is something else to keep in mind. There is considerable interest and energy behind parent involvement. The Canadian Teachers' Federation 2004 national issues poll asked a sample of Canadians about "increasing parents' involvement in their children's education." The summary of major findings states that this issue was "ranked as the highest priority among the four issues surveyed with respect to improving how well children are doing in school." And, "Two-thirds of Canadians surveyed consider this issue a high priority giving it a rating of one to three on a scale of 10, including 34% who consider it a top priority" (*Economic and Member Services Bulletin,* 2004 -3, p. 5). This view may be driven by a sense that parents ought to live up to their responsibilities, but as I have sketched out earlier, parents have been pushing for some years to have a greater decision-making role in the education of their children even if they have very mixed feelings about being more directly involved in the schools. "In short, what parents want is not so much involvement in schools as involvement in their child's learning" (*The Learning Game,* p. 107).

The advent of the Third Schools responds, in part, to an emerging new situation in family life. The reality for many families is that the home is becoming a centre for learning for adults as well as children and young people. The more obvious reason is that adults in those families either have careers or are looking to careers that require learning, whether new kinds of knowledge and skill, or upgrading existing credentials. People in professions are constantly under pressure to keep up with reading and research. The less obvious reason is that in the Third Schools, many parents will make a serious commitment, to be captured in the learning plan, to become ongoing learners about learning and human growth. This will take its place alongside the need to be learning, or at least conversant, in other areas of family life such as personal health and financial planning.

There will be little need to fill in time in front of the computer or TV screen. There will be much to learn and do, and it might even end up being a whole lot of fun. Let us start with the home as a learning centre.

The Family Learning Centre

This section could be titled The Home: The *Real* Learning Centre. The term "learning centre" has been appropriated over the years for many purposes, from special education to private counseling and tutoring services. The home is returning to the centre of our lives in many ways. A lot of that has to do with dwindling public resources and for some, streets and playgrounds that are less than inviting. But for many, it is a natural outcome of changes in values and lifestyles that lead people to being manufacturers and suppliers of experiences central to the quality of their own lives. The home is becoming a recreation centre and is being further centred for home-based business and home-schooling. Learning at home is becoming a multi-aged pursuit.

It is appropriate to turn our attention to the organization and layout, maybe even remodeling, of the home as a learning centre. After all, in the Third Schools, the home will be the base camp and maybe even the advanced camp and summit of learning careers in the family. Even for families that choose a learning plan that emphasizes learning centre-based group instruction, the home will be a key environment for practicing the art of co-creating learning.

Many families have already taken steps to increase the effectiveness of the home as a study or homework centre for those 10 minutes per grade per day. These include a well lit and comfortable work area and a daily quiet time or, at least, the removal of the TV to a distant room where it doesn't dominate the living space. Basic steps such as these will occur in any home where a young person's learning is valued and supported. In cases where a family wishes to create a centre for learning together, much more can be done.

We need to keep in mind that even with traditional homework, the ways that the parents work with the child are more important than the qualities of the study space. In the Third Schools, the supportive processes will be critical and a driving force in the parents' learning about learning. So I will try to balance a look at the spaces for learning with some ideas about ways to be together around learning as a family.

There are excellent resources available for parents in books, magazine articles and on the Internet. Many are written specifically for parents and examine issues such as home and school, and parent and teacher relationships, homework, tests and discipline from a parent's perspective. The earliest example on my bookcase is John Gasson and Paul Baxter's *Getting the Most out of your Child's School*. Others are Paul Kropp and Lynda Hodson's *The School Solution* and Laurence Steinberg's *Beyond the Classroom*. I have drawn upon them for the ideas that follow. Resources like these will be indispensable to the pioneering parents who first venture into the new territory of the Third Schools. Building on these writers with a few ideas of my own, let me sketch some things that might make sense:

1. Set a room aside for learning.

The location and set-up will vary from family to family but should tilt toward the more "fragile" learning styles in the family. Some can handle, or may even prefer, a noisy space where there are people talking and music playing. Some need a quiet retreat-like space. "Buzzing with activity" style learners are more likely to survive in a "could hear a pin drop" space than the reverse. Some children and teens will want to retreat to their own rooms. Compromises will occur, but create a space that is inviting, with warm non-classroom-fluorescent lighting, perhaps with maps, posters, and other displays on the walls. Decorate together. Have a work bee. And then…

2. Equip the space.

Some families will be able to afford more than others. Stores that sell second-hand office furniture are a great resource. Some school systems sell unneeded furniture and equipment. A large desk or work table invites project and collaborative work. The computer may need its own desk, but that will depend on the number and kinds of electronic devices being used.

Throw a couple of old armchairs and a low table into a reading alcove. The television should not be in the learning space. Like other areas of the home, such as the kitchen and the workshop, the TV room will be useful for certain kinds of learning as well as time out.

3. Be bookish – and magazinish.

In the age of IT, print still matters. Make books and magazines a fixture in all the living areas of your home, but especially in the family learning centre. This need not be a big expense. Libraries are a good resource, but trips should be made to second-hand book stores and thrift shops where there are treasures to be found. Ask friends and relatives to save their *Canadian Geographics and National Geographics.* For Third Schoolers who have some experience in home schooling, there will be stocks of books that get passed on from family to family. Read from them out loud when there is something interesting. Leave post-it notes in them to remember favourite passages and to flag good material for projects. Save pictorial magazines for scrapbooks, collages and illustrations.

4. Use technology.

I have mentioned computers and suspect that although we seem to be moving to an era when everyone in the family has their own portable device, it may evolve that families save their money to purchase one fully featured big-screen computer that is upgraded regularly to serve the learning needs of the whole family. More and more formal and informal communicating with friends and colleagues is being done with smart phones and tablets, so the family computer needn't be tied up for long periods with e-mail and social networks. It should be available for research, projects and publishing.

5. Talk. Have good conversations.

For many families, dinner hour is not an hour but a squeezed-in time between places to go and a brief chance to catch up on calendars and appointments. Try to slow this time down. In a Third Schools family, instead of "what did you do at school today?", the question, from those who weren't at home, may be "what did you (or everyone) work on today?" Let the interests and preoccupations of the day come forward.

Look for opportunities to bring some current events, pet projects, and puzzles and brainteasers into the conversation. Sports heroes and pop-culture icons are natural territories for conversation to head into, but ensure everyone can join, and look for those occasions where natural interests can shed light on the deeper challenges of learning. Do not force it. Do not let it become eye-rolling boring. A *Globe and Mail* article on the importance of mealtimes reports that "by adolescence, the more often a family eats together the less likely children are to smoke, use alcohol and drugs, suffer from an eating disorder or consider suicide. Family meals have also been linked to higher self-esteem and better performance at school" (September 12th, 2009). All right! Please pass the spaghetti.

6. Manage the time.

There is good advice in an article in the September 2004 issue of *Canadian Living* entitled, "Kids 201: Parenthood Primer". The article suggests ways to help children handle major projects with research and time-management skills. It suggests a daily time for homework (pp. 143-144). In the Third Schools, homework may be part of the "day job" of learning in which time will be allocated carefully to a number of learning activities. Time could also be scheduled that brings the family together in the family learning centre at a number of times during the week, probably in the evening, so that everyone can be in on the reading, study, and projects that are underway. Other family activities can be suspended during this time – a new version of the old Uninterrupted Sustained Silent Reading (USSR) that many schools once used. Or schedule Time Out Of Time (TOOT) sessions, an idea from Barry Oshry's book *Seeing Systems*, where there is honest sharing, careful listening and feedback to each other about the issues arising in everyone's learning journeys (pp. 21-24).

7. Model learning.

It makes a big difference if parents, family, friends, and other caregivers and mentors are seen reading and enjoying talking about it. Often there are opportunities to bring reading home, whether a new procedures manual or background reading and research. If work must be brought home, adults can share their "homework" with the young learners and share the space in the learning room. Model balance and taking time off. Look for novelty and adventure, opportunities to take the family beyond the usual visits with family and friends, and sports and recreational activities. The *Canadian Living* article warns about over-scheduling, and the examples given are those things that draw a family apart. Schedule time to watch a movie or go hiking and camping together.

The above suggestions are examples of what might be done. Each family will tailor its own response to these possibilities.

In the list above, I mentioned balance briefly, so a bit more on that topic. If the learning plan emphasizes home learning to the exclusion of almost all other activities, there will be an unhealthy imbalance. The family learning centre could become a cocoon, which is not a natural situation for healthy and inquisitive people. The learning design centre will have guidelines and checklists, but parents and learners need to make sure that there is sustained and appropriate interaction with other learners and families, neighbours and communities. Social cohesion will slip away if there is no effort to learn from other communities and systems of values and beliefs. The family learning centre should expand at times to accommodate groups of various kinds, working, learning, enjoying shared challenges and just having fun together. Parents will find ways to collaborate on the hosting of special learning events quite apart from the myriad of learning opportunities that exist in all communities and cities.

Learning Matters

As I pointed out in chapter four, good learning creates connections to community. Learning that matters and is relevant will, even at an early age, have some active connection with that intricate linkage between the health of the family and the local community. This is not learning about the community or imbedding little bits of curriculum in the community. This is a two-way street of participation and mutual learning. It means getting out of our homes, libraries, arenas, and school buildings and being with others in our community. It especially means that communities bend over backwards to become safe and welcoming places for learners to grow and develop, and to pursue their plans. David Orr, in responding to the accusations of school failure from the corporate world, expresses the challenge for communities very well.

> The answer to poor schools is to create better communities that take their children and their long-term prospects seriously regardless of the cost (Orr, *Earth in Mind*, p. 39).

These new connections into community are more than a new twist on the old "expanding horizons" of the elementary social studies curricula, referenced in Claire's story. Children first learned about their family, then their neighbourhood, then their city, town or community, then their country and finally the world. Sometimes there were even more stages in between, such as a look at regional economies. Sometimes there were field trips, but more often, the teaching was classroom-based, even though there were topics such as how to handle traffic and street crossings safely, or what postmen, firemen and policemen do (as we called them back then) and why they are our friends, or how stores work, with lessons on purchasing and counting change. The message seemed to be, "We'll describe how your world works and what you must do to thrive in it. The rest is up to you – when you get out there."

This challenge is different. It is about the miniature but gradually enlarging communities that children and young people engage with interactively and help create as they grow older, make friends and add their energy to community and youth activities. It is about early and small-scale engagements with the commons and the public good where even very young children can see themselves contributing at home and on the playground as they deal with issues of caring, fair play, and shared expectations. It is about children's learning being expressed in and influencing their lived lives at the earliest possible age. It is also about the development of communities that actively and intentionally support learning, even in the face of our rapid urbanization and preoccupation with safety and security. This means finding new ways to cultivate, nurture, and safely shelter good learning in the sometimes cold and harsh wildernesses that many communities have become.

So, it is time to fill in some moats.

The image of a school as a castle is an old one in public education. More than one observer has pondered the irony that children, for so many decades, have been required every day to leave the surrounding "village" and cross the moat into the "castle" of learning. The castle-moat mentality has weakened a bit in recent years as schools have turned themselves inside out to get the students out of the inside and into the community for field trips and international travel.

But it is still remarkably persistent. The simple explanation is that the "castle," the school, for many decades, was seen and accepted as the only place where education could and should happen. It was designed to deliver education, the teachers were trained to teach, and school was seen as the only place where education could occur, just as a bank was seen as the only place that saving could occur. The moat came to make sense in a way that was as powerfully taken for granted then as it is being challenged now.

In the Third Schools, the moat will be filled in, and learning and the community will slowly become each other's best partners. A new form of community development will arise, fueled by the excitement of communities transforming into human spaces that are resources for learning and experiencing the great gifts that learners can bring. The communities we live in, new and old, urban and rural, wealthy and poor, are all too rich a resource to go untapped in this new way of scaffolding learning. The connection will be two-way, as noted above. Learners will engage with and have a lasting impact on communities. Communities will actively support learners and their families and will participate in the co-creation and detailed design of places and processes to learning plans. As Thomas R. Berger says, addressing the shortage of Inuit teachers in his report *The Nunavut Project*, "School would become the business of the whole community" (p. vii).

The Learner Supports the Community

The positive impacts that learners will make on their communities can start at a very young age. The nature of this learner engagement with community can be an important part of the family's learning plan right at the outset. This key element of the learning plan will include some direct statements about outcomes. What new competencies, attitudes and elements of character are the family and the learner looking for? What forms of engagement and support with the community are most likely to call forth these outcomes? These questions will be addressed in the family and individual learning plans. Some serious thought will be required as the community support strand will continue right through the learner's journey to graduation. A deeper sense of what it means to support their community will develop in children who are truly engaged and will be expressed in growing satisfaction and pride in volunteerism and participatory citizenship.

That first sense of contribution or community building often comes through a formal group such as Brownies and Cubs. A look at the leadership and program manuals of volunteer organizations that work with youth will reveal an emphasis on character and service as well as crafts, recreation and fun-filled evenings around campfires. I have a 1955 edition of the Canadian Boy Scout's Handbook, *Tenderfoot to Queen's Scout*. It is from my scouting era, dare I admit. And dare I claim to remember the Scout Law as taught to me back in the early 1950s? Well no, but the words do evoke strong memories of boisterous meetings in the Lakeview United Church Hall in Regina. Although much in the Handbook is somewhat quaint and dated now, words like "honour," "friend," "courteous" and "thrifty" are a reminder of youth organizations that still take a strong stand on a well-articulated set of values. The resources of these organizations will be of great help in creating the community engagement parts of the learning plans and should be referenced in and accessible through the learning design centres.

Perhaps of more importance is the role of parents and close family and friends as guides and mentors. Many parents are volunteers and serve in a variety of roles in the community, often in groups of family and friends. Our children were drawn in (their Mom and Dad really didn't give them much choice) to community work in a variety of ways. They helped carry supplies, set tables and decorate, wash dishes and sweep floors and assist with lighting and sound, but more importantly, they also got in on the conversations that drove a lot of the organizing and witnessed firsthand the transformation that occurs when people have fun together as they make their community a better place. Sometimes they couldn't wait for the chores to end. Other times they watched, listened and chimed in as the adults figured something out and made plans.

As children get older, they become capable of partnering over a longer term with a person in their community, perhaps a senior or a disabled person. With help from staff in a non-profit or volunteer organization, they can design the personal contributions that will enrich and assist with a person's daily life. This kind of commitment over a longer term should be encouraged so that a deeper two-way relationship of caring and learning can be achieved. There are organizations in communities, such as long-term care centres, that are set up to not only incorporate children and teens into their programs as with other volunteers but also to help track their use of time, the contributions they make, and the skills and understandings they develop during the experience.

This dimension of learning by supporting the community can have its fullest expression in a series of personal challenges, commitments and relationships in the more senior years. This might mean working directly with disabled or elderly persons to fulfill roles directly related to their ability to live independently and to have a better quality of life. It might mean cooking, cleaning, repairing or even making personal assistive devices of the type that the Tetra Society volunteers make for the disabled in some of our Canadian cities. This type of approach is most suitable for an older learner in the mid- to late teens and could become part of a "year of challenges" program as described by Paul Ray and Sherry Anderson and referred to above (*The Cultural Creatives*, p. 280).

Older children and teens have been known to contribute enormous energy and enthusiasm to community campaigns in areas such as public health, the environment and social issues. The organizing, talking and debate, efforts to clarify the objectives and issues, problems of trust and communication, and working with others in often intense situations are powerful learning opportunities. There are always risks that enthusiasm will outrun balance and that young people will be treated unscrupulously and used to meet the agendas of others. In spite of this, significant and lasting learning occurs when learners make a commitment to help their own community understand and take action on the need for clean water, a safe habitat for an endangered critter, recycling, tree planting and green space, traffic controls, heritage preservation, and the list goes on. This does not mean that Third Schoolers will all become social activists and alienate themselves from their own communities. It means that there is always important work to be done in any community; work that people support but often lags or lapses for lack of energy, commitment and good thinking; work that could be a very good source of learning, particularly when background research is needed and public debate must occur.

Modeling by parents, family and friends of a purposeful and engaged community and civic life will be a central part of the designs for learning in the Third Schools. The commitment of learners to projects will grow out of the attitudes and support of the family. Meaningful engagements with the community do not usually divide by age group, gender, ethnicity or other arbitrary criteria. They bring people together around shared meanings of "the good" in community life. The whole family can be involved. The experiences should be thoughtful, planned and the subject of many conversations about what happened and what was learned.

The Community Supports the Learner

It is time to take a closer look at how the community can be cultivated, developed and even researched to provide multiple centres and possibilities for learning. The goals and outcomes, and learner and parent preferences in many of the learning plans, will call for intensive community-centred learning. While some learning plans will direct learners to more traditional group learning, many more will see the learners spending most of their time in home and community learning with only occasional periods of time spent in formal groups. Learning engagements and activities will occur in local communities and will use the resources of surrounding cities and regions, with the participation of family and friends and community-based groups and volunteers. And it should be noted, community-based learning may be an important way that Third Schools are able to work effectively with the resources that will be available.

There is a wise elder who would approve. As David Orr reminds us, "Dewey proposed that the immediate vicinity of the school be a focus of education, including the study of food, clothing, shelter and nature" (*Earth In Mind*, p. 110). A century has passed since Dewey made these observations, and the "immediate vicinity" now includes his list and much more.

Communities are too rich a resource to be left out of the learning equation. It is hard to imagine a community so monochrome, insular or intensely private that there would be no opportunities for engagement with a rich array of learning opportunities. The history of school and business partnerships gives many examples of the kinds of knowledge, skills and areas of interest that groups of employees have been able to bring into the schools. Expand the possibilities out to the hundreds, or even thousands, of people in an urban community and many good things become possible for learners. The trick is to design not only for good learning, but also for safety and consistency. The community learnists will play an important leadership role here.

For those Third Schoolers who find that they are pioneers in working with a community learnist and the design of community learning, the following may provide a start.

A good first step would be to do a community profile. Some cities, such as Calgary, already have published basic profiles. More detailed community profiles are fairly easy to create in a portion of a daylong meeting of parent and community representatives. Some very good processes for community profiling are used for participant selection in the planning of Search Conferences. They call it the community reference system. Merrelyn Emery and Ronald Purser describe a social network map of a system, in our case, a community, that will "typically cover such variables as key interest groups, demographics, different types of institutions, such as small businesses and large corporations, social services, schools, government offices, religious groups and so forth" (*The Search Conference*, p. 157). I have created such "maps" in workshops by drawing circles on large sheets of paper and inviting the participants to think about their community and begin giving the circles names such as seniors, strip mall, public library, arena, home businesses, and so on. As soon as some names appear, they act as prompts for other groups, and the complete map emerges. Then a list of key contacts can be created and discussions opened up to reveal potential learning engagements and activities for children and young people in the community.

A map can be created (a geographic one) that shows the boundaries of the community being studied, the major features of the community, such as waterways, environmental reserves, safety-related features such rail and roadways, and major buildings and complexes. Along with the map, and as people are contacted, logs can be kept and lists created of important information such as organizational profiles, including mission statements, policies related to learning, availability of meeting and work space, and kinds of knowledge, skills and employee interests that can be made available. Records can also be kept as individuals are interviewed, specifying the time they can give and the kinds of interests and experiences that they can bring to the learning effort. Seniors are an especially valuable resource and frequently have personal histories that can fill out the abstract outlines of a period of history, local or otherwise. They will have traveled, lived in other parts of the world and have had time to develop interests such as art and music.

Funds of Knowledge

Without question, one of the most exciting developments in expanding the community's role in learning is the work done by Luis C. Moll and his colleagues in the Funds of Knowledge Project at the University of Arizona. The research was done to enrich and empower classrooms and teachers in public schools who were working with more traditional assumptions about curricula and organization. However, there are powerful and promising implications for community-based learning that will be part of the shift to the Third Schools.

The Funds of Knowledge Project found fertile and abundant resources for learning hidden in the homes and communities that were studied. According to the U.S. North Central Regional Educational Laboratory (NCREL), Moll and his colleagues "have studied Mexican-American families who have survived successfully in spite of debilitating circumstances such as poverty and discrimination. Particular constellations of cultural patterns – strategies if you will – that value learning and the transmission of knowledge to children distinguish these families" (NCREL, Luis Moll).

> Moll and his colleagues discovered that Mexican-American households are clustered according to kinship ties and exchange relationships. These clusters of households develop rich funds of knowledge that provide information about practices and resources useful in ensuring the well-being of the households. Each household in the cluster is a place where expertise in a particular domain can be accessed and used; examples of domains include repair of vehicles and appliances, plumbing, knowledge of education, herbal medicine and first aid. Together, the households form a cluster for the exchange of information and resources. Often, everyone seems to congregate at one core household (NCREL, *Luis Moll*).

In other words, households have become integrated into learning networks with important nodes where know-how is concentrated and shared. Another NCREL online article adds:

> ...his research team performed what he calls an "ethnographic analysis" of Tucson's Latino community. Interviewers gathered data about the origin, use, and distribution of the knowledge and skills in the community. They also talked with individual family members to learn the personal and labor history of the family. Moll is quick to point out that any teacher or school member can perform this kind of analysis.

The home investigations revealed that many families had abundant knowledge that the schools did not know about – and therefore did not use in order to teach academic skills. In general, the barrio families knew about agriculture and mining, economics, household management, materials and science, medicine, and religion.

Various families with rural backgrounds knew a great deal about the cultivation of plants, animals, ranch management, mechanics, carpentry, masonry, electrical wiring, and medical folk remedies. They also had some entrepreneurial skills and were familiar with archeology, biology, and mathematics.

More important, the families shared what they knew (NCREL, *Funds of Knowledge: A Look at Luis Moll's Research Into Hidden Family Resources*).

It turns out that the families studied had significant and relevant funds of knowledge. Another article calls them "impressive and diverse" and adds that they "may include such areas as farming and animal husbandry, construction, trade, business, and finance" (ERIC *L & L Digest*, February 1994).

Some of the exciting findings revolved around the transformation of teachers' work and the high level of trust and understanding created with the households that were part of the project. The Third School community learnists will almost certainly want to have training in some of the attitudes and skills of anthropology and ethnography that Moll's teacher researchers acquired. As the teachers in the project pointed out, the extra work involved in field notes, journals and follow-up meetings was more than a typical teacher's workload can handle. The Third School's approach to learning is intended to capitalize on these kinds of possibilities and accommodate crucial learning and developmental commitments on the part of the learnists.

And by the way, just in case readers had concluded that the Third Schools could operate in upper-income communities only, this work on funds of knowledge should set such a conclusion aside. Especially in our large cities, communities have huge resources for learning even where there is poverty and a number of minority groups. Many communities that have been labeled by educators as "high need" have a remarkable and potent diversity: immigrant populations, a wide range of work experience and a myriad of enterprises from home-based to large scale. And like many of the Mexican-Americans in Moll's study, significant numbers of our immigrants have come from advanced training and education in their own countries to cab driving and fast food operations in Canada. They frequently show a greater respect for learning and the institutions that deliver it than their recently acquired fellow citizens – the rest of us. Our recent Canadians and many others in their communities have much to offer. We just haven't studied and tapped into them, or moved past simplistic views of culture and diversity, in ways like the Funds of Knowledge Project illustrates.

Many years ago, a remarkable piece of imaginative research came to our attention at the Calgary Board of Education. It was a 1970 thesis prepared for the School of Architecture at the University of British Columbia by Ron Ellis and was entitled *Learning and the Inner City*. Using a combination of text and graphics, Ellis's thesis documented in vivid detail how learning could be constructed in the inner city of Calgary. Ellis's learning resources included theme clusters such as history, agriculture, ecology, religious studies and communication, all linked by the then new idea of educational television. Specific resources, some general and some tied to the theme clusters, included the Glenbow Museum archives, municipal greenhouses, public library, central YWCA, IBM data centre, courthouse, livestock pavilion, swimming pools, poultry hatchery and so on. Learning was to be supported by learning centres and resource islands, multi-purpose mini-libraries and demo areas, and mobile classroom units. Although Ellis modestly subtitled his work "a direction for the improvement of the educational facilities in the central Calgary area," it was a remarkably thorough and imaginative look, for 1970, at a new world of possibilities for learning imbedded in community. But it was also a very small straw caught up in the freshening school reform breezes of the '70s.

The larger community, a city or region, will have excellent resources and, in all likelihood, experience and a track record in hosting learning. Obvious examples are zoos, museums and outdoor or environmental learning sites. Their experience may be helpful in creating smaller-scale learning networks and nodes in a local community. The key will be willing volunteers, people who sense the importance of this kind of engagement between learners and their communities and the responsibility to be screened and to help create processes and procedures to ensure that learning occurs in safe and secure environments. Inevitably, there will be a number of logistical issues to sort out, such as making transportation arrangements, putting learning groups together, and creating schedules and procedures for checking in and out.

If We Do It Well

We may feel that the barriers on the road to family and community-based learning loom like giant standing stones blocking the way forward. The effort to get over or around them will require a large investment in time, energy and ingenuity. In fact, the journey is already underway, and inevitably so.

> But after all, what would lead a sensible person to conclude that a human child – the descendant of tens of thousands of generations of people who spent their days actively working to secure their subsistence – would find it congenial to sit in a room with one adult and twenty-five or more other children for six hours a day over twelve or sixteen or eighteen years? Our ancestors learned by doing, by taking on tasks under the intimate guidance of more experienced persons who could impart knowledge, concepts and skills (Greenspan, *The Growth of the Mind,* p. 228).

> Fred Emery…observed from many experiments in the education system, and from many failures, that there were two layers of assumptions about education. The first contained the assumption that bureaucratic structure was necessary. The second layer contained the assumption that people are unable to learn from their experience.

> Others, too, have noted that the assumptions on which the education system is based have become beliefs. It is now an axiom that "learning is the result of teaching. And institutional wisdom continues to accept this axiom, despite overwhelming evidence to the contrary. (Emery, *The Future of Schools,* p. 157, quoting I. D. Illich).

Some frames need to be broken. The assumptions that adhere to the old ways of framing how learning works have obscured our view toward different kinds of futures. Projects such as Funds of Knowledge have a frame-breaking energy, and are like signposts pointing to the possibilities of the future. There are probably many other frame-breaking efforts that the magnetic force of a serious rethink effort along the lines of this Third Schools scenario would draw out into the light. Once these changes are underway, there will be an outpouring of practical ways of creating new contexts for learning in the home and the community. And many of the changes that schools have been trying to implement, such as building partnerships into the community and bringing real life experiences into the classroom, will at last come to fruition.

If the Third Schools succeed in creating these connections within the family, to the community, and to achieving learning in community, we will create the opportunity for children to not only "fall in love" with their parents, their families and their own lives, but also to feel passionate caring toward the health of their communities, societies and our increasingly endangered planet.

CHAPTER 11: THE ADULT LEARNER

Give and Take Learning

Imagine an adult learning system that lives at the heart of a large community such as a city or densely populated region and creates a space where those seeking learning and those with learning to offer can quickly and easily become part of each other's lives and learning. Imagine a system that, like an effective e-2-e design, effectively connects the supply and demand sides of learning and allows people to earn and bank tuition credits so that providing learning creates the resources to acquire learning. Imagine a system that, because of its openness and freedom of access, encourages many more people to vacate the comfortable couches of their lives and both add to and share in the store of knowledge and experience in their community. Imagine a system that ensures that those who are serious about deep, vital and extended learning will create and fulfill a personal plan for learning, while others who want to explore something new or enhance something old can do so with a minimum of bureaucratic structure and wasted time and effort. And imagine this system working so well that it invites people with good minds to live within its embrace and become part of a self-created adult learning community.

Our beliefs and capacities as adults and learners and the requirements of the communities and organizations we live our lives in may be pushing us toward a system just like this. As with the traditional trappings of the public schools, the old systems of prerequisites, required courses, credits and credentials won't soon melt away. But we are invited to this new, wilder and more tangled garden of learning, rich with possibility and ripe for exploration. It will grow up beside the old and familiar geometry, tidy, clipped and orderly, of the existing gardens we have. And, it can be brought into being without the wastelands of trivia and back alleys of sinister intent that bedevil the Internet as a source of learning.

Now is the time for such a system. What I am about to describe, an adult learning exchange as a civic or municipal enterprise, could come to a rich and colourful reality within a few years. We need only to turn attention and resources to its development.

The Adult Learner in the Third Schools

As I bring the adult learner into this extended scenario of learning in the future, I need to acknowledge that significant changes are underway, even for our traditional credentialing institutions: the colleges, technical schools and universities. Many of these large and complex post-secondary schools are anticipating change and are deploying a variety of innovations to test the ground ahead. Their efforts to make learning more learner-convenient, let alone learner-designed and -directed, will ease their entry into the era of the Third Schools. However, whether they choose to or they must, many adults will be looking for learning outside the halls and walls of higher learning. Some remarkable Third School possibilities are presenting themselves. The adult learning future can be as exciting and rewarding as that of the child and adolescent.

The Third Schools will provide a natural home for adult learners, especially if they are already mature and self-directed people in their careers and home-lives. Many find it frustrating to bump up against the confines of traditional learning: the rules and procedures of course selection, graduation requirements, and traditional grading and assessment. Many have demonstrated their capacity to be reflexive and self-managing as they create learning in their homes, careers and communities. They bring books, research reports and self-help material home to a den, kitchen table or coffee table. They study endless pages of information on the Internet. They go out to lectures, book clubs and conferences. They are increasingly ready for a support system that would assist in the creation and maintenance of a coherent personal program of learning.

But who is an adult learner? It might be time to evolve a new definition, something related to learning rather than a mixture of chronological age and funding formulas, as satisfying as that might be for our inner bean-counter. We are used to categories such as student and teacher, even though we know there are boundary cases. Examples are student teachers who are teachers in training, students who instruct, such as teens who teach swimming, and teachers who are researchers, perhaps learning about reading. There are cross-age teaching programs where older students assist younger students in specific ways through defined bits of coaching, tutoring and role modeling under the close direction of a teacher. For the purposes of this chapter, I'd like to take our thinking in a slightly different direction toward a new boundary, more appropriately seen as a transition. As a springboard, let's recall Claire Chappell's interest in helping children to learn.

Earlier, in Claire's story and elsewhere, I described how a mature and academically advanced high school-age learner might assist younger learners as a junior learning assistant or para-learnist. The challenge here is to avoid creating an exact dividing line between the two roles, learner and learnist. At some point though, a distinct enough role shift from a learner just doing learning to a learner who is assisting others to learn will need to be identified so that formal recognition in the form of payment, a record of service, and perhaps a certificate can occur. This shift from a single-role learner to a blended one, a learning assistant, will be carefully planned and implemented and will occupy a significant portion of that young learner's time. There will be a careful preparation to assume a longer term and closely supervised responsibility for assisting another learner or a group of learners and their efforts to reach specific learning outcomes or implement defined learning plans and processes. It is in this transition, the role shift that Claire wants to initiate, that we can see how, taken further, the shift to being an adult learner in the Third Schools will occur.

An adult learner in the Third Schools is someone who, because of their maturity, knowledge and skills, has learning to offer as well as learning still to do. We can define an adult learner as one who has significant learning to put into a learning system as well as clear learning outcomes they would like to get out of a learning system.

Adult learners in the Third Schools will understand they are on a two-way street. Adult learning systems in the Third Schools will make it possible for learners to create and implement learning that would not be possible within the traditional age and credential boundaries.

With this definition in mind, the question becomes: how will adult learning unfold as a marketplace or learning exchange?

Learning to Work, Working to Learn

There are a number of forces acting on our assumptions about learning in our workplaces, families and communities. These forces are signals that change is coming with new possibilities. Let us take a look at two of the most powerful and significant forces at work in our current world of adult learning and ask how they might point to a different future. The first is the increasing likelihood and importance of prior learning, the knowledge and experience that people bring into a learning situation. The second is the pressure on people, mostly in the workplace, but also in areas like parenting and volunteering, to continuously learn.

The first, prior learning and experience, is loaded with potential, especially for Canada's significant immigrant population and our aging workforce or "junior seniors." Some years ago, my wife Joanie told me about a remarkable adult student who was enrolled in a continuing education program which she taught. I was also able to meet and talk with him, so I learned a bit about his circumstances. This young family man was from Africa, a filmmaker, fluent in at least two languages, married and raising a family. In order to pay for his tuition, books and other costs as well as help support the family, he was working at the usual minimum wage jobs with little intellectual challenge, security, or opportunity to learn or advance, a familiar story for immigrants to Canada and many other places. As I learned more about his background, it became obvious that he had much learning to offer. I could imagine a short course for business people on what one needs to know, say and do when visiting and doing business in his home country. I thought about the powerful resources he would bring to a junior or senior high school social studies classroom. Instead, this knowledge and experience was locked up inside him and his family, and he was working at a mindless job in order to afford that all-necessary high school credential.

Another facet of prior learning is the importance of the knowledge and experience that employees carry around in their heads. This know-why and know-how is now regarded as an asset that adds significant value to a business or organization. It is given names such as human or intellectual capital. It becomes an important issue when layoffs occur, or when valued employees leave. This personal store of knowledge, experience and competencies is also an asset to the individual. It is portable and of great importance in advancing one's career. It is an asset that employees will seek to grow and enhance. The responsiveness and willingness of an employer to support personal growth plans is a major factor in an employee's decision to stay or leave. Many employees have been well coached and mentored and are ready to coach and mentor others.

As for the second force, much has been spoken and written about the importance of continuous and life-long learning over the past few decades. Back in 1996, Dr. Roger Selbert, looking at the steep growth trend in information technology and training and education, observed in his newsletter, *Future Scan*:

> Training. Education. Retraining. Updating of skills. Professional development. Lifelong learning. Career strategizing. We've been preaching these "preparation-for-change" themes for 15 years, and businesses have been listening…(*Future Scan*. No. 845, May 20th, 1996).

The article goes on to suggest that learning how to learn trumps technical training as the most important adult learning objective. Various reports through the '90s and on into this century have documented the distinctive learning demands of the quality movement as well as many other pressures to increase productivity and profits. Investment in employee development has grown steadily in importance, but perhaps a bit more slowly in reality. The Conference Board of Canada points out that "Canada's record on employer-sponsored training is weak" compared with leading European countries, such as Sweden, Norway and Finland (The Conference Board of Canada, March 20th, 2014).

What about adult education?

> Nearly half of Americans aged 25 and older – 92 million people – take part in some form of continuing education… Some just want to learn how to paint a Maine coastal scene, but the majority is enrolled in work-related training, and many are earning degrees.

> No matter who they are, though, their openness to lifelong learning shows that individuals have a great capacity to adapt, learn, and contribute – at any age. Adult Ed reflects an American belief in reinventing one's self through education, and it contributes to the country's competitiveness.

> Continuing education is also a growing business. One hot niche market – people over 50 – is now a $6 billion business, up from $4 billion only two years ago (*The Christian Science Monitor*, December 1st, 2006).

The desire to be "reinventing one's self through education" is probably universal. Lifelong learning and personal development for career advancement and engaging with change remain high in the minds of employees. Add to that the growing expectation of employees that they will learn and increase their own stock of skill, knowledge and experience – and that their employers will assist them with more than narrowly focused job-specific skills. Indeed, had better assist them if employers want the good ones to stay.

What we have here are some of the essential ingredients for the emergence of an adult learning marketplace.

The Learning Marketplace

We have a potent mixture in our society of people with learning to offer and people wanting and needing learning. Imagine a new kind of classified ad online or in your local paper – Learning 4 Sale, or Learning Wanted. But these exchanges cannot be just the informal barter of know-how that goes on around us all the time, as valuable as that may be. These learning transactions will need to be screened, assessed and evaluated in ways that ensure that commitment and quality are always there. In other words, they will be subject to wise and thoughtful organization, leadership and governance.

We need to create a parallel but connected channel to formal systems of training, credentialing and certifying, one that brings the participants in this new learning game together in a learning exchange. Every day, in our cities, municipalities, communities and medium to large organizations, there is a vast array of good- to high-quality learning on offer and being consumed – especially if you are among those fortunate ones who are connected and networked with the right people. Much of this learning is available through existing programs of staff training and development, course offerings, and formal systems of coaching and mentoring. This will continue. But much more of this learning, this froth of knowing and seeking, can be tapped to bring significant benefits to people, organizations, communities and society, and create new players in the learning game.

Let us imagine a situation where those who have learning to offer are able to formally register their background, credentials and learning offerings into a formal learning registry and exchange system that makes the information available to many others. Some learning proposals may come from people who are essentially "free agents," such as my wife's continuing education student mentioned above. Other offerings may come from corporate resource people, such as technical support staff or leadership development specialists in H.R. departments. They would, hopefully with the support of their organization, or on their own time, enter the learning exchange. Entrepreneurs and business people also could be a powerful resource.

Stretching our imaginations even further, let's imagine that those seeking learning are also able to formally register their need or interest in this learning registry and exchange system. This is the Learning-Wanted side of the equation. Some adult learners might be very clear about the learning they are after, even specific about the kind of content and resources, or even the credentialed source they are looking for. Others may be deliberately more open and flexible because theirs is a general interest that can be met in a variety of ways. Others will be uncertain and vague and will need assistance to make any kind of an effective entry into the system.

If these processes have any basis in reality, we have reason and opportunity to design a support system for a remarkable new adult learning exchange, a system that brings together adults who are seekers of learning and adults who are providers of learning, while enabling them to take charge of their own learning in a way that is similar to the deep intentions of the Third Schools. This effort will likely be brought to life outside the walls of the traditional post-secondary system. Like the relentless duality of oil and water, the emphasis on accreditation, requirements, credentials and competitiveness, not to mention a shortage of time and resources, will likely keep post-secondary systems out of such a new and experimental venture. It will be those who have a consuming interest, time, expertise, and a degree of impatience with the formal systems in the higher halls that now deliver adult learning that will be attracted to pioneering a learning exchange system.

The support system will need to be very flexible. The idea of a voluntary exchange will be at its very core. It will allow adults to offer learning, to seek to learn, to work and earn to learn, to serve or volunteer to learn, or to pay to learn. Such a system will be the learning analogue of local currencies that are appearing in many communities. They allow for a valuing and exchange of localized goods and services. That same creativity and energy will unfetter the learning capacities of communities. The voluntary learning exchange will likely be confined to a city or region. It will encourage entrepreneurship and a flourishing of learning. It will focus the rich resources of information technologies such as the Internet not only on the needs and interests of individuals but also on the shared needs and interests of communities.

So, what needs to be done?

The Calgary Learning System (Shhh – They Don't Know About It)

I will use my former neighbouring city of Calgary, Alberta, as the blissfully unaware subject of a rough sketch or straw design, but a design that has some essential process elements that we can imagine and foresee. Just for fun, let's pretend this new system exists and call it Learn Calgary. Remember, it could as easily be Learn Vancouver…or Learn Atlanta…or Learn Liverpool.

This is the Third Schools for adults. The idea is that adults can or should be able to take charge of their own learning consistent with the shift toward conscious learning discussed earlier. In Calgary, as in other population centres, this shift is increasingly likely and timely because:

> - People in low-wage jobs, wishing to upgrade their skills, must take the initiative and are often lacking the time and resources to get a basic credential such as a post-secondary diploma or certificate.

> - People in careers can expect their employers to support work-related training and development, but it is less likely they will be supported when they seek new careers or to modify their qualifications.

> - Seniors seeking upgrading and renewal in order to remain productive or to attract clients and contracts must look for appropriate sources of learning.

> - New immigrants often enter the work force over-educated and over-qualified for the positions they get and must go back to working on a high school diploma in order to recover their career path or start a new one.

> - Changes in the more specialized or technical areas of employment are occurring faster than the traditional institutions can keep pace with.

Add to this, all the enchanting and truly useful meta-skills that employers would like and our own life plans may require; Selbert's learning how to learn, creativity, initiative, ingenuity, and social and emotional intelligence. Add also a greater capacity to thrive in fast-paced and complex systems.

On the other side of the coin, and partly because of these same forces and social and work pressures, there are people of all ages who have the knowledge, skills, ideas and passions to offer to others:

> ➢ People are learning for personal interest and recreation far more often than they used to, whether it's sailing, rock climbing, financial management, gardening or parenting.

> ➢ As the planet has shrunk, our capacities have had to enlarge as we have learned how to do business, deliver health care or volunteer in different places and cultures.

> ➢ We have brought the planet home, expanding our repertoire from cooking to belief systems, from Tuscan bean soup to the Tao Te Ching.

> ➢ People have become serious students of the places they visit, often adding books and formal coursework to their traveler's understandings of a place.

> ➢ A glance at our local community newsletters and newspapers reveals many people who have stepped forward to offer their coaching, mentoring, healing and counseling skills.

> ➢ Skills and knowledge gained in obtaining diplomas and degrees are constantly being expanded and pushed to a cutting edge in areas as diverse as electronic systems, computer software, management, health and wellness, human relations, and communications.

In this entire feast of learning on offer, expectations may be much higher than in the old days of "night school." In some cases, it will be good enough to be a talented and entertaining amateur or retiree. In others, one's capacity to fulfill the learning commitment offered will be tested in the same way that matchmaking is different from promoting a club or special interest group.

What are some of the likely essential design features of Learn Calgary?

Assessment Upon Entry
When the adult Third Schooler approaches the Learn Calgary system, the system needs to know one of two very basic things:

> - If seeking learning: Is the adult learner able to put a credible and educationally valid (à la Glickman's "pedagogically valid") learning plan together?

> - If offering learning: Is the adult learner's offer of learning substantive and backed by evidence of knowledge and experience, if not a formal credential?

This suggests that there is a professional role known as an adult learnist whose skills are similar to the community learnist described earlier.

Those seeking learning do so within the framework of an adult learning plan. The adult learnist determines whether a satisfactory learning plan exists or is required, and if required, launches the process. Those unable to craft a learning plan are referred to an entry or preparatory program. It engages the learner in developing the skills and strategies of an adaptive learner who can create effective learning plans, not to mention life plans. The learning plan, once ready and approved, moves the learner to the next stage.

If learning is on offer, the adult learnist uses means such as interviews, protocols, checklists and follow-up checks of references and credentials to ensure that those offering learning are well prepared to do so and can fulfill their commitments. If there is some uncertainty about the capacity of a learning provider or the quality of the experience, a panel of qualified people may be convened and consulted or a demonstration session may be required. Once the adult learnist has determined that the learning on offer is a valuable and viable addition to Learn Calgary, it is placed into an information system.

Entering the System
We now have two kinds of qualified adult learners: Those who seek learning within the framework of a well-constructed learning plan; and those who offer learning that has been judged to be educationally valid; sometimes both may be embodied in the same person. Let us take both of these people a step further

and enter their data into an information system that covers Calgary and its surrounding urban and rural region.

Those seeking learning now have a personal learning plan that may vary all the way from a few specific skills or knowledge areas to a multi-year effort that represents a major shift in competencies and/or career direction. What do those seekers have to choose from? The Learn Calgary system has an array of courses, workshops and programs offered by people with a range of backgrounds. Many are solo operators, but some may represent larger organizations, whether business, public or not-for-profit, which choose to contribute to the Learn Calgary system. If what the learner seeks to learn is not available, a "learning wanted" ad is placed on the system's website and into its learning match-making software which may encourage people to step forward and offer their knowledge and experience by creating just that learning opportunity.

Those who have learning on offer have their proposed classes, course, workshop or other experience placed onto the same website and into the match-making software. There is a brief description with an online source for more information and a way of making contact. If the learning on offer is in demand, or perhaps has been offered before, there is information on times and locations. The cost of the learning experience is given both in cash and in Learn Calgary credit units. How does one earn those credits? Read on.

Meeting and Learning
Those offering learning and those needing learning have now found each other online in the Learn Calgary information and registration system. They must arrange to meet and to establish a routine of meetings and sustained communication, whether virtual or physical, so that the learning may be exchanged. Some arrangements are a bit more formal and conventional. Going back to my wife's continuing education student described earlier, the learning space for his cross-cultural business offering might be a meeting room provided in the offices of a corporation, public service or international agency in order to provide that learning more conveniently to their own employees or clients. Some learning places may be "found" places where space is not in use full-time, such as public school classrooms or corporate training facilities that have been made available to the Learn Calgary system. Other spaces may be

studios, workshops, conversation cafés or online. As the system matures, many more options will appear.

Obviously, if specialized space or equipment is required, the person or agency offering the learning incorporates that need into the arrangements and the cost. Generally we will find that a large city or a well-populated region is filled with suitable spaces that are not fully utilized and can be made available for this ongoing shared feast of learning.

Accounting for Learning
The plan for adult learning in the Third Schools, in most, if not all, cases, addresses how to know that learning has occurred. Those offering the learning build in an assessment process with a specification of the evidence of learning and the tools and techniques to gather that evidence. With adults, much of the assessment is anecdotal, that is, arises from the ongoing work itself, and is built right into the learning. The learners take responsibility too, and help to define the outcomes of the learning experience, and help gather the evidence that assures all that the outcomes have been reached. The Learn Calgary system similarly puts in place monitoring systems that ensure that learners are fulfilling their learning plan. Some sort of a journal or log book as a requirement helps achieve the general objective of assisting the adult learners to take responsibility for their own learning and adapt their personal learning plan to their growing and changing awareness and expectations.

This is a rough outline of some of the possible elements of a Third School's adult learning exchange system. I have talked as though there really is a Learn Calgary system. What does it look like?

The Learning City
Before I push the City of Calgary any further as an unwitting accomplice in the learning of many adults, I need to push our imaginations a bit further. I foresee the emergence of a civic infrastructure, a community and regional framework and network that will bring a city's learning exchange to life. Just for still more fun, here are some elements that might make up the Learn Calgary Adult Learning Exchange.

Ideally, this kind of grassroots, broadly based community learning is an overarching project for the whole city and its region. The benefits to its citizens, organizations, families and communities are substantial, so why not a multi-partner governance group operating as a learning commission, with a mixture of appointed and elected members – the Calgary Learning Commission? To add to the fun, let's fold the public libraries and maybe even some of the learning functions of museums and galleries into this governance group.

Problem! This suggests an infusion of tax revenues to fund the system. But since participation is voluntary, unique to individuals and groups, with variations throughout the system, costs are kept low. Varieties of sources of revenue, corporate, government, individual and not-for-profit, emerge and add up to a sizable and sufficient amount of cash. The Calgary Learning Commission embodies the civic interest in and ownership of Learn Calgary and represents all the major interest groups committed to making the new system work. The Learning Commission also ensures that all the major sectors in the community: Business, seniors, health care, volunteers, arts, education and others are represented for their advice and contributions. Learn Calgary increasingly is seen as a considerable civic asset adding to the quality of life and the desirability of Calgary as a place to live, work and learn.

The leadership of the system requires a very small management team and a number of part-time workers. Specific responsibilities include the core learning processes, information systems, logistics and finance. The heart of the system is a web-based civic learning engine that connects the demand and supply sides of learning in an exciting, novel and flexible way. Breaking this open a bit more:

> ➢ Core learning processes – besides the assessment, personal learning plan development, system entry, learning, and accounting stages referred to earlier, a counseling process refers people to existing post-secondary institutions in cases where packaged learning better meets their needs. Conversely, these same institutions contribute some of their courses and faculty to the civic learning exchange.

> ➢ Information system – keeps track of the learning supply and its specifics, the status of the personal learning plans, and the learning and financial credits earned and expended. It maintains a bureau, like a speakers' bureau, of all those who offer learning, with brief bios and descriptions of the learning on offer – to be maintained at the source.

> Logistics system – seeks out, catalogues, tracks and updates all the spaces and places where learning can occur, in addition to the innumerable informal places, such as parks and coffee shops. This system could also support the community based learning for younger students as described in previous chapters.

> Financial system – collects revenues, budgets and disburses as in any organization but also finds new sources of revenue, fund-raises, and processes the hopefully modest fee paid by all learners who subscribe to the system. This system also prices the learning credit units that are earned and expended by providing and acquiring learning.

Having slipped into this valley of detail, let us explore a brief version of how such a system might work and involve the continuing education student introduced earlier.

Our recent Canadian and Calgarian has just dropped his open newspaper onto his table at Tim Hortons as he looks out into the street and thinks about what he has just read. He hopes this Learn Calgary opportunity is as good as it sounds. There have been brochures that have caught his eye, but this is the most detail he has read. He is excited. He sees a way to earn the tuition credits that will help him pay for the high school courses that will qualify him to enter a college or university. He grabs his cell phone and makes a call. Soon he has an appointment with a Learn Calgary adult learning adviser who works in a learning design studio close to his home.

When the adult learning advisor, or learnist, hears about our new learner's qualifications and experience, she invites him to describe his proposed offer of learning as part of a personal learning plan that will include some hours of presenting and workshopping the culture, history and customs of his own country to interested travelers, business people and those with a general interest in his part of the world. He leaves the first meeting with a workbook and some ideas about how to fill it out. He does so quickly and feels ready for his next meeting with his advisor.

But no one has placed a request for this particular slice of learning into the Learn Calgary information system, so once the adult learnist has the personal learning plan in hand, she submits the offer of learning to the system. It turns out (in this tidy example) that a Calgary energy company, also a subscriber to

Learn Calgary, has just signed a contract to undertake a construction project in our adult learner's home country. Corporate and contract staff are being trained to work and recruit workers in that country. The timing is perfect. Someone notices the posting on the Learn Calgary web site, a phone call is made, and an interview is arranged with the energy company human resources staff.

Once the energy company determines that our adult learner can deliver the learning experience as advertised and that it meets their needs, details are ironed out quickly. It's agreed that two sessions, each lasting a full day, will be offered. This is a generous and progressive company, so they decide to invite other Learn Calgary corporate subscribers to send employees to the two learning sessions.

The sessions go well. Our adventurous and willing adult learner opts for tuition credits instead of cash payment. He finds, to his great pleasure, that his two days of work have earned him enough tuition credits to pay for two high school credit courses at a nearby adult learning centre. And best of all, he has met some new acquaintances and maybe even made some new friends.

There are many potential variations on this little example. Our cultures are full of rich, promising, and humane stories of people talking, sharing, showing and training others in significant ways, both small and large. Cancer patients speak to and meet with teenagers about the risks of smoking, recovered addicts share their stories of helplessness and strength and hope and despair, laid-off middle-aged executives explain how they created their own next career, care-givers explore ideas with families on how to care for the elders, neighbours acting as tutors help teenagers survive algebra – the list is endless.

As I have stressed, there will be no need for any action to replace the traditional institutions providing adult learning. For one thing, some credentials depend on a very high level of skill, training and specialized facilities. Extensive, certified, stable and predictable knowledge bases and skill sets will still be required. Alongside those systems of learning there will be enough lovers of learning, giving and receiving, to encourage us to open up a whole new world of learning containing all kinds of communities and anywhere from a few hundred to several million people.

CHAPTER 12: IMPLEMENTING THE THIRD SCHOOLS

No, Let's Not!

Please read on.

CHAPTER 13: WE NEED TO TALK

Not So Fast

Yes, we need to talk. It is about those new maps and all the thinking, imagining and creating we are invited to do.

I have suggested that our First Schools, the schools I went to as a child, disappeared sometime in the late '50s and early '60s. Our Second Schools, the schools I taught in, appeared about then, are still around doing a heroic job but are dealing with increasing expectations, complexity, challenges and constraints. Their successor, the Third Schools, is signaling its arrival. And so we find ourselves on the edge of a new frontier.

Our explorations will take us into framing beliefs and assumptions about the next era of learning. Our explorations will take us into imagining and debating the essential elements of new systems of learning. Then we will begin bringing them to life. The Third Schools is the name I have given to that new era and the systems that we will build as we struggle with our beliefs and assumptions about the reflexive mind and self-conscious learning, and why and how we will do it as a major societal endeavor. Sure, I would like to think that the learning systems that emerge will look like my brave little scenario. I suspect they will, in many important ways. But the fact is I don't know because, although this book gathered in many voices, it is just one-way talk. More minds are needed, better than mine, to gather and share our images and beliefs about the future of learning and to support, challenge and extend one another's ideas. How important is the talk?

Many years ago, I attended a workshop in the U.S. on strategic planning in schools. The leader was Dr. Bill Cook, a seasoned expert in the area and a skilled consultant who had worked with many school systems. He was a good teacher who devised ways for us to live the lessons he was trying to teach. After some hours of working and getting to know one another, Bill Cook launched a key task. It is long ago, but I think the task was to build a statement of beliefs as though we were the senior staff of a school system. So we brainstormed for a while and wrote some impressive-sounding ideas up on flip charts. After some positive comments about our initial work and some cautions about how easy it is to create a bad product, Bill suggested we nominate our "best minds" to go away and write a statement to be brought back for discussion and approval.

Best minds! I think a lot of us shrank in our seats, but we nominated some of the more articulate and mentally agile among us. They went away for a while and we got on with other work. When they returned, we, with some prompts from Bill, asked questions and challenged our shared understanding of the statements written on our behalf. We ended up tearing them apart. Bill then said, "Let's ask our second-best minds to go away and work on this." We nominated, they did, and they came back with a new draft. It fell apart fairly quickly as we realized how hard it was to write statements of belief that could stand the challenge of conveying non-trivial thinking quickly and with clarity. We nominated our third-best minds, they went away, and I think you get the idea. I forget who finally nailed it, our fourth- or fifth-best minds; but we all hammered away, listening to and arguing with one another until our last-best minds had what they really needed to do the job. The point was made. We needed all of our minds!

This is the music that powers the dance of change, intense conversation and debate.

It is true that at times it is better to act our way forward to new ways of thinking than the reverse. But it would be wrong to treat a scenario as if it were a plan and jump into writing about its implementation. My conviction, shared many pages ago, is that we have important thinking to do together as citizens concerned about the future of learning in our societies. My declared commitment was to step out of the school crisis and reform mindset and provide compelling reasons to think our way forward together. This does not rule out action. We need to invoke the spirit of the creative change as developed in F. David Peat's powerful book *Gentle Action*. We need to take the long view, interrogate our future, and ask what vision of learning we most fundamentally want for our children and ourselves. At the same time, we need to launch straw designs, mini-initiatives and well-crafted pilot projects that will, if we slow down to listen to one another and learn from what we are doing, become our teachers. Along the way, a scenario like my version of one possible Third Schools system may be valid and useful. It may even offer an initial map. The odds are it will quickly be superseded by better ideas.

So were the preceding chapters from Claire's story onward just fantasy? Embroidery? No. First of all, I owed readers an answer to the question, "All this talk of a new era of learning is fine, but what might it look like?" More importantly, I wanted to try working through a response to the invitation I identified in the early pages of this book: The times we are in invite us to serious work, work that challenges us to get out of our rut of crisis-driven reform and restructuring and explore novel and substantial possibilities for moving from the "DNA of schooling" to new modes of learning. Claire's journey and the following futuristic and, hopefully, thoughtful expansion of the scenario was my response.

In striving to make my story of the future plausible, I picked up on many themes and initiatives that are happening in our schools right now, such as personalizing learning and teachers working with students over longer blocks of time. I added detail and illustrations to make the highly improbable sound attractive and doable. If I learned anything, it is that the work is challenging and intriguing. It would be all that plus more fun to have a group around a table tossing these ideas around. I hope you were drawn into my imaginative journey, perhaps thinking about other Third School possibilities I missed. I believe that something like the Third Schools is on its way and will happen sooner than we think. I hope so and would gladly jump into the discussions, debates and planning.

Creating a brand new public learning system would be very exciting. There are serious voices urging us to get on with it.

Early on, I quoted from a 2001 *Maclean's* piece by Diane Francis calling for a "learning revolution." Her key words were "its very *modus operandi* must change." Back then, her call was a lonely one and went unheeded. Since then, a few other voices have issued similar calls. Linda Darling-Hammond is not calling for a revolution, quite, but hers is an important and authoritative voice that speaks, I think, from the boundary between transition and transformation.

> Today's expectation that schools will enable *all* students, rather than just a small minority, to learn challenging skills to high levels creates an entirely new mission for schools. Instead of merely "covering the curriculum" or "getting through the book," this new mission requires that schools substantially enrich the intellectual opportunities they offer while meeting the diverse needs of students who bring with them

> varying talents, interests, learning styles, cultures, predispositions, language backgrounds, family situations, and beliefs about themselves and about what school means for them (*The Flat World and Education*, p. 237).

Darling-Hammond calls for a redesign of public education to address inequality in America's schools. Her book is rich in international research and evidence about the many things schools do that work. System redesign may not mean a learning revolution, but as I suggested earlier, we are in a two-track world in responding to change. In one track, echoing the spirit of W. Edwards Deming, we "constantly and forever" improve what we have. Darling-Hammond's "entirely new mission" is very similar to Francis' call but is more evolutionary than revolutionary and essentially calls on us to radically renew the existing system. In the other track, we are called to fundamentally reconsider what we mean by learning, its social value and deep purpose, and the systems we might fashion to create and sustain it. On that more transformational track, and echoing Francis, here is Richard Florida writing about financial recovery and restarting economic growth.

> Human capital investments are the key to economic development. But many of our schools are giant creativity-squelching institutions. We need to reinvent our education system from the ground up – including a massive commitment to early-childhood development and a shift away from institutionalized schooling to individually tailored learning. This will require a level of public and private investment of a magnitude larger than the wide-spread creation of public schools and modern research universities a century ago (*The Globe and Mail*, November 29th, 2008).

So while we continue to give attention and support to track one and efforts to make the existing system substantially, even radically better, let us get to work on track two, "from the ground up." After all, there is so much already happening and so much more that can be done.

Before I wrap it up, I would like to briefly touch on a few more issues that bear on the creation of new systems in the era of our Third Schools.

A Matrix That Mirrors and Envelops

One of the issues is: Who will such a new learning system be for? I write in the belief that all young learners are capable to some degree of doing the new kind of learning that we are moving toward. It would be a very bad outcome if we all worked hard to design a system that ended up being a gigantic special program for the independent learner. I am proposing we think together about a new era of learning and the possible designs of systems than can support all learners.

As our talk helps the new possibilities for learning become clearer and as the Third Schools begin to form distinct shapes on the horizon, some venturesome parents and learners will create small islands of change, experimentation and innovation. They will be the explorers and early settlers of the new territory, creating the more detailed maps that allow other pioneering learners to follow. As this occurs, our existing public schools will be around, perhaps for some years to come. These schools should not, by default, become the safety net for those who cannot make the transition. The eventual transformation must produce learning systems that are accessible, secure, and effective for all learners, not just the precociously adaptive and self-managing.

On occasions when I have discussed the ideas and proposals in this book, one issue has been raised more than any other. It is about the families and children that not only need more structure, but are often characterized as needing a stronger, firmer version of the existing institution of schooling. I am warned that many parents and students will be simply unable to become the co-creators and designers of their learning. For many reasons, they will not have the time, skill or inclination to make learning so intense and constant a pursuit in their lives.

Earlier I cautioned against throwing out the traditional schooling bathwater having snatched the learning baby out of its warm suds. I said that for some learners, more traditional learning designs, still responsive to that learner and family, but with an emphasis on directed group learning, will be an important entry-level strategy that is appropriate to their narrower repertoire of learning interests and skills. Although the professional staff will have a responsibility to urge parents and learners toward greater autonomy, self-management and reflexivity, no learner can be allowed to fall through the cracks. This can be prevented. Let us look at the range of design options.

On the one hand, as depicted in my extended scenario, the Third Schools era opens up the possibility for uniquely personalized learning journeys. Distinctive and pedagogically valid learning plans will combine group-, community-, home- and technology-based modes of learning appropriate to each learner and their family. Learning plans will evolve into a learning matrix that mirrors and extends the capabilities of self-management and self-direction. Learning plans will take the learner and the learning into the family's and the community's life and history, and will summon the resources of the wider civic or regional community.

So what's on the other hand?

The Third Schools will also be about unique designs that accommodate greater system dependence and minimal family involvement. They will focus less on self-management and self-direction and more on intensive direction and guidance. These learning plans will provide a different kind of matrix that envelops the learner and engages the family, contains low or no ambiguity about what comes next, and provides sensitive but all-encompassing prescriptions for the sum of the learning activities. Most of these activities will take place in groups, some having the features of a traditional classroom, and will be located in a learning centre.

The requirement for such a range of learning designs will be consistent with the role of the Third Schools professionals. Although their long-term core mandate will be to foster reflexively conscious and self-managed learning, they will, as educators always have, seek to start where the learner is. They will, if required, employ more directive and restrictive options at the lower end of the self-management spectrum. The family will be encouraged to move the student into a more open and flexible learning design and plan as soon as he or she is able to handle greater autonomy. If the problem is financial and/or demanding parental work schedules, or other stress factors that make the family less able to move into the Thirds Schools' co-creative mode, the learning advisors and designers may be able to create connections with community supports and the extended family to help get the learner on track with additional coaching and mentoring. And finally, if the learner is just not at a stage of mental and emotional maturity where conscious and co-creative learning is an option, then the appropriate structure and "training wheels" will be provided, perhaps with significant family involvement, until the learner is ready to start being involved in mapping his or her own learning path.

If the new learning system is properly designed and led, no one will be allowed to fall through the cracks, or more appropriate to the Third Schools, get lost in the vast open spaces where the design options for learning are drawn from. It is not 1935, or even 1955. We have new options. The bandwidth of ways of doing learning is much enlarged as are the technologies which may assist us. Over time, we will increasingly be able to draw from well-tested portfolios of learning activities that represent established patterns or templates as well as build uniquely personalized learning designs out of an infinite universe of design variables, including degree of autonomy.

Oil and Water and the Hardness of the Nose

An issue that will become acute in the next era of learning is the oil and water mixture of high-stakes testing and highly personalized designs for learning. Is it necessarily true that the former must always drown the latter; that the standardized cannot find a way to live with the personalized?

It is safe to assume that any system using public funds will be required to be thoroughly and publicly accountable. The public's interest in holding public systems accountable, whether health care, elder care or education, is very strong and will likely stay that way for some time. Even though many influential researchers and educators regard high stakes tests and scores as "desperate measures" and attempts to "fatten a goat by weighing it," quite beside the point of assessing a child's learning; I will assume that the tests and the testing programs will be with us for many years to come. They will likely be rather hard-nosed requirements. The results will be published and the Third Schools will be compared with the traditional ones.

Can the hardness of the testing-nose be softened to accommodate the advent of the Third Schools? It may end up depending on the type of tests and testing programs, and in particular, the weightiness of the schedules of grade-specific tests. Those tests that assess the general knowledge of students at an age-grade level and benchmark student levels of competence through time will likely continue to be administered to all students. The Third Schools, while they are developing new modes of learning, may alter test results until a new pattern and set of benchmarks emerges. Of course, there's always a possibility that a system that lets people learn in their own way, at their own pace, and toward their own purposes, will push the benchmarks up. In any case, it will be better for our health if we do not hold our breath until the tests melt away.

The accountability-nose may soften when we come to content. In the jargon, we may be able to move from norm-referenced tests, comparing individual learners with flocks of other learners, to criterion-referenced tests, comparing the learning acquired with the learning yet to be acquired. As this shift happens, standardized tests can be broken out into their component parts, relating clusters of test items to specific learnings, helping learners assess their own progress in a specific content or skill and knowledge area. Used this way, and in the traditional content areas, a grade nine math or grade six social studies test will help rather than hinder learners who likely have no way of knowing what grade they would be assigned to in a traditional school. They will want to know what they have actually learned in a domain, not what their grade-equivalent score would be.

So the purpose and flexibility of tests will be important. Learning plans will include various forms of assessment, with "multiple measures of student learning," as Darling-Hammond calls for in *The Flat World and Education* (p. 298), including testing. Hopefully, the learner and those who are designing learning plans and guiding the learning will get to determine when it will be time to challenge the test and what is to be learned from the test when the results are in.

No Running with Scissors

If you plan to change schools in Canada, you may want to carry a large pair of scissors. But you will be perfectly safe; there is no risk of breaking into a run with them dangerously in hand. The scissors are for the red tape. Schools everywhere, even in small systems, are captives of twin monsters called myriads and labyrinths; myriads of rules and regulations within labyrinths of bureaucracy. Some rules are out-of-date and rarely applied. Others are for special situations, such as particular kinds of student excursions or eligibility to get a bus ride to school. Some are essential for things like the safety and security of young people and ensuring that the system is effective and accountable. And as for bureaucracy (I lived a long time in one), after many years of tight budgets, it has been somewhat trimmed and tamed, but the shadows of the labyrinth still lurk.

The myriads and the labyrinths must not be allowed to stand in the way of the desired changes that are gathering in the minds and hearts of students, parents and teachers. Bureaucrats and their rule books would be seriously vexed with all the unpalatable decisions, unthinkable thoughts and opposing twin monsters of untidiness and uncertainty. They would become distracted and exhausted from sandbagging the dangerous levels of creativity and energy required to move toward a new way of learning I am calling the Third Schools. We will need a new and coherent philosophy of trusteeship and a consistent model of governance. It will be built on a base of parental involvement and community integration rarely achieved in traditional school systems.

A philosophy of trusteeship will centre on the answer to questions like: On whose behalf do we hold this trust? Whose interests are being served? What will success look like for learners and in the quality of their learning? How do we address accountability, trust, and open communication? Some of these issues will relate more to the model of governance, which I will not go into here.

I have always found John Carver's question very useful: Who constitutes the "moral ownership" of the system? (*Boards That Make a Difference*, pp. 130-133). Public education has struggled with the issues raised by this question. The legislation or school acts of the Canadian provinces have, over the years, tended to see the provincial governments as the moral owners, acting on behalf of the public. Some trustees I have observed have seen themselves as the moral owners, acting on behalf of local needs and a common good that they have struggled to define in public meetings and in debate. And at times, public educators have acted as though the parents are the moral owners, turning decisions over to parent committees and trying to embrace parents' and students' interests as decisions are being made. Some administrators I have worked with have seen themselves as the moral owners of the system, struggling, alone and thankless, to preserve and protect the heritage and traditions of the public schools. Put simply, there were too many self-appointed moral owners with differing views about the purpose of the public schools.

These issues should not be allowed a rerun in the Third Schools. The effects of the silos and power struggles would be too damaging. There should be no question about moral ownership haunting the trustees of a system of Third

Schools. The moral ownership is vested in the learners and their families; simply that and no more. This basic belief will reside at the core of governance and leadership. Others, like the provincial and municipal governments, may be stakeholders, and important ones with legal prerogatives, but to confuse them with the moral ownership leads back to command and control systems, schooling instead of learning, and the imposition of wrong-headed accountabilities. Trustees who understand that they are acting on behalf of the learners and parents who *are* the moral ownership will exercise better stewardship of emerging systems for co-creating good learning – learning that leads to reflexive approaches and self-management. They will be accountable for ensuring that an authentic and effective Third School system emerges that is not a rerun of the 20th century, let alone with bits of the 19th.

It is likely that current electoral processes of selecting trustees or governors will be used. I hope that some consideration will be given to using a jury system similar to that proposed by Fred and Merrelyn Emery. I will only sketch out a modified version of the idea. For a more complete explanation, readers should take a look at Fred Emery's discussion in *The Jury System and Participative Democracy*. (*Participative Design for Participative Democracy*, pp. 207-211). The first step is to create a pool of eligible and committed Third School constituents who might be selected for governance duty. The process starts with developing parent, business and community leadership through direct involvement and volunteer service in the Third Schools. All parents, older and adult learners, and community and multi-sector volunteers would be advised of their "duty of service" and automatically have their names placed in a pool of candidates for local, perhaps community-based, councils. Only those who have served on local councils would have their names placed in the pool of candidates to serve on a regional council that might serve several communities within a city or a rural region. Similarly, only those who have served on both councils could be selected to serve as a governor or trustee of a city or regional Third School system.

Like the courtroom jury system, people could be excluded because of a criminal record or mental incompetence. Any person wishing to argue that a candidate's previous service was of a low enough standard to make him or her ineligible could challenge any name drawn. At that point, a process of open hearings and secret ballots would occur. There are other features of this system, but one I particularly like is Emery's suggestion that those who serve receive no financial reward, but be eligible for as many years of state-supported education as years of service – in this case, probably restricted to service at the level of governor or trustee. Emery argues that such a system creates a culture of responsibility or taking your turn, discourages lobbying and the intrusion of political parties, and encourages service for community rather than selfish ends. It nourishes participative democracy.

Participative democracy matters. The trust being held will be about establishing, nourishing and protecting the mandate of their particular locally developed variety of the Third Schools.

Leading in a Co-creating Learning Community

Will there be paid leadership? Probably, but what will it look like? It is clear that the new learning systems, the Third Schools, will be complex and evolving operations requiring leadership that emphasizes orchestration with room for improvisation, rather than traditional management. The old hierarchies and distinctions of traditional school administration would be deadly for everyone and likely frustrate many of the desired outcomes. Many schools and school systems know this now and are trying to drape the soft fabric of "community" and "collaboration" over the skeletal structure of the traditional organization of schools. On the other hand, how much structure can we let go of before people are simply unable to comprehend their job, let alone do it? New and more flexible approaches to old ideas such as superior and subordinate, line of reporting and span of control will be invented. It will be a delicate balance. Too much fear of uncertainty and ambiguity at the beginning with the wrong antidotes will significantly distort the resulting patterns of leadership in the Third Schools for the long run.

Effective leaders, who will be urgently required early on in the game, will bring clarity to the new roles and support the professional growth of individuals, networks and teams. They will foster and focus the high energy and creativity that will be essential for the many different assignments arising from the design and implementation of diverse learning plans. They will handle a rapid flow of tasks and decisions, many of them non-routine, and evolving assignments within a complex learning support system that never loses track of a learner. They will be skilled communicators and will collaboratively develop and implement appropriate accountabilities for a remarkable variety of responsibilities.

A responsive and integrative approach to leadership will be required. As the Third Schools emerge and are staffed, collegial professional learning networks will evolve. An important and deepening connection between the learners and their families in a community or region and an associated group of professional staff will begin to occur. As these democratic, collegial and mutually supportive professional networks develop, their initially fuzzy boundaries will gel into enduring associations with communities and clusters of communities. They will become learning communities that embrace places as well as people: homes, learning centres, community facilities, and other locations where distinctive kinds of learning will occur. We will see a gradual transformation of former schools into integrated learning and design centres, including resource centres, learning design studios, and a variety of working and meeting spaces. Eventually, most communities and regions will have some kind of learning centre and offer the services of a team of learning professionals on site. Each of these clusters of people and places will exert its own distinctive pull toward innovative and adaptive learning leadership.

What about the principle of having a principal? This role always included the idea of being a head or principal teacher. It evolved into school administration in more than just name, and then management and leadership were layered on. These old layers of expectations will fade away and some very different ones will emerge. Instead of having a principal, which would be a disorienting title in the Third Schools in any case, we may find a "first among equals" role emerging that provides leadership in learning in the clusters of people and places described above. It may be term-specific and subject to approval or even selection by the professional staff. However it shapes up, this leadership will need operational support. There could be a separate but related role of business manager serving each cluster of professional staff. This person would administer and manage in the traditional senses and would be responsible primarily for the buildings, technologies and budgets. This role could well be filled by people we used to airily refer to as support staff, but who were very capable of managing the routine business of a large school or group of schools. Some senior and head secretaries I remember from my school board experiences, if offered appropriate training, would be perfect for the job.

And lastly, there would be a very small central staff. I will not try to guess at structure or roles here, but I expect that it will be very small compared to today's central offices as most of the money will have to be directed to the learners and their learning-support professionals.

A Learning Commons

Moving beyond these crude recipes for governance and leadership, I would like to tie learning and citizenship together. For young learners especially, this is not about the familiar exercises in schooling and democracy, such as student councils or mock parliaments. It is about the emergence of a learning commons and the learner as an increasingly engaged citizen contributing to the co-creation of learning.

I am making some tolerably ambitious claims for the Third Schools. For example:

- All are capable of giving and receiving learning.
- Hierarchy is minimal, often temporary and informal.
- Roles have soft boundaries and can become indistinguishable.
  - Some volunteers will be competent to instruct, mentor and coach learners.
  - Parents will support the learning; learning designs will support the parenting.
  - Leadership will be distributed, mostly horizontally.
- The adult learner is a creator, provider and a consumer of learning.

These characteristics open up the possibility for citizen learners to share in the creation of a new common or indivisible good, in this case, a new way of doing good learning together, and new opportunities and commitments arising from a passion for learning expressed throughout a community.

A commons in a democracy is a place where multiple perspectives are shared. Citizens accept the responsibility to voice a point of view with the expectation of persuading others and being persuaded to alter their point of view. A learning commons could arise from the evolving networks and associations of learners, their families, learning professionals, and volunteers where multiple perspectives on creating learning will be shared. Citizens who are passionate about learning will share their views, enrich the debate about co-creating learning and enlarge the space of possibility for all learners. Those grey words, "social capital" and "capacity building," will be embodied in real people who put their commitment to good learning on the table in the form of face-to-face engagements with one another.

This will be the true learning community of our future.

Toward Strategic Optimism

Clearly this is not a story about a failure of public education or failure on the part of the rest of us. Several generations of children and young people and legions of adults have been well taught and have received a good education in our public schools. The little learning that is a dangerous thing is the failure to do the kind of learning that prepares us for life in the 21st century.

Are we so captive that, as Leonard Shlain describes in *Art and Physics*, we are like the pioneer thinkers in the early Renaissance experiencing intellectual strife and emotional pain as they try to imagine a heliocentric reality in the midst of many rigid, doctrinal beliefs about an earth-centred cosmos? I don't think so. I think we have a much greater and more accessible cognitive space in which to explore. Yes, we are still constrained by old assumptions and beliefs, but they are fewer and less binding, and we are readier to suit up and head out into less familiar territories of the mind and heart. We need to be relentlessly learning-oriented, not schooling-bound, as we approach this continental divide of change. We need to defy the evidence of our experience and create a parallel track to the public education track we are on, trusting that in a curved space-time world, they will meet.

I began by using the language of possibility and would like to exit on that note. I began by laying out the case for creating a second track of discontinuous change beside the current track of continuous improvement with occasional lurches into large-scale reforms. I built the case upon our growing sense of having reached the limit of our attempts to fix up what we have and our willingness to contemplate the signals telling us to seek radical new ways of creating a fundamental public good – a flourishing of learning in our society. Doing this work without just doing more tinkering will require the vision, courage and commitment that leads to confident and deft steps into the new territory of learning. Soon, some brave public educators, parents, and students will begin the journey into an era of new learning systems I have called the Third Schools.

The question that drove me into beginning, "What will our next public education look like?" cannot be answered by this book. This probe into the future can only be the beginning of the search for a complete and satisfactory answer. It may be an act of what Thomas Friedman calls "strategic optimism," designed to invite others to the conversation and to gently detach our thinking from a set of driving assumptions so that we can look to the future with clearer eyes. The good minds and the best thinking will surely follow.

BIBLIOGRAPHY

Alberta's Commission on Learning, *Every Child Learns. Every Child Succeeds*, Alberta Learning, Edmonton, 2003

Alberta Teachers' Association, *The ATA News*, August 27th, 2002

Anderson, Walter Truett, *Reality Isn't What It Used to Be*, Harper and Row, New York, 1990

Arendt, Hannah, "Labor, Work, Action," in Baehr, Peter, *The Portable Hannah Arendt,* The Viking Portable Library, Penguin Putman Inc., 2000

Badran, Margot and Cooke, Miriam, Eds., *Opening the Gates: A Century of Arab Feminist Writing*, Indiana University Press, Bloomington and Indianapolis, 1990

Barber, Michael, *The Learning Game*, Indigo, London, 1997

BBC News, *Call for weapon checks in schools*, February 25th, 2004

BBC News, *Five-year-olds short on skills*, November 10th, 2007

BBC News, *'Last chance saloon' for schools*, April 16th, 2007

BBC News, *Pupils ready to learn outside school,* December 30th, 2002

BBC News, *Teachers face violence from pupils and parents*, February 10th, 1999

BBC News, *Truancy levels 'under-estimated,'* September 6th, 2005

Beck, Don Edward and Cowan, Christopher C., *Spiral Dynamics*, Blackwell Publishing, 1996

Berger, Thomas R., *Conciliator's Final Report, "The Nunavut Project,"* March 1st, 2006

Berliner, David C., Glass, Gene V., *50 Myths and Lies that Threaten America's Public Schools*, Teachers College Press, New York, 2014

Birmingham, John, Ed., *Our Time Is Now: Notes From the High School Underground*, Praeger Publishers, Inc., New York, 1970

Black, Erin; DeBerjeois, Jim; Hood, Annice; Lane, Pat; *School Safety: What's Being Done and Where Is It Going? Issues Challenging Education*, Horizon Site, University of North Carolina at Chapel Hill, http://horizon.unc.edu/projects/issues/papers/Lane.html

Botkin, James W., Elmandjra, Mahdi, Malitza, Mircea, *No Limits to Learning: Bridging the Human Gap, A Report to the Club of Rome*, Pergamon Press, Oxford, 1979

Buzzell, Chris A., *Investment Strategies, The Family Mission Statement*, High Country News, May 2005

Callahan, Raymond E., *Education and the Cult of Efficiency*, The University of Chicago Press, Chicago, 1962

Calgary Herald, *Bulletproof backpack a big seller*, August 21st, 2007

Calgary Herald, *New research key to early childhood development*, December 3rd, 2006

Calgary Herald, *School system given failing grade*, September 6th, 2005

Calgary Herald, *Schools taking aim at bullies*, April 20th, 2002

Calgary Herald, *Skills, not behaviour predictor of success*, November 13th, 2007

Canadian Institutes of Health Research, http://www.cihr-irsc.gc.ca/e/45838.html

Canadian Living, *Kids 201: Parenthood Primer*, September 2004

Canadian Teachers' Federation, , *The 2004 CTF National Issues in Education Poll, Summary of Major Findings, 2004-3*, Economic and Member Services Bulletin, September 2004

Carroll, John, A Model of School Learning, *Teachers College Record*, 1963, 64: 723-733

Carter, Gene R. and Cunningham, William G., *The American School Superintendent: Leading in an Age of Pressure,* Jossey-Bass, San Francisco, 1997

Carver, John, *Boards That Make a Difference*, Jossey-Bass, San Francisco, 1990

CBC News online, *Bullying among school children declining: study*, March 4th, 2010

CNN, *A closer look: How many Newtown-like school shootings since Sandy Hook?*, June 19, 2014

CNN Staff, *Maryland university buying bulletproof whiteboards*, August 17th, 2013

Cochran-Smith, Marilyn, and Lytle, Susan L., Relationships of Knowledge and Practice: Teacher Learning in Communities, *Review of Research in Education*, #24, American Educational Research Association, Washington DC, 1999

Cohen, Jack and Stewart, Ian, *The Collapse of Chaos*, Viking, New York, 1994

Darling-Hammond, Linda, *The Flat World and Education*, Teachers College Press, New York, 2010

Darling-Hammond, Linda, *The Right to Learn: A Blueprint for Creating Schools That Work*, Jossey-Bass Publishers, San Francisco, 1997

Dewey, John, *Experience and Education*, Collier Books, New York, 1966

Drucker, Peter F., *Post-Capitalist Society*, HarperCollins Publishers, New York, 1993

Edmundson, Mark, *The Teacher Who Opened My Mind*, Utne, Jan-Feb 2003

Ellis, Ron, *Learning and the Inner City*, Thesis, University of British Columbia School of Architecture, May 4, 1970

Emery, Merrelyn, *Participative Design for Participative Democracy*, The Australian National University, Canberra, 1993

Emery, Merrelyn, *The Future of Schools: How Communities and Staff Can Transform Their School Districts*, Rowman & Littlefield Education, Lanham, Maryland, 2006

Emery, Merrelyn, and Purser, Ronald, *The Search Conference*, Jossey-Bass Publishers, San Francisco, 1996

ERIC L & L (CAL) Digest, EDO-FL-94-08, February 1994

Fastcompany, *How Startl Is Hacking Education From the Outside In*, February 16th, 2010

Flavelle, Christopher, *Ignatieff's Challenge*, The Walrus, May 2005

Francis, Diane, "A Learning Revolution." *Maclean's*, March 5th, 2001

Franklin, Ursula, *The Real World of Technology*, CBC Enterprises, Toronto, 1990

Garrett, Sandy, America's Smallest Schools: Families, *Vital Speeches of the Day*, 1995, v61, 742-8

Gasson, I. John, and Baxter, E. Paul, *Getting the Most out of your Child's School*, McGraw-Hill Ryerson, Scarborough, 1989

Gell-Mann, Murray, *The Quark and the Jaguar*, W. H. Freeman and Company, New York, 1994

Glickman, Carl D., *Renewing America's Schools*, The Jossey-Bass Education Series, Jossey-Bass, San Francisco, 1993

Godet, Michel, *Scenarios and Strategic Management*, Butterworth Scientific Ltd., London, 1987

Goffman, Erving, *Asylums*, Anchor Books, Garden City, New York, 1961

Gonzalez, Norma; Moll, Luis C.; Floyd-Tenery, Martha; Rivera, Anna; Bendon, Patricia; Gonzales, Raquel; Amanti, Cathy; Teacher Research on Funds of Knowledge: Learning from Households, *Educational Practice Report 6*, National Center for Research on Cultural Diversity and Second Language Learning, 1993

Goodlad, John I., and Anderson, Robert H. *The Nongraded Elementary School*, (Revised Edition). New York: Teachers College Press, 1987.

Goodman, Paul, *New Reformation*, Random House, New York, 1970

Graff, Keir. Is This Revolution for Real? *Chicago Tribune Magazine*, February 4th, 2001

Greene, Maxine, *The Dialectic of Freedom*, Teachers College Press, New York, 1988

Greenspan, Stanley I., *The Growth of the Mind*, Addison-Wesley, Reading Massachusetts, 1997

Greenfield, Baroness, The Way We Are Going, quoted in *The Economist* Book Review, 9/10/03, courtesy Innovation Watch Website

Harper's Magazine, *Grand Theft Education*, September 2006

Harper's Magazine, *Harper's Weekly*, May 3rd, 2005

Heilbroner, Robert, *The Nature and Logic of Capitalism*, W. W. Norton & Company Inc., New York, 1985

Hillis, W. Daniel, *Close to the Singularity*, in Brockman, John, *The Third Culture*, Touchstone, New York, 1995

Hock, Dee, *Birth of the Chaordic Age*, Berrett-Koehler, San Francisco, 1999

Homer-Dixon, Thomas, *The Ingenuity Gap*, Alfred A. Knopf, New York, 2000

Huitt, W., Overview of Classroom Processes, *Educational Psychology Interactive*, December 2, 1997

Institute for Information Technology, National Research Council Canada, www.iit.nrc.ca

Jacobs, Jane, *Dark Age Ahead*, Random House Canada, 2004

Janigan, Mary, It's All About School, *Maclean's*, April 5th, 2004

Kegan, Robert, *In Over Our Heads – The Mental Demands of Modern Life*. Boston: Harvard University Press.

Kennet, Wayland, Futures and Government, *Futures*, 1984

Kingwell, Mark, *Better Living: In Pursuit of Happiness from Plato to Prozac*, Penguin Canada, Toronto, 1998

Kropp, Paul and Hodson, Lynda, *The School Solution*, Random House of Canada, Toronto, 1995

Kurzweil, Ray, *The Age Spiritual Machines*, Penguin Books, New York, 1999

Kohn, Alfie, Choices for Children: Why and How to Let Students Decide, *Phi Delta Kappan*, September 1993

Kostash, Myrna, *The Next Canada*, McClelland and Stewart, Toronto, 2000

Langer, Ellen J., *The Power of Mindful Learning*, Perseus Books, Cambridge Mass., 1997

Law, Danielle, *The New Cyberbullies*, The Tyee, thetyee.ca, May 21st, 2007

Leader-Post, *Lockdown*, April 20th, 2007

Lessig, Lawrence, *The Future of Ideas: The Fate of the Commons in a Connected World*, Random House, New York, 2001

Lifton, Robert Jay, *The Protean Self*, Basic Books, New York, 1993

Lindstrom, Martin, Fast Company, *Generation Y Is Born To Startup*, November 16, 2011, http://www.fastcompany.com:80/1795255/gen-y-entrepreneurial-rebels?partner=homepage_newsletter

Maclean's, *Canada's Best Schools*, August 29th, 2005

Maclean's, *Homework is Killing Kids*, September 11th, 2006

Maclean's, *How We Live*, November 4th, 2002

Maclean's, *Ready for School*, September 27th, 2004

Maclean's, *Stalked by a Cyberbully*, May 24th, 2004

Maclean's, *Stop Brainwashing Our Kids*, November 5th, 2012

Maclean's, *Stressed Out*, November 22nd, 2004

Maclean's, *They'll come to your house and fix your kids*, March 13th, 2006

Maclean's, *This is not a field trip*, June 24th, 2013

Maclean's, Special Report, *What's Wrong At School?* January 11th, 1993

Maclean's, *Why England is Rotting*, June 11th, 2007

Maclean's, *Why is it your job to teach your kid math?* March 19th, 2012

Maclean's, *Your mission: just don't blow it all*, November 19th, 2007

Marcus, David L., Mulrine, Anna, and Wong, Kathleen, How Kids Learn, *U.S. News & World Report*, September 13, 1999

Markham, Beryl, *West With the Night*, North Point Press, New York, 1983

Marsh, James H. (Ed.), *The Canadian Encyclopedia*, Hurtig Publishers, Edmonton, 1985

Masuda, Yoneji, *The Information Society*, Institute for the Information Society, Tokyo Japan, 1980

McGregor, Roy, *The Globe and Mail*, October 28th, 2003

Michael, Donald N., *Learning to Plan and Planning to Learn*, Second Edition, Miles River Press, Alexandria Virginia, 1997

Mitchell, W. O., *Who Has Seen The Wind*, Laurentian Library, Macmillan of Canada, Toronto, 1972

Morgan, Evan, Dead Students Society, *Maclean's*, September 2nd, 2002

Morgan, Gareth, *Images of Organization*, SAGE, Thousand Oaks, 1997

Morton, Desmond, *A Short History of Canada*, McClelland and Stewart, Toronto, 1997

National Research Council, Institute for Information Technology, Ottawa, Ontario, www.iit.nrc.ca

Naisbitt, John, *High Tech/High Touch, Technology and our Accelerated Search for Meaning*, Nicholas Brealey Publishing, Boston, 1999

Neatby, Hilda, *So Little For The Mind*, Clarke, Irwin & Company Limited, Toronto, 1953

Nelson, Ruben, *Three Views of the Future*, various sources

Newsweek, *America's Best High Schools*, May 18th, 2005

Newsweek, Special Edition, *How to teach our kids*, Fall/Winter 1990

Noddings, Nel, *The Challenge to Care In Schools*, Teachers College Press, New York, 1992

North Central Regional Educational Laboratories, *Luis Moll, Pathways Home* and *City Schools, Funds of Knowledge: A Look At Luis Moll's Research Into Hidden Family Resources*, online articles

Orr, David W., *Earth in Mind*, Island Press, Washington D.C., 1994

Oshry, Barry, *Seeing Systems*, Berrett-Koehler Publishers, San Francisco, 1996

Owen, Harrison, *The Power of Spirit*, Berrett-Koehler, San Francisco, 2000

Peat, F. David, *Gentle Action: Bringing Creative Change to a Turbulent World*, Pari Publishing, Grosseto, 2008

Postman, Neil and Weingartner, Charles, *The Soft Revolution*, Dell Publishing Co., Inc., New York, 1971

Program Development Center of Northern California, *Educational Goals and Objectives*, Commission on Educational Planning – Phi Delta Kappa Inc.

Ray, Paul H. and Anderson, Sherry Ruth, *The Cultural Creatives*, Three Rivers Press, New York, New York, 2000

Reich, Robert, *The Future of Success*, Alfred A. Knopf, New York, 2001

Rocky View Adult Education, Spring 2001 Catalogue

Sarason, Seymour B., *How Schools Might Be Governed and Why*, Teachers College Press, New York, 1997

Sarason, Seymour B., *The Predictable Failure of Educational Reform*, Jossey-Bass, San Francisco, 1990

Saunders, Doug, The Irate Parent Industry, *This Magazine*, September-October, 1994

Saturday Night, *The Ignorant Canadians*, October 1976

Schmidt, Sarah, Teachers finding happiness in private tuition, *Victoria Times Colonist*, March 27, 2005

Selbert, Dr. Roger, *Future Scan*, No. 845, May 20th, 1996

Shlain, Leonard, *Art & Physics*, HarperCollins Perennial, New York, 2001

Silberman, Charles E., *Crisis in the Classroom*, Random House, New York, 1970

Starobin, Paul, Dawn of the Daddy State, *The Atlantic Monthly*, June 2004

Statistics Canada, *Fifty years of families in Canada: 1961 to 2011*, http://www12.statcan.gc.ca/census-recensement/2011/as-sa/98-312-x/98-312-x2011003_1-eng.cfm

Statistics Canada, *Portrait of Families and Living Arrangements in Canada*, http://www12.statcan.gc.ca/census-recensement/2011/as-sa/98-312-x/98-312-x2011001-eng.cfm

Statistics Canada, *The Daily*, Wednesday April 20th, 2005

Stein, Janet Gross, *The Cult of Efficiency*, House of Anansi Press, Toronto, 2001

Steinberg, Laurence, *Beyond the Classroom*, Simon & Schuster, New York, 1996

Taylor, Charles, *Sources of The Self: The Making of the Modern Identity*, Harvard University Press, Cambridge Massachusetts, 1989

Tenderfoot to Queen's Scout, The Canadian General Council, The Boy Scouts Association, Ottawa, 1953

Time, *How To Build a Student for the 21st Century*, December 18th, 2006

Time, *Is Getting Tough The Answer?* February 1st, 1988

Time, *So You Want To Raise A Superkid...* April 30th, 2001

Time, *What Makes A Great Student?* October 19th, 1998

The ATA Magazine, excerpt from *A Brief History of Public Education in Alberta*, Winter 2005

The Atlantic Monthly, *Murder in the Schoolroom*, June 1970

The Atlantic Monthly, *Dawn of the Daddy State*, June 2004

The Christian Science Monitor, *American youths bridge religious divides*, October 24th, 2007

The Christian Science Monitor, *Hitting the books at any age*, December 1st, 2006

The Christian Science Monitor, *Needed in class: a few good men*, March 15th, 2005

The Christian Science Monitor, *Today's News In Brief, USA,* August 17th, 2007

The Christian Science Monitor, *Today's teens are less selfish than some adults think*, March 5th, 2007

The Christian Science Monitor, *Tracing the benefit of preschool, 36 years later*, November 23rd, 2004

The Christian Science Monitor, *When the school bus becomes a scary place*, April 19th, 2005

The Christian Science Monitor, *Why school violence is declining*, December 6th, 2004

The Conference Board of Canada, *Developing Skills: Where Are Canada's Employers?*, March 20th, 2014, http://www.conferenceboard.ca/topics/education/commentaries/14-03-20/developing_skills_where_are_canada_s_employers.aspx

The Globe and Mail, *'America's Worst Mom' strikes back*, April 21st, 2009

The Globe and Mail, *An age-old question about school*, November 28th, 2006

The Globe and Mail, *Crime rate falls to lowest point since 1972*, July 26th, 2013

The Globe and Mail, *Everyday war zone*, March 30th, 2002

The Globe and Mail, *Family unit now defined by function, not just form*, November 29th, 2004

The Globe and Mail, *Financial recovery needs money – and a massively different mindset*, November 29th, 2008

The Globe and Mail, *Girl's harrowing ordeal in a Catholic school's halls*, November 14th, 2005

The Globe and Mail, *Grandparents take active role in households*, December 10th, 2003

The Globe and Mail, *Mealtimes offer consistent check-ins with children*, September 12th, 2009

The Globe and Mail, *Nine U.S. teens charged with bullying Irish girl who later committed suicide*, March 31st, 2010

The Globe and Mail, *Ontario dropout rates soar: Enter the magicians*, November 12th, 2005

The Globe and Mail, *Ontario students bullying teachers, poll finds*, September 26th, 2005

The Globe and Mail, *Saying goodbye to childhood*, May 27th, 2006

The Globe and Mail, *School gives teen's makeup failing grade*, March 9th, 2004

The Globe and Mail, *Sikh student who won kirpan case now considers leaving Quebec*, October 22nd, 2013

The Globe and Mail, *Social Studies*, March 11th, 2004

The Globe and Mail, *Taser-armed police patrolling U.S. schools*, September 27th, 2004

The Globe and Mail, *Teaching a new generation to duck and cover*, October 18th, 2004

The Globe and Mail, *The age of uncertainty*, September 11th, 2007

The Globe and Mail, *Thinking is not a priority in schools*, October 10th, 2007

The Globe and Mail, *Tracking the teacher*, September 3rd, 2005

The Globe and Mail, *Where's the danger in a student's kirpan?* March 9th, 2004

The Globe and Mail, *Why tolerance for 'zero tolerance' is running out*, January 13th, 2007

The Guardian Weekly, *Alaska boys arrested over 'school massacre plot'*, April 28th – May 4th, 2006

The Guardian Weekly, *Bullies blight online*, November 20th, 2009

The Guardian Weekly, *Fear of teenagers on rise, study warns*, October 27th – November 2nd, 2006

The Guardian Weekly, *Week in Britain, Bonus and bouncers at the chalkface*, April 17th, 2009

The New York Times, *In Age of School Shootings, Lockdown is the New Fire Drill*, January 16th, 2014

The New York Times, *In Middle School, Charting Their Course to College and Beyond*, February 28th, 2010

The Premier's Commission on Future Health Care for Albertans, *The Rainbow Report: Our Vision For Health,* Queen's Printer, Edmonton, 1989

TheTyee.ca, *Unschooling*, December 16th, 2005

Theobald, Robert, *Reworking Success*, Participation Press, New Orleans, 1996

This Magazine, Special Issue! *Back To School*, September-October, 1994

Tough, Paul, *How Children Succeed*, Mariner Books, New York, 2013

Trueman, Anne, School can be scary for victims of bullies, *Vancouver Sun*, August 15th, 2002

Tyack, David and Cuban, Larry, *Tinkering Toward Utopia*, Harvard University Press, Cambridge Mass., 1996

Ungerleider, Charles, Support where it's needed, *The Globe and Mail*, September 2nd, 2003

USA Today, *Poll: Kids worry about school violence*, March 15th, 2001

U.S. News & World Report, Special report, *Outstanding American High Schools,* January 18th, 1999

Utne Reader, *Crackdown on Kids*, September-October, 1998

Utne Reader, *School's Out*, January-February, 2002

Utne Reader, *The Protean Self*, May-June, 2003

Vancouver Sun, *Teens find better way of dealing with bullying and vandalism*, November 19th, 2009

Waks, Leonard, *Choice, Charters and the Common School*, Presentation, American Educational Research Association Annual Meeting, 1996

Webster's New Universal Unabridged Dictionary, Barnes and Noble Books, New York, 1989

Wilson, Edward O., *Consilience*, Alfred A. Knopf, New York, 1998

Whitman, Walt, *Leaves of Grass*, Cassell and Company Ltd, London, 1909

Wright, Ronald, *A Short History of Progress*, House of Anansi Press, Toronto, 2004

Wyn, Johanna, *Education for the New Adulthood: implications of youth research for education*, Paper presented at the American Educational Research Association Annual Meeting, New Orleans, April 2000